Target America

Target America

Dr. Lloyd Stebbins

To: Milbrey & Tom

Lloyd & Lou

XULON PRESS

Xulon Press
2301 Lucien Way #415
Maitland, FL 32751
407.339.4217
www.xulonpress.com

© 2020 by Dr. Lloyd Stebbins

All rights reserved solely by the author. The author guarantees all contents are original and do not infringe upon the legal rights of any other person or work. No part of this book may be reproduced in any form without the permission of the author. The views expressed in this book are not necessarily those of the publisher.

Unless otherwise indicated, Scripture quotations taken from the English Standard Version (ESV). Copyright © 2001 by Crossway, a publishing ministry of Good News Publishers. Used by permission. All rights reserved.

Scripture quotations taken from the King James Version (KJV)–*public domain*.

Printed in the United States of America.

ISBN-13: 978-1-6312-9276-7

To my beautiful, thoughtful, and understanding wife, Lou who lovingly put up with the long hours required to write this book and ever so graciously volunteered to review endless manuscript drafts of each chapter. She is my gift from God; she is my personal miracle.
To her, I am and will be forever grateful.

What Happened?
What Now?

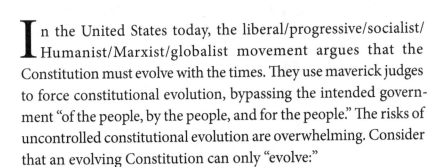

In the United States today, the liberal/progressive/socialist/Humanist/Marxist/globalist movement argues that the Constitution must evolve with the times. They use maverick judges to force constitutional evolution, bypassing the intended government "of the people, by the people, and for the people." The risks of uncontrolled constitutional evolution are overwhelming. Consider that an evolving Constitution can only "evolve:"

- Away from God
- Away from freedom
- Away from the roots of America's spiritual history

All three are precisely what the Constitution was designed to prevent. The same liberal/progressive/ socialist/Humanist/Marxist/globalist movement (all derived from a similar no-god philosophy) is aggressively dedicated to denying your freedom. The movement targets YOU and all freedom's anchors (protections), including the United States Constitution, the free enterprise economic system, democracy (actually a representative republic), Judeo-Christian values, and the traditional family.

Why? Simply this. Everything distinctly American that has made America great and distinctly different from the rest of the world is diametrically opposed to the goals of this extreme anti-American movement. **Abraham Lincoln** said, "*We shall nobly save, or meanly lose, the last best hope of earth* (freedom)."

Today, we are witnessing and directly experiencing a vicious battle fought between believers in God's magnificent wisdom and man's severely incomplete and flawed wisdom. Scripturally, "<u>For we do not wrestle against flesh and blood, but against the rulers, against the authorities, against the cosmic powers over this present darkness, against the spiritual forces of evil in the heavenly places</u>." [**Ephesians 6:12 ESV**] The battle in heavenly places has become graphically and inescapably apparent in earthly places, that is, in our world, before our very eyes. The battle dominates the 24-hour news cycle every single day.

Freedom is a gift from God and God alone. American colonists were given the greatest gift of freedom since the Garden of Eden. Nevertheless, there have been those throughout history determined to take away the freedom of others. Man's "wisdom" relentlessly seeks power, justifying it by claiming that the self-proclaimed "best and brightest" (whoever they are) should have the power to make important life decisions for all others. Man's perceived utopia has always produced tyranny (dictatorship in one form or another). **Power can only be consolidated when freedom is denied.** The liberal/progressive/socialist/Humanist/Marxist/globalist movement can only successfully deny freedom after first destroying freedom's anchors, which are all manifestations of the faith of the colonists and the Founders.

What Happened? What Now?

Heritage inescapably determines destiny. A cultural memory is one of the most important anchors and also a foundation for sustaining any culture. If Christians do not hold up Christian history for others to see, no one else will. If we lose Christian history our culture will lose Christianity.

A silent church and hosts of silent believers beg for calamity. Whether ordered by God or simply allowed by God as a natural result of individual and collective sin, catastrophe is inevitable. It can ONLY be avoided by 1) the greatest awakening of all time OR 2) a fervently praying body of believers willing to stand up, stand out, and speak out in support of all things good and in opposition to all things evil.

> **ONLY GOD CAN FLOAT A SINKING AMERICAN CULTURE. CHRISTIANS ARE THE CONSCIENCE OF THE NATION. IF CHRISTIANS FAIL TO STAND UP, STAND OUT, AND SPEAK OUT SUPPORTING ALL GOOD AND OPPOSING ALL EVIL, AMERICA HAS NO CONSCIENCE.**

> "Freedom is never more than one generation away from extinction. We didn't pass it to our children in the bloodstream. It must be fought for, protected, and handed on for them to do the same, or one day we will spend our sunset years telling our children and our children's children what it was once like in the United States where men were free." ***President Ronald Reagan***

> "The philosophy of the schoolroom in one generation is the philosophy of government in the next." ***President Abraham Lincoln***

Further development of vitally important concepts is accompanied by an abundance of quotations by people extremely well-known and influential in American history and beyond. Some quotations provide stand-alone support; others are referenced in the narrative.

The Founders

Before proceeding, consider an important word about the Founders. History is what it is, the good, the bad, and the ugly. For the benefit of people today, history must be recorded and passed from generation to generation without being biased by historians, teachers, politicians, the media, or anyone else. "Those who fail to learn from history are doomed to repeat it." [***Sir Winston Churchill***, 1948 speech to the British House of Commons] Nevertheless, accurately recording and communicating history down through the ages is a virtually unattainable ideal, because of the inherent personal biases in every word, written or uttered.

The remedy is to avoid being beguiled by the experts' "interpretations of history." Otherwise, communication of the flow of history becomes a bit like the well-known party game where a story is told to the first person in a line of five. It is quietly passed through the line. By the time the fifth person tells the story, it is unrecognizable compared to the original version.

Of course, "scholarly" historians attempt to prevent such gross oral inaccuracies by performing so-called scholarly research. However, the historians tend to rely on quoting each other (often peers who know each other), creating an "official" version of groupthink, ratifying today's popular view of history.

How can average folks who have not devoted their lives to studying history deal with such an intellectual mess? The answer lies in forming opinions about historical figures based on exactly what they said, wrote, and their actions, recorded at that time, i.e. first person accounts and quotations. Avoid relying on modern interpretations. Even the original first person records must be understood in the context of the time.

For reference, modern sources of historical information should rely heavily on first person quotations and records with just enough background material to establish context for the quotations. Two modern historians who use the quotations/minimal context approach superbly are David Barton, *Wallbuilders* and William Federer, *American Minute*. Both are prolific writers who have published many exciting books. They are easily found on the Internet.

Relying on the first person-primary source/minimal context approach reveals a fresh, wholesome view of the Founders that has not been taught in the public schools for a very long time. They were not "just Deists;" most were men of profound Christian faith. Of course, the Founders had faults and weaknesses like everyone else. However, those personal faults and weaknesses do not in any way detract from their astonishing, mind-boggling accomplishments. Overwhelming, first-person evidence confirms:

THE FOUNDERS WERE MEN OF UNCOMMON WISDOM, UNCOMMON KNOWLEDGE, UNCOMMON LOVE, UNCOMMON COURAGE, AND UNCOMMON COMMITMENT.

Such uncommon strength of character can only come from God. The Founders included many ministers and other leaders who might be called politicians today. Most were supported actively and eagerly by wives with the same strength of character. They too are considered to be among the Founders. God's abundant blessings on the colonies and later the nation were readily visible and unmistakable.

> "Of all the dispositions and habits which lead to political prosperity, Religion and Morality are indispensable supports. In vain would that man claim the tribute of Patriotism, who should labor to subvert these great Pillars. Let us with caution indulge the supposition that morality can be maintained without religion. Reason and experience both forbid us to expect that national morality can prevail in exclusion of religious principle…Morality is a necessary spring of a popular government…Who that is a sincere friend to it can look with indifference upon attempts to shake the foundation?" **George Washington**, Farewell Address

NOTE: Bible quotations are from the versions indicated. Quotations attributed to other famous figures are from:

1) David Barton (2011), *Original Intent: The Courts, The Constitution, and Religion,*

2) William Federer (2003), *American Minute: Notable Events of American Significance Remembered on the Date they Occurred* or

3) William Federer (1996), *America's God and Country: Encyclopedia of Quotations.* Appendices from outside sources

feature an Internet link to the original source at the end of each one.

Certain elements of the narrative were inspired by Rev. George Whitefield, Rev. Jonathan Edwards [both leaders of the Great (spiritual) Awakening that drove the War for Independence—known at the American Revolution today], Charles Spurgeon, and many ministers of the Puritan movement in the 16th, 17th, and 18th centuries. They bequeathed to us whole libraries of material that project oceans of God's unconditional love without a single line of legalism. A rediscovery of their writings in the last 50 years may yet trigger another awakening today, the awakening for which millions are praying.

The following chapter headings feature poignant clarifying quotations and parenthetical page numbers.

Table of Contents

What Happened? What Now? (1)

America's Cultural Breakdown (13)
In a declining culture, evil is progressively defined away. That which was formerly called evil is no longer seen as evil. In 1993, U.S. Senator Daniel Patrick Moynihan called it "defining deviancy down." As evil becomes increasingly acceptable, personal accountability fades, reinforcing pride and removing most vestiges of guilt

Excessive Materialism Caused the Death of Every Great Civilization (46)
Obsessive runaway materialism facilitated the replacement of God's real, infinite wisdom with man's finite imitation of "wisdom."

Heritage Determines Destiny (54)
A cultural memory is an anchor and foundation for sustaining any culture. If Christians do not hold up Christian history for others to see, no one else will. If we lose Christian history our culture will lose Christianity.

Astonishing Silence of Believers (76)
All cultural problems have spiritual roots. *No* political action can ever resolve deeper spiritual problems. Believers have and are the

only solutions. They have been enabled by the power of the Holy Spirit. Believers MUST NOT quench that power or that Spirit.

Cultural Impact of Liberal Churches (90)

The most liberal churches are called upon to endorse sin, first by replacing an explicit term with a euphemism, then by declaring the euphemistic (still sinful) behavior as acceptable, later even desirable, camouflaging the behavior in carefully crafted Bible-speak. The mockery of atheists is clear and easily avoided or ignored by believers. However, the deceit of religious liberals, liberal-leaning evangelicals, false Christians, and lapsed Christians is subtle and grossly misleading. It sugar coats sin. The deceit appears to put God's stamp of approval on sin.

Cultural Danger of "Christian" Hypocrites (95)

Atheism typically affects one person, but each false conversion leads many others down the same path.

Politics is the Struggle to Protect & Promote God's Matchless Gift of Freedom (102)

Thomas Jefferson codified the "pursuit of happiness" in the American Declaration of Independence as an unalienable right (truth), "**endowed by our Creator**." That Declaration honored and proclaimed to the world an ironclad commitment to the original announcement of the gospel, "peace on earth" and "good will toward men"

Holy Spirit-Empowered Christians Must Act Now! (130)

A silent church and hosts of silent believers beg for calamity. Whether ordered by God or simply allowed by God as a natural result of individual and collective sin, catastrophe is inevitable. It can ONLY be avoided by 1) the greatest awakening of all time OR 2) a body of believers willing to stand up, stand out, and speak out in support of all things good and in opposition to all things evil.

THE GREATEST AWAKENING OF ALL TIME MUST BEGIN WITH ME (170)

Salvation in Christ is powerful; it is exciting. It MUST be shared. I MUST share it. All history is the story of redemption. It is His story! Remove Jesus and history collapses into chaotic clusters of facts, without significance or meaning. Include Jesus and history reveals infinite beauty and harmony as an expression of His infinite love. All the tragic moments of history are rebellion against God. I MUST be part of a historic awakening!

Appendix I
Fall of Rome: Are there lessons we can learn? (180)

Appendix II
America's Spiritual Heritage (196)

Appendix III
Conservativism v. Liberalism (261)

Appendix IV
What Are the 8 Types of Jihad? Former Radical Muslim Explains (270)

Appendix V
The High Price of Forgetting God (274)

Appendix VI
10 Reasons Why the Church Should Not Abandon Politics (279)

Appendix VII
Importance of Thoughtful Planned Voting (285)

About the Author (289)

America's Cultural Breakdown

Righteousness exalts a nation, but sin condemns any people.
PROVERBS 14:34 NIV

In an utterly fallen world, the United States has been an island of God's special blessing. Most of the early American settlers were fleeing religious persecution in Europe. In some forms, the persecution was violent up to and including death. Following several waves and centuries of Protestant Reformation only the hardiest of the hardy and the most spiritually committed had the faith, courage, and strength to abandon everything they had ever known and face the uncertainties of a high-risk ocean crossing.

Why? They sensed God's blessing as an analog or type of the ancient Israelites. God freed the Israelites from the physical bondage of Egypt.

> "Freedom is a need of the soul, and nothing else. It is in striving toward God that the soul strives continually after a condition of freedom. God alone is the inciter and guarantor of freedom. He is the only guarantor. *External freedom is only an aspect of interior freedom.* Political freedom, as the Western world has known it, is only a political reading of the Bible. *Religion and freedom are indivisible.* Without freedom the soul dies. Without the soul there is no justification for freedom."
> **Whittaker Chambers**, [Journalist, author, former Communist defected to the West] 1952, *Witness*

He was freeing the colonial settlers from the spiritual and sometimes physical bondage of Europe. They sought *both spiritual and political freedom*, and much more. They were committed to forming a minimal government that would protect that hard-won freedom for their children, grandchildren, and continuing on to posterity.

The freedom for which they yearned was a gift from God and God alone.

God told the Israelites of old that He would lead them to their Promised Land, Canaan. Similarly, the Christian settlers viewed the New World as their "promised land." They were driven by their faith and a missionary zeal to spread God's gospel message. They longed to spread God's Word to anyone who would listen, especially to the Indians (later known as Native Americans) who had never before been exposed to it. The missionary zeal is found in nearly all the colonial charters as well as in the writings of many of the settlers and their leaders.

The comparison of colonial America to ancient Israel was far more than a passing, convenient analogy. It was deeply embedded in the American culture. One of the best and most powerful explanations of the connection was provided by President John Quincey Adams at *The Jubilee of the Constitution: A Discourse*, delivered at request of New York Historical Society, April 30, 1839:

> *When the children of Israel, after forty years of wanderings in the wilderness, were about to enter the promised land, their leader, Moses...commanded that when the Lord their God should have brought them into the land, they should put the curse upon*

Mount Ebal, and the blessing upon Mount Gerizim. This injunction was faithfully fulfilled by his successor Joshua. Immediately after they had taken possession of the land, Joshua built an altar to the Lord, of whole stones, upon Mount Ebal. And there he wrote upon the stones a copy of the law of Moses, which he had written in the presence of the children of Israel…

*Fellow citizens, the **ark of your covenant** is the <u>Declaration of independence</u>. **Your Mount Ebal**, is the <u>confederacy of separate state sovereignties</u>, and **your Mount Gerizim** is the <u>Constitution of the United States</u>…*

Lay up these principles, then, in your hearts, and in our souls…teach them to your children…cling to them as to the issues of life—adhere to them as to the cords of your eternal salvation. So may your children's children…[celebrate the] Constitution…in full enjoyment of all blessings recognized by you in the commemoration of this day, and of all the blessings promised to the children of Israel upon Mount Gerizim, as the reward of obedience to the law of God.

The intimate harmony of Christianity and the American form of government has been blessed by God and sustained our country for hundreds of years. But today, the *liberal progressive movement* works tirelessly to paint Christians as rebels to the government, some even labeling Christians as "terrorists" or "haters."

The United States government is the only government ever created by the body of Christ, relying on God for direction. God has blessed our government and people more than any other. We MUST NOT, by the sin of neglect, allow the original form of our government to continue to deteriorate and self-destruct.

A man's conscience tells him to abhor the worst of evil, i.e. murder, robbery etc. Historically, people have been held personally accountable for wrongdoing (evil). ***But in a declining culture, evil is progressively defined away. That which was formerly called evil is no longer seen as evil. In 1993, U.S. Senator Daniel Patrick Moynihan called it "defining deviancy down." As evil becomes increasingly acceptable, personal accountability fades, reinforcing pride and removing most vestiges of guilt. The barriers to receiving Christ become psychologically higher. Fewer are saved.*** "*Woe to those who call evil good and good evil, who put darkness for light and light for darkness, who put bitter for sweet and sweet for bitter!*" [***Isaiah 5:20 ESV***]

FREEDOM IS A GOD-GIVEN GIFT; GOVERNMENTS CAN ONLY TAKE FREEDOM AWAY

Director, **Cecil B. DeMille** billed the classic movie, *The Ten Commandments* as the story of the birth of freedom. The Israelites of the Biblical "Exodus" had been held captives (slaves) of the Egyptians for 400 years.

A few hundred years after being freed from Egyptian bondage, Israel increasingly disobeyed and when they became a "*stiff-necked people,*" insisted on having a king like other nations. The Israelites perceived that life would be easier if someone else makes the tough decisions. However, shirking personal responsibility produces slothfulness, a pathway to moral chaos. God warned the Israelites that a king would take away their precious gift of freedom. The Lord said, to the Israelites:

> This will be the manner of the king (**head of any government other than a representative republic, a.k.a. democracy**) that shall reign over you:
>
> - *He will take your sons*, and appoint them for himself, for his chariots, and to be his horsemen; and some shall run before his chariots. And he will appoint him captains over thousands, and captains over fifties; and will set them to ear his ground and to reap his harvest, and to make his instruments of war, and instruments of his chariots. and
>
> - *He will take your daughters* to be confectionaries, and to be cooks, and to be bakers. and
>
> - *He will take your vineyards and your olive yards* (wealth), even the best of them, and give them to his servants (bureaucrats). And
>
> - *He will take the tenth (or more) of your seed* (taxes), and of your vineyards, and give to his officers (politicians), and to his servants (bureaucrats). and
>
> - *He will take your menservants, and your maidservants, and your goodliest young men, and your asses, and put them to his work. He will take the tenth of your sheep* (wealth); and

YE SHALL BE HIS SERVANTS (tyranny to totalitarianism). And ye shall cry out in that day because of your king which ye shall have chosen you; and the Lord will not hear you in that day. [*1 Samuel 8: 11-18 KJV, emphasis and parenthetical updates added*]

In later Biblical times, the disobedient Israelites of the Northern Kingdom of Israel became captives of the Assyrians and still later the Israelite of the Southern Kingdom of Judah were captives of the Babylonians. Freedom lost from without or within inevitably leads to tyranny.

In most conflicts between nations after biblical times, the vanquished became captives—often slaves—of the victors. Christianity freed people for the first time since ancient Israel at the time of the Judges. Modern Christianity freed slaves in the predominantly Christian European countries. Ultimately Christianity freed the slaves in the United States.

> "Proclaim Liberty throughout the land unto all the inhabitants thereof." [*Leviticus 25:10 KJV*] Inscribed on the *Liberty Bell*, August, 1752
>
> "It was wonderful to see...From being thoughtless or indifferent...it seemed as if all the world were growing religious, so that one could not walk thro' the town in an evening without hearing psalms sung in every street." *Benjamin Franklin* on the Great Awakening, circa 1750
>
> "Atheism is unknown there; Infidelity rare and secret; so that a person may live to a great age in that country without having their piety shocked by meeting with either an Atheist or an Infidel. And the Divine Being seems...pleased to favor the whole country." *Benjamin Franklin*, *Information to Those Who Would Remove to America*, 1754

Early modern freedom was initially codified in the **Magna Carta** (June 15, 1215), the **Fundamental Orders of Connecticut** (January 14, 1639), and finally in the **Declaration of Independence** (July 4, 1776) and the **United States Constitution** (September 17, 1787).

The pathway to achieving and sustaining both spiritual and political freedom has always been undergirded by Judeo-Christian faith and associated moral, ethical and life standards.

Most American wars were battles for freedom versus tyranny (good versus evil). WWII was the ultimate earthly battle between good and evil. A man will sacrifice his life and die ONLY for a sacred soul-deep cause. The civil war was two variations of good commingled with some evil. *Both sides subscribed to the values of the Founders; both sides sought and revered freedom.* Slavery was the trigger, but not the sustainer of the Civil War.

- **The South fought a second revolutionary war** to achieve freedom and independence from federal persecution. The southern goals were to preserve states' rights (good) and preserve slavery (evil). Nevertheless, the underlying driving force was the collection of Christian values that sustained the American Revolution.

- **The North believed that God blessed the United States as a whole** and that one successful secession would be followed by others, splintering the sacred union, resulting in the utter failure of the *Great American Experiment* in self-government. The North fought to free the slaves (good) and solidify federal power (evil), thereby removing power from the people. The North too was driven by the Christian values that sustained the American Revolution.

Most modern American "wars" are or have been driven by earthly politics and left unfinished.

The American colonists and the Founders knew that spiritual freedom thrives best when the host government champions temporal (civil, political) freedom. *True **spiritual freedom** and true **political freedom** are so intertwined that they cannot be separated without seriously damaging both.*

Freedom is a gift from God and God alone. To protect freedom and prevent it from being incrementally or suddenly taken away, the wise and astute Founders tethered freedom to numerous anchors, including the United States Constitution, democracy (actually a representative republic), free enterprise economy, Judeo-Christian values, and the traditional God-created family. The Founders and many successors, repeatedly proclaimed that the Great American Experiment and the U.S. form of government could be sustained only as long as the anchors and values held firm. To the extent that the anchors are compromised, freedom is lost and the American culture declines. Unchecked, the current move toward socialism would ultimately destroy all the anchors.

> "A patriot without religion in my estimation is as great a paradox as an honest Man without the fear of God. Is it possible that he whom no moral obligations bind, can have any real Good Will towards Men? Can he be a patriot who, by an openly vicious conduct, is undermining the very bonds of Society, corrupting the Morals of Youth, and by his bad example injuring the very Country he professes to patronize more than he can possibly compensate by intrepidity, generosity and honour?" ***Abigail Adams***, wife of John Adams and mother of John Quincy Adams, November 5, 1775 (Letter to Mercy Otis Warren)

Today's believers must flee from the liberal progressive wolves who seek ultimate power for themselves. ***The farther government gets away from local towns and villages, the further government gets away from God.*** America today is experiencing God's limited wrath as His hand of blessing is removed, but America is risking God's ultimate temporal wrath, virtually complete loss of the greatest freedom since the Garden of Eden.

Today, the American culture is rapidly collapsing. Christianity is declining and atheism is growing. Atheism is tacit license for all manner of evil, chaos, and cultural collapse. "If God does not exist, everything is permitted." [***Fyodor Dostoevsky*** in *The Brothers Karamazov* (1880)] Only, Jesus, can save America. Please God, sweep our beloved country with the greatest awakening of all time!

To unbelievers, Satan (sin) is a false refuge from the convicting power of the Holy Spirit. Sin is a false comfort that sears the conscience. As sin becomes increasingly commonplace, the American culture is hating God, more and more. Only believers or a Great Awakening can slow or turn the tide. The conscience of America is becoming increasingly seared.

Natural men are natural enemies. They flee from God seeking to benefit only self by cheaply earning or outright taking whatever they desire. Among individuals or small groups we call it robbery. Among nations, we call it war. As done by the government to its own citizens, we call it taxation, which is simply legalized plunder. Regardless of the context, love is pre-empted by brute force.

The unbelieving Hedonist (modern Humanist/liberal/progressive/socialist/Marxist/globalist) seeks pleasure and avoids pain. His focus is only the physical; he neglects the emotional, and is ignorant of the spiritual. <u>*The believer*</u> understands that the greatest pleasure and least pain is through a life of continual unhindered holiness which satisfies ALL needs, physical, emotional, and spiritual.

What is America's current condition?

1. Many Americans rebel against God.
2. God is withdrawing His hand of blessing
3. America continues to self-destruct.
4. Believers, the conscience of the nation, seem to be overcome by terminal apathy and quarantined by the cultural pressure of political correctness to within the walls of their home and the walls of their place of worship.
5. The only real and lasting remedy? The greatest spiritual awakening of all time, led by spiritually available believers.

The conditions existing in the United States today are a frightening and astonishing parallel to the conditions existing when the Roman Empire fell. Appendix I, *Fall of Rome: Are there lessons we can learn?* provides a detailed comparison.

Future generations can learn from the ***factors that led to the fall of Rome***:

- open borders
- loss of common language
- welfare state
- violent, sensual entertainment and sex-trafficking
- ***church withdrawal from cultural and political involvement***
- birth control, "planned parenthood" and fewer children
- immorality, infidelity and loss of virtue

- class warfare
- high taxes
- out-sourcing
- exploding debt and coinage debasement
- deep state, establishment politicians
- defense cuts and over-extended military
- loss of patriotism
- terrorist attacks

Refer to Appendix I for a detailed discussion of each factor.

The trends exposed on **Figure 1:** *America' Changing Religious Landscape* graphic are alarming. Every category, save one, is declining markedly. The Percent of Population claiming no religion has been rising nearly exponentially for over 25 years, from about 7% (1992) to over 23% (2018). For now, the short cause or one of the greatest contributors to America's cultural and religious decline is widespread apathy among believers and their local leaders. Before exploring the details of America's cultural decline and practical remedies, first consider the nature and power of the Great American Experiment.

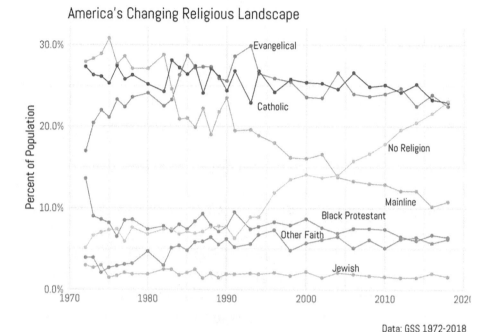

https://www.christianpost.com/news/religious-nones-now-as-big-as-evangelicals-in-the-us-new-data-shows.html Samuel Smith, *Christian Post*
Wednesday, March 20, 2019

Figure 1: *America's Changing Religious Landscape*

The Great American Experiment

The Great American Experiment simply poses the question, "*Is it possible for a people to be self-governing, from the nation's founding to posterity?*"

The Founders contended that:

1) **only a virtuous people of strong moral character could be self-governing** and further that

2) **virtues emerge and are sustainable only by a religious people.**

3) **Religion is the ONLY foundation of virtues that are held so strongly they can be reliably passed on from generation to generation.** Finally,

4) **the strongest foundation of virtues is Christianity, anchored in the Bible.**

The underlying source of ALL conflicts in marriage, family, neighborhood, workplace, government entity, or between nations is the conflict between humility and pride. The same conflict perpetually jeopardizes the Great American Experiment.

Humility is one of the greatest virtues specifically because it is the opposite of pride. It is maintained in a godly Judeo-Christian culture. Humility tends to place others before self. Unbelievers are generally controlled by *pride*, self before others. Many have proclaimed pride the mother of all sins. If so, humility is the mother of all virtues. Believers call the tendency to make decisions for the benefit of self a <u>sin nature</u>. The secular term is <u>egoism</u>. Believers are taught and commanded in Scripture to seek a humble nature. Humility breeds a culture of competitive givers; pride

> "When exiting the last meeting of the Constitutional Convention, Franklin was asked, 'Well Doctor, what have we got, a republic or a monarchy?' Franklin quickly replied, 'A republic, if you can keep it.'"
> ***Benjamin Franklin***
>
> "The *Declaration of Independence* gave liberty not alone to the people of this country, but <u>hope to all the world for all future time</u>. It was that which gave promise that in due time the weights would be lifted from the shoulders of all men, and that all should have an equal chance…This is the sentiment embodied in the Declaration of Independence…I would rather be assassinated on this spot than surrender it."
> ***President Abraham Lincoln***, Independence Hall, February 22, 1861

breeds a culture of competitive takers. The former feeds and perpetuates cultural harmony; the latter feeds and perpetuates conflict.

Freedom requires ultimate personal accountability to God and others. "Jesus replied: <u>Love the Lord your God with all your heart and with all your soul and with all your mind</u>. This is the first and greatest commandment. And the second is like it: '<u>Love your neighbor as yourself</u>. All the Law and the Prophets hang on these two commandments.'" [**Matthew 22:36-40; Mark 12:28-34; Luke 10:27; Deuteronomy 6:5; Leviticus 19:18 NIV**] Prayer and significant personal effort are required to sustainably maintain the freedom bequeathed by the Founders.

Consider carefully, the unusually long two-page quotation from **President Calvin Coolidge's** powerfully inspiring *Independence Day speech*, 1926 (150 years after the signing of the *Declaration of Independence*). It loudly proclaims the intimate and inextricable link between Christianity and the American culture, a link which was purposely and deliberately anchored by the *Declaration of Independence* **and** the *United States Constitution*.

> "At the end of 150 years the **four corners of the earth** unite in coming to Philadelphia as to a <u>**holy shrine**</u> in grateful acknowledgement of a service so great, which a few inspired men here rendered to humanity, that **it is still the preeminent support of free government throughout the world...** It is little wonder that **people at home and abroad** consider <u>Independence Hall</u> as **hallowed ground** and revere the <u>Liberty Bell</u> as a **sacred relic**... They are the framework of a <u>**spiritual event**</u>.

The **world** looks upon them, because of their associations of one hundred and fifty years ago, as it looks upon **the Holy Land** because of what took place there nineteen hundred years ago. Through use for a righteous purpose they have become sanctified... There is something beyond the establishment of a new nation, great as that event would be, in the **Declaration of Independence** which has ever since caused it to be regarded as one of the great charters that <u>**not only was to liberate America but was everywhere to ennoble humanity**</u>...

When we take all these circumstances into consideration, it is but natural that the first paragraph of the **Declaration of Independence** should open with a reference to Nature's God and should close in the final paragraphs with an appeal to the Supreme Judge of the world and an assertion of a firm reliance on Divine Providence.

Coming from these sources, having as it did this background, it is no wonder that **Samuel Adams** could say "The people seem to recognize this resolution as though it were a decree promulgated from heaven..."

No one can examine this record and escape the conclusion that in the great outline of its principles the Declaration was the result of the religious teachings of the preceding period... the immediate conception of the **principles** of human relationship which went into the **Declaration of Independence** we are not required to extend our search beyond our own shores. *They are found in the texts, the sermons, and the writings of the early* **colonial clergy** *who were earnestly undertaking to instruct their congregations in the great mystery of how to live.*

They preached equality *because they believed in the <u>fatherhood of God</u> and the <u>brotherhood of man</u>. They justified freedom by the text that we are all created in the divine image, all partakers of the divine spirit...* **In its main features <u>the Declaration of Independence is a great spiritual document.</u> It is a declaration not of material but of spiritual conceptions.** *Equality, liberty, popular sovereignty, the rights of man — these are not elements which we can see and touch. They are ideals.* **They have their source and their roots in the religious convictions.** *They belong to the unseen world.*

Unless the faith of the American people in these religious convictions is to endure, the principles of our Declaration will perish. *We cannot continue to enjoy the result if we neglect and abandon the cause."*

*"***The people have to bear their own responsibilities. There is no method by which that burden can be shifted to the government. <u>It is not the enactment, but the observance of laws, that creates the character of a nation.</u>***

About the Declaration **there is a finality that is exceedingly restful.** *It is often asserted that the world has made a great deal of progress since 1776,* *that we have had new thoughts and new experiences which have given us a great advance over the people of that day, and that we may therefore very well discard their conclusions for something more modern. But that reasoning cannot be applied to this great charter. If all men are created equal,* **that is final.** *If they are endowed with inalienable rights,* **that is final.** *If governments derive their just powers from the consent of the governed,* **that is final.** <u>No advance, no progress can be made beyond these propositions</u>.

If anyone wishes to deny their truth or their soundness, the only direction in which he can proceed historically is not forward, but backward toward the time when there was no equality, no rights of the individual, no rule of the people. Those who wish to proceed in that direction cannot lay claim to progress. They are reactionary. Their ideas are not more modern, but more ancient, than those of the Revolutionary fathers...

We hold that the duly authorized expression of the will of the people has a **divine sanction.** *But even in that we come back to the theory of* **John Wise** *that "Democracy is Christ's government."* **The ultimate sanction of law rests on the righteous authority of the Almighty...** *Ours is a government of the people. It represents their will. Its officers may sometimes go astray, but that is not a reason for criticizing the principles of our institutions.*

The real heart of the American Government depends upon the heart of the people. It is from that source that we must look for all genuine reform. It is to that cause that we must ascribe all our results... *No other theory is adequate to explain or comprehend the* **Declaration of Independence.** <u>It is the product of the **spiritual insight** of the people.</u> *We live in an age of science and of abounding accumulation of material things. These did not create our Declaration. Our Declaration created them.* ***The things of the spirit come first.*** *Unless we cling to that, all our material prosperity, overwhelming though it may appear, will turn to a barren sceptre in our grasp. If we are to maintain the great heritage which has been bequeathed to us, we must be as like-minded as the fathers who created it. We must not sink into a pagan materialism.* <u>We must cultivate the reverence which they had for the things that are holy</u>. *We must follow the* **spiritual and moral leadership** *which they showed. We must keep replenished, that they may glow with a more compelling flame, the altar fires before which they worshiped."* **Calvin Coolidge,** *July 5, 1926*

THE STABILITY OF THE WHOLE WORLD RESTS ON THE SUCCESS OF THE GREAT AMERICAN EXPERIMENT.

<u>Is the United States a Christian Nation? Absolutely!</u>

The United States of America was founded as a Christian nation, has always been a Christian nation, and continues to be a Christian nation today, despite massive, relentless assaults on America's history and culture.

The evidence is overwhelming. America has far deeper roots than the original founding. In reverse chronological order, America's spiritual roots extend beyond the *Declaration of Independence*, beyond the arrival of the early settlers, through several waves of the Protestant Reformation in Europe, all the way to the origin of the first Protestant Reformation itself.

Near the turn of the 20th Century, United States Supreme Court Justice David J. Brewer wrote one of the most remarkable opinions in the history of the Supreme Court, *Church of the Holy Trinity v. United States, 143 U.D. 457 (1892) No. 143*. The entire second half of the ruling chronicles the inescapable evidence that the United States of America is and always has been a Christian nation. After reviewing 80 exhibits, the ruling of the Supreme Court was unanimous. The unanimity of justices' view that the United States is a Christian nation supported ruling in favor of the Church of the Holy Trinity with regard to the specific, disputed legal issue.

Much more can be cited today. Since the *United States Constitution* was ratified on June 21, 1788:

- Every United States President has been a visibly devoted, outspoken Christian, except Barak Obama (For details regarding Barak Obama, refer to Appendix VII, *America's Most Biblically-Hostile U.S. President*, https://wallbuilders.com/americas-biblically-hostile-u-s-president/).
- Every President has enjoyed a stellar career ahead of the Presidency.

- Every President has been an outstanding role model, despite occasional personal failures.
- Every President was confident and proud to publically proclaim their faith in God and uncompromising belief in Jesus Christ as savior.
- Since virtually all presidents have been visible outspoken Christians, they had to be elected by a predominantly Christian electorate that desired a Christian President and a culture-wide promotion of the stable Christian values represented by the President.
- The *United States Senate* has always had a chaplain. All chaplains from the nation's founding to the present have been Christians.
- The *United States House of Representatives* has always had a chaplain. All chaplains from the nation's founding to the present have been Christians.
- All *military branches* have chaplains. Until recently, they have been predominantly Christian and a few Jewish. Today, there are some Muslim Chaplains.
- About 93% of all *United States Supreme Court* justices have been Christian; about 7% have been Jewish.

Historians have recognized *four great spiritual awakenings*, beginning with the first one that immediately preceded and propelled the Revolutionary War. In this context, a spiritual awakening is a profound reconnection with God that visibly transforms the lives of individuals and spreads rapidly throughout the American culture. Altogether, the four great spiritual awakenings total 170 years, much of the life-to-date of this country. In between great awakenings, there has always been sufficient spiritual momentum to maintain the Judeo-Christian values that drive the American culture.

Many presidents have issued proclamations for days of humiliation, prayer, fasting, or any combination thereof. In addition, there have always been enormous numbers of churches, missionary organizations, para-church organizations. The famous circuit riders took the gospel message westward. Christian holidays are the most celebrated holidays of all. Most early universities were founded as Christian universities, schools at all levels were founded as Christian schools, and hospitals were founded as Christian institutions.

What is the evidence for these bold statements? Let the historic leaders speak for themselves. The 35 pages of direct quotations in Appendix II, *America's Spiritual Heritage* provide undeniable proof of the veracity of the truths above. Presidential terms are cited along the right margin; spiritual and temporal milestones are indicated by centered subheadings. No other commentary is necessary.

ALTHOUGH STRAINED IN MANY WAYS, THE UNITED STATES OF AMERICA IS STILL A CHRISTIAN NATION.

Greatest Pinnacle of Freedom since the Garden of Eden

The *Declaration of Independence* and the *United States Constitution* codified the highest level of freedom since the Ancient Israelites at the time of the Judges, second only to the virtually unlimited freedom enjoyed by Adam and Eve in the Garden of Eden. Freedom is greatest when it is exercised within the boundaries commanded by God. Governments have a long history of restricting freedom or licensing chaos by sanctioning behavior outside of God's limits.

The Founders clearly understood the difficulty of keeping and maintaining the new government and succeeding at the *Great American Experiment* in self-government.

The two founding documents were and are intended to be a combined cultural anchor, changeable only by the deliberately cumbersome process of Constitutional amendment. The Constitution was intended to put the federal government in a very tight box. What is in the box?

- *Three Branches of Government (Legislative—U.S. Congress; Executive—White House & agencies; Judicial—U.S. Supreme Court)*: The Founders were wisely aware of the worldwide history of the tendency of power to concentrate, at the expense of personal freedom. Ego seeks power and influence. Believers know that power concentration results from man's sin nature. Secular philosophers call it egoism. Regardless of the label, it is the tendency of people to make decisions for the benefit of self. To prevent the inevitable and relentless concentration of power, the Founders chopped the federal government into three pieces or branches, 1) legislative (make the laws), 2) executive (administer the laws), and 3) judicial (guardian of the Constitution and interpret the laws to settle disputes).

- *Checks and Balances*: For similar reasons, the Founders were very concerned that throughout the passage of time, each branch of government would attempt to expand its power and influence at the expense of the other two branches. Once again, freedom of the people would become the ultimate sacrifice. To prevent the continuous erosion of freedom resulting from inter-branch competition, the

Founders erected tough barriers, which became known as *checks and balances*. The checks limited the authority of each branch to assure a balance or political equilibrium among the branches. The goal was coordination without consolidation.

Despite the very tight box and the powerful barriers to infighting within the box some Founders insisted there were still insufficient protections to guard individual freedoms from government intrusion. A group known as the Anti-Federalists insisted on the <u>Bill of Rights</u> as ten chains around the already tight box. *The **"chains"** were intended to provide **absolute** protection of individual freedoms from federal government abuse.*

Finally, the Founders clearly understood that ***the farther any government is from the people the less accountability it has to the people***. The greatest illustration of the principle is the British attempt to govern the colonies, from several thousand miles away. Later, politicians in Washington had similar difficulties governing the "wild west," thousands of miles away. The vast distances produced frequent misunderstandings of the remote American subcultures and the widely varying cultures of Indian (Native American) tribes. Since that time, communications and transportation have improved dramatically and advanced information technology has emerged. Nevertheless, distance and lack of accountability continue to provide an incentive for federal abuses of freedom and public funds. *O*NLY *an active, vibrant faith in God can shackle the powerful temptations for such abuses.*

MAXIMUM FREEDOM IS GOD'S FREEDOM WITHIN HIS RESTRAINTS VOLUNTARILY OBEYED.

When a culture is at the pinnacle of freedom:

- There are many individuals, groups, and nations anxious to take away part or all of the freedom. Throughout world recorded history, vanquished states consistently became the slaves of the victors.
- Sadly, today many individuals are still willing to let *freedom* incrementally drift away. They have lost sight of the preciousness of God's great gift.

Seeds of Destruction

For over a century, there has been an emerging and growing view that the Constitution must be flexible and change with the times. A rubber constitution is no constitution at all. Evolving away from the Constitution is evolving away from God, because of His influence on the founding documents.

Despite supposed intellectual arguments to the contrary, the writers of the *Declaration of Independence* and the *United States Constitution* bequeathed to us an abundance of materials, written in their own hand, attesting to their profound, life-driving faith in God, through His Son Jesus Christ, enabled by the Holy Spirit. The common assertion that the Founders were "just deists" does not survive even the barest scrutiny. As such, deviation from the founding documents nearly always replaces God's perfect wisdom with man's flawed imitation of "wisdom."

The government "...of the people, by the people, and for the people" is being progressively lost by:

1. Activism by a runaway unelected federal judiciary
2. Bloated executive branch bureaucracies outside the reach of the voters
3. Political view of a rubber constitution (must change with the times), arbitrarily changed by all three branches of government (Executive, Legislative, and Judicial) without using the constitutional amendment process
4. Increasing power of the federal government at the expense of state and local governments.
5. Ill-advised constitutional amendments.

<u>Devastating Consequences of Lack of Christian Diligence</u>

The Founders knew with abundant certainty that <u>spiritual freedom</u> and <u>political freedom</u> are so strongly integrated that they cannot be separated. Together, they are a precious gift from God and God alone. Freedom is NOT, in any sense, a grant from government.

> "It has long, however, been my opinion, and I have never shrunk from its expression, ...that the germ of dissolution of our federal government is in the constitution of the federal Judiciary,...working like gravity by night and by day, gaining a little today and a little tomorrow, and advancing its noiseless step like a thief, over the field of jurisdiction, until all shall be usurped."
> **President Thomas Jefferson**

> "In the first place, there is not a syllable in the plan under consideration which directly empowers the national courts to construe the laws according to the *spirit of the Constitution*, or which gives them any greater latitude in this respect than may be claimed by the courts of every State."
> **Alexander Hamilton**, *Federalist No. 81*

The world is replete with people constrained by the bondage of sin who have collectively, forcefully, and repeatedly deprived people of their *God-gifted freedom*. It is taken away by progressive government restriction or enslavement. Even today, the harshest penalty ordered by government for wrongdoing is confinement in a jail cell, i.e. total loss of freedom. The only harsher penalty is capital punishment.

Unless voluntarily restricted, by a culture widely committed to abiding by the as-written Constitution, a runaway government will progressively expand the arbitrarily defined sphere of wrong doing (cancerous expansion of a stifling network of laws) at the expense of progressively shrinking the sphere of freedom. Tyranny or totalitarianism becomes inevitable.

Tyrants include monarchs, dictators, feudal barons, and strong men emerging from the residue of fallen democracies. They often declare themselves to be gods, actually or tacitly. Such a belief or declaration becomes license for a power grab.

> "Our free government was a happy, but a costly purchase; let it not be lost by drowsy inattention, and implicit confidence. How a free government may be preserved, is a just inquiry." **Joseph Lathrop, D.D.**, July 4, 1794
>
> "I have sworn upon the altar of God eternal hostility against every form of tyranny over the mind of man." **President Thomas Jefferson**
>
> "The *tree of liberty* must be refreshed from time to time with the blood of patriots and tyrants. It is its natural manure." **President Thomas Jefferson**

Chaos results from a lack of moral restraint. As God is abandoned, His restraints are discarded. Orderly culture quickly declines into chaos. A denial of God becomes license for all manner of unbridled behavior. A chaotic culture has no restraints, no laws (except a tyrant's decrees), no morals, and no ethics.

The antidote presented by the Founders was enthusiastic and aggressive protection of God's precious gift of freedom undergirded by strong families, a virtuous culture, and an educational system all committed to raising children to become Christian adults of strong character.

FREEDOM, IN THE UNITED STATES, WILL CONTINUE TO COLLAPSE IF THERE IS A CONTINUED LACK OF DILIGENCE AMONG CONSERVATIVE BIBLE-BELIEVING CHRISTIANS.

***Figure 2**, Freedom is a gift from God and God alone, not a grant from government*, clearly illustrates the vital importance of everyone participating in the protection of freedom. God's antidote for a decaying culture is *"Render to Caesar the things that are Caesar's; and to God the things that are God's."* [**Matthew 22:21 KJV**] Ultimately, very little belongs to "Caesar" (government).

Like the early church at Ephesus America has "*left your first love*," [***Revelation 2:4 NKJV***] the love of God. The exhilaration and tribulation of founding a new nation, based on the love of God and gift of freedom have faded into the past. **We have forgotten God. We have forgotten that America is great, not because the people are great, but because God is great.** Lord, return us to the Judeo-Christian values responsible for the love and cohesiveness of the American culture.

"The Declaration of Independence...claims...the ultimate source of authority by stating... they were...'appealing to the Supreme Judge of the World for the rectitude of their intentions'...The foundations of our independence and or government rests upon basic religious convictions. Back of the authority of our laws is the authority of the Supreme Judge of the World to whom we still appeal...It seems to me perfectly plain that the authority of law, the right to equality, liberty, and property, under American institutions, have their foundation reverence for God. If we could imagine that to be swept away, these institutions of our American government could not long survive." *President Calvin Coolidge*

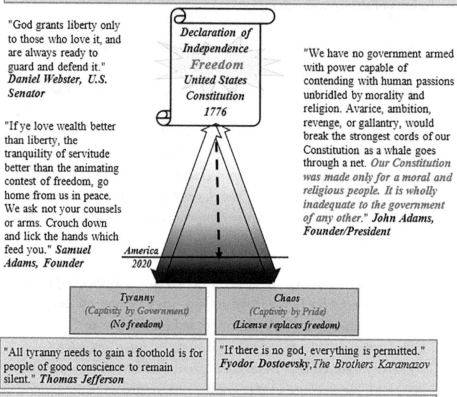

Figure 2: *Freedom is a gift from God and God alone, not a grant from government!*

> The United States is only one superpower. Today they lead the world. Nobody has doubts about it. Militarily. They also lead economically but they're getting weak. But they don't lead morally and politically anymore. The world has no leadership. The United States was always the last resort and hope for all other nations. There was the hope, whenever something was going wrong, one could count on the United States. Today, we lost that hope. ***Lech Walesa*** (former President of Poland and Noble Peace Prize winner) ***circa 2011***

"<u>Pride goes before destruction, a haughty spirit before a fall</u>" [***Proverbs 16:18 NIV***] *applies to both believers and unbelievers. It applies to individuals and nations. Widespread cultural pride has enabled and facilitated the fall of the American culture.*

We are constantly fed the unbelieving (no god) lie 1) by the culture, 2) by the devil himself, and sometimes, 3) by a poor upbringing, or even by 4) "friends." But Jesus says, "<u>Come to me</u>." [***Matthew 11:28 ESV***] The rewards are priceless. Failure is ultimately terrifying.

As in the Biblical days of old, God's modern miracles in the Revolutionary War, World War II, and rescue of Apollo 13, and many others are quickly forgotten. Believers are notoriously fickle,

> ***PURPOSE OF THE UNITED STATES CONSTITUTION AND PURPOSE OF LIBERTY***
>
> "…we have been enabled to establish constitutions of government…<u>*particularly the national one now lately instituted, for the* **civil AND religious liberty**</u> with which we are blessed…*to promote the knowledge and practice of true religion and virtue.*" **President George Washington**, first National Thanksgiving Proclamation

especially when their religious affections are superficially emotional and not deeply spiritual.

There is Only One Sustainable Remedy: Virtuous, Vocal Christians Empowered and Driven by the Holy Spirit

The military protects the United States from foreign attempts to take away freedom. ONLY CHRISTIANS can and MUST protect freedom within the United States.

When freedom collapses, humility defaults to pride leading to tyranny and chaos. Power concentrates at the top of the culture to control increasing disorder among the masses. Tyrants progressively control the masses.

A common Revolutionary War battle cry was, "No king but King Jesus." Unbelievers, especially today, simply do not understand the vital importance of *God-gifted freedom*. For a culture to be orderly and stable, someone must be in charge. The very best leader is the all-knowing, all-loving, all-powerful, and always present God made visible through Jesus Christ. Such a culture is enabled and secured by God's infinite Holy Spirit.

> "*An enlightened people will not easily be brought under despotism.* They will foresee and prevent the evil. **Great attention should therefore be paid to the education of youth, to the culture and diffusion of knowledge, and to the means of public information.**
>
> '*Righteousness exalts a nation.*' **To preserve our liberty and independence, and to increase our importance and respectability, we must attend to the interest of virtue, as well as knowledge.** This we must promote in our private station, while we expect that our rulers pursue it in their larger sphere. *Industry, frugality, temperance, justice, benevolence and peaceableness, are virtues, in every nature, essential to the happiness of every community. The promotion of these in smaller societies (homes), will spread and strengthen their influence in the nation at large.*" **Joseph Lathrop**, July 4, 179

In contrast, unbelievers view the man-made government in charge. Such a government becomes a highly inefficient, prideful competition among the participants for power and influence.

The Founders were well aware of the weaknesses of prideful men and women. Nevertheless, some form of earthly government is necessary to protect freedom from external and internal encroachment and provide for the safety and security of the people.

The *Declaration of Independence* and the *United States Constitution* were written to achieve those goals in a way that is not easily compromised by future generations. Hence, the abundance of bold checks and balances. Since then, America's founding documents have been revered by the world.

Following the example of the ancient Israelites, America's earliest settlers, America's Founders, and generations of subsequent Americans, America's story of freedom MUST be retold frequently by parents, teachers, and politicians. As unlikely as it may seem today, America's story must be regularly reinforced by the media and those in the sports and entertainment fields. In short, *saturation evil* must be replaced by *saturation good* in the American culture, as it has been for over 400 years, save the last few decades. Godly patriotism must be restored. Judeo-Christian believers must take the lead. "*Seek first the kingdom of God and His righteousness, and all these things shall be added to you.*" [**Matthew 6:33 NKJV**]

> "*To you, ye citizens of America, do the inhabitants of the earth look with eager attention for the success of a measure on which their happiness and prosperity so manifestly depend…On your virtue, patriotism, integrity, and submission to the laws of your own*

making (and the government of your own choice) do the hopes of men rest with **prayers and supplications** for a happy issue. ***Be not therefore careless, indolent, or inattentive in the exercise of any right of citizenship***. Let no duty, however small or seemingly of little importance, be neglected by you... <u>**Good government generally begins in the family and if the moral character of a people once degenerate, their political character must soon follow**</u>..."
Elias Boudinot, (1793)

"Is it not that, in the chain of human events, the birthday of a nation is indissolubly linked with the birthday of the Savior? That it forms a leading event in the progress of the gospel dispensation? <u>Is it not that the ***Declaration of Independence*** first organized the social compact on the foundation of the Redeemer's mission upon earth?</u> That it laid the corner stone of human government upon the first precepts of Christianity, and gave to the world the first irrevocable pledge of the fulfillment of the prophecies, announced directly from Heaven at the birth of the Savior and predicted by the greatest of the Hebrew prophets six hundred years before?...

...This was indeed a great and solemn event. The sublimest of the prophets of antiquity with the voice of inspiration had exclaimed, "<u>*Who hate heard such a thing? Who hath seen such things? Shall the earth be made to bring forth in one day? Or shall a nation be born at once?*</u>" [*Isaiah 66:8*]. In the two thousand five hundred years, that had elapsed since the days of that prophecy, no such event had occurred. It had never been seen before. In the annals of the human race, then, for the first time, did one People announce themselves as a member of that great community of the powers of the earth, acknowledging the obligations and claiming the rights of the Laws of Nature and of Nature's God. The earth was made to bring forth in one day! ***<u>A nation was born at once!</u>*** " *John Quincy Adams*, *July 4, 1837* [Note: One hundred years later, modern Israel was similarly born.]

"***Democracy is Christ's government in church and state.***" **Rev. John Wise, *The Churches Quarrel Espoused, (1710)* His works were reprinted in 1772 and have been declared to have been nothing less than a textbook of liberty for our Revolutionary fathers.**

As America drifts away from God, the culture has lost its sense of personal accountability, from the individual to the national level. Someone else is always to blame, never self. The blame game is greatly magnified by the current tsunami of sexual harassment claims. <u>Humility accepts personal responsibility; pride blames others</u>. The shift from humility to pride is as clear in modern American culture as it was in Adam and Eve. "<u>Against you (God) only have I sinned and done what is evil in your sight, so that you may be justified in your words and blameless in your judgment</u>." [**Psalm 51:4 ESV**]

Historian Arnold Toynbee studied 26 of history's greatest civilizations. He concluded that no great civilization dies my murder; they die by suicide. The warning is inescapably clear.

> "The evil was not in bread and circuses (Roman government's efforts to appease the masses), per se, but in the willingness of the people to sell their rights as free men for full bellies and the excitement of games which would serve to distract them from the other human hungers which bread and circuses can never appease." **Marcus Cicero**

For now, God's wrath is restrained by His love—in general for everyone—in particular, eternal love for those who believe and commit wholly to Him—those who are saved! Spiritual gravity pulls towards hell because of man's fallen sinful nature. The Gospel provides the power to achieve escape velocity to reach the blessed destination of heaven.

> "The diminution of public virtue is usually attended with that of public happiness, and the public liberty will not long survive the total extinction of morals. 'The Roman Empire,' says the historian, 'must have sunk, though the Goths had not invaded it. Why? Because the Roman virtue was sunk.'" **Samuel Adams (1776)**

EXCESSIVE MATERIALISM CAUSED THE DEATH OF EVERY GREAT CIVILIZATION

Those who want to get rich fall into temptation and a trap and into many foolish and harmful desires that plunge people into ruin and destruction.
1 TIMOTHY 6:9 NIV

You shall not covet…anything that belongs to your neighbor.
EXODUS 20:17 NIV

There is no problem with working hard to provide for family and to enjoy nice things that are the fruit of the hard work. Actually, it is highly desirable to provide for the family's needs, some wants, and even a few luxury desires as the Lord enables. Serious problems arise when the excessive pursuit of material goods interferes with God's higher priorities. For example, consider, in order, life's highest priorities:

1. <u>Salvation</u>, a free gift from God that assures an eternity with Him.

2. <u>Growing and maturing in godly character</u>, a prerequisite for other priorities.

   *And Jesus increased in wisdom and in stature and in favor with God and man. [**Luke 2:52 ESV**] Now the young man Samuel continued to grow both in stature and in favor with the Lord and also with man. [**1 Samuel 2:26 ESV**] All Scripture is breathed out by God and profitable for teaching, for reproof, for correction, and for training in righteousness, that the man of God may be competent, equipped for every good work. [**2 Timothy 3:16-17 ESV**]*

3. <u>Selection of God's best for a spouse</u>, unless specifically called by God to lifetime singleness—marriage is a lifetime commitment, hence an extremely high priority.

4. <u>Having children, God's greatest gift to married believers</u>. The more children, the happier the believers.

   Behold, children are a heritage from the Lord, *the fruit of the womb a reward. Like arrows in the hand of a warrior are the children of one's youth. Blessed is the man who fills his quiver with them! He shall not be put to shame when he speaks with his enemies in the gate. [**Psalms 127:3-5 ESV**]*

5. <u>Raising children to become adults of strong godly character</u>. Since having children are God's greatest gift to parents—each is truly a miracle—their greatest responsibility is to raise the children to be humble, godly adults.

These commandments that I give you today are to be on your hearts. Impress them on your children. Talk about them when you sit at home and when you walk along the road, when you lie down and when you get up. Tie them as symbols on your hands and bind them on you foreheads. Write them on the doorframes of your houses and on your gates. **[Deuteronomy 6:6-9 NIV]** *Children, obey your parents in the Lord, for this is right. 'Honor your father and mother' (this is the first commandment with a promise), 'that it may go well with you and that you may live long in the land.' Fathers, do not provoke you children to anger, but bring them up in the discipline and instruction of the Lord.* **[Ephesians 6:1-4 ESV]** *Shepherd the flock of God (children) that is among you, exercising oversight, not under compulsion, but willingly, as God would have you; not for shameful gain, but eagerly; not domineering over those in your charge, but being examples to the flock.* **[1 Peter 5:2-3 ESV]**

Notice that the top five life priorities have nothing to do with career choice or chasing materialistic goals. Regretfully, many believers today routinely invest the best, most creative, and highest number of waking hours each day (quality AND quantity) for material gain at the expense of the five higher priorities. Wrong priorities for a day easily become wrong priorities for a lifetime. Career and excessive materialism are the _world's_ highest priorities, not suitable for the body of believers. *Come apart and be separate.* **[2 Corinthians 6:17 ESV]**

Excessive Materialism Caused the Death of Every Great Civilization

Obsessive runaway materialism facilitates the replacement of *God's wisdom* with *man's "wisdom,"* a condition fraught with undesirable consequences. The loss of God's wisdom produces 1) a progressive lack of self-control, 2) a denial of God and the spiritual realm in fact or in practice, and 3) a reduction of the beautiful range of emotions to the binary Hedonistic notion of seeking pleasure and avoiding pain.

In particular, excessive materialism consumes massive amounts of time. Further, it:

- Distracts from the joys of a personal relationship with God and godly pursuits
- Distracts from the joys of family as well as family obligations and responsibilities
- Becomes a false god in violation of the first of the Ten Commandments
- Reinforces pride, an even more powerful false god than materialism itself
- Weakens spiritual commitment
- Creates an excessive number of ethical and moral temptations
- Increases the frequency of sinful yielding to temptations by self and others
- Sets a poor example for family and others, a contagion that causes unnecessary temptations to ripple through many others

Collectively, a wide gateway opens, unleashing an aggressive pursuit of materialism to maximize perceived pleasure and physical security and to assure the least possible amount of pain. Interpersonal aggression mounts, because of eroding social values and the perception that time-consuming relationships hinder material pursuits. Civilizations die from terminal materialism-induced apathy which breaks down relationships, families, organizations, and ultimately nations.

Between a *total commitment to God* and a *total commitment to self* lies a spectrum of mixed commitments. Maturity is a measure of nearness to God, light, and love. God IS all three. Nearness to self is a measure of immaturity, extent of withdrawal from God, and default commitment to the darkness of sin and pride.

A *materialist* (most Americans today, including many believers) seeks to satisfy pride by personal gain and status. A *hedonist* (many Americans today) seeks to satisfy the body with lustful pleasures. Both are equally frivolous, risking their eternal souls. "*For what is a man profited, if he shall gain the whole world* (ultimate materialistic goal), *and lose his own soul? Or what shall a man give in exchange for his soul?*" [**Matthew 16:26 KJV**]

The futility and shallowness of excessive materialism is glaringly illustrated with every listing of the current year's celebrity deaths and moral failures that appears on the Internet. Excessive materialism repeatedly sells Christ for "twenty pieces of silver." "*Buy the truth and sell it not*; *also wisdom, and instruction, and understanding.*" [**Proverbs 23:23 KJV**] Jesus said, "I am…the truth…" [**John 14:6 ESV**]

> "The most fundamental fact of all is that the spiritual forces which have motivated our nation in its periods of greatness have been too frequently forgotten; we can see all too clearly the devastating effects of Secularism on our Christian way of life.

> The period when it was smart to 'debunk' our traditions undermined high standards of conduct.
>
> A rising emphasis on *materialism* caused a decline of 'God-centered' deeds and thoughts. The American home…ceased to be a school of moral and spiritual education…When spiritual guidance is at a low ebb, moral principles are in a state of deterioration.
>
> Secularism advances when men forget God. And it is in these periods that the godless tyranny of atheistic Communism (*or Socialism*) has made its greatest inroads" **J. Edgar Hoover,** Director of the FBI, introduction to Edward Elson's book, *America's Spiritual Recovery*, 1954 (parenthetical clarification added)

To God, earthly material things are worthless. His views are abundantly clear. *He who loves money will not be satisfied with money, nor he who loves wealth with his income; this also is vanity.* [**Ecclesiastes 5:10 ESV**]

And he (Jesus) said to them, "Take care, and be on your guard against all covetousness, for one's life does not consist in the abundance of his possessions." [**Luke 12:15 ESV**] They are major distractions that hinder men from coming to Him in whole or in part. He seems content to let unbelievers amass extraordinary wealth. It is temporary! **God lovingly and graciously limits the wealth of many believers because of the damage it causes to their relationship with Him and the relationships with others.**

Material wealth is often a great distraction from God. Lot's wife looked back the material things she loved [**Genesis 19:26**]. Becoming a pillar of salt was a tragic end, similar to the fate awaiting those who devote their lives to the unquenchable pursuit of excessive materialism. A man's heart may become as hard as a pillar of salt, a 21st Century Ebenezer Scrooge. It is a heart that shuts out the richness of interpersonal relationships and greatly hinders the richness of a relationship with God.

Excessive materialism is evil in part because of the massive amount of time it requires. It substantially limits the time available for more godly pursuits, especially interpersonal family relationships.

We MUST NOT continue to be wounded by excessive materialism. *Life's richness is in relationships, NOT in material riches.* Christian character produces unbounded *liberty*. I MUST use that liberty to consistently and conspicuously choose that which is good. The Hedonist (Humanist) longs for something more, but is often unable to identify the "something."

The American culture must NOT be allowed to die from the effects of excessive materialism. America may be in the winter of its captivity to materialism, but a great awakening is coming.

Compared to most around the world, Americans enjoy abundant prosperity. Yet, the prosperity itself is killing our culture, because prosperity distracts from God. Without His abundant graces no man can bear abundant prosperity. Paul wrote, "*I know how to abound.*" [**Philippians 4:12 KJV**] It is a divine lesson to know how to be full. It is impossible to learn and retain that lesson without God.

"Civilizations die from suicide, not by murder... So what does the universe look like? ...It looks as if everything were on the move either toward its Creator or away from Him. The course of human history consists of a series of encounters... in which each man or woman or child...is challenged by God to make the free choice between doing God's will and refusing to do it. When Man refuses, he is free to make his refusal and to take the consequences." ***Historian Arnold Joseph Toynbee***, *Study of History*, 1961

"It is not our duty to leave our children wealth, it is our duty to leave our children *Liberty*." ***Chaim Solomon*** – Financier of the American Revolution

"Have you ever found in history, one single example of a Nation thoroughly corrupted that was afterwards restored to virtue?...And without virtue, there can be no political liberty. Will you tell me how to prevent luxury from producing effeminacy, intoxication, extravagance, vice and folly...I believe no effort in favor of virtue is lost." Former ***President John Adams*** letter to Thomas Jefferson, 1819

Heritage Determines Destiny

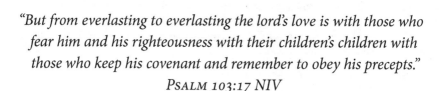

"But from everlasting to everlasting the lord's love is with those who fear him and his righteousness with their children's children with those who keep his covenant and remember to obey his precepts."
Psalm 103:17 NIV

Every culture has a cultural memory and a powerful cultural inertia that tends to persist unless confronted with overwhelming forces such as war or total economic collapse. Otherwise, change tends to occur very slowly over a long period of time. Understanding America's cultural foundation and history enables its strengthening and secures propagation to posterity.

Far too often, our ignorance of the past leads to our own spiritual impoverishment. "<u>The destiny of this country is inseparably bound up with loyalty to its national heritage …apart from faith in God the history of America has no meaning</u>. The greatest spiritual task that confronts us consists in interpreting for our time the meaning of the motto inscribed on each copper penny, *In God We Trust*, and in applying that interpretation to our national and international policy." **John A. Mackay** President, Princeton Theological Seminary in *Heritage and Destiny*, (1943)

A CULTURAL MEMORY IS AN ANCHOR AND FOUNDATION FOR SUSTAINING ANY CULTURE:

- Judeo-Christian culture
- Organizational culture
- Family culture
- Church culture
- National culture

America's most important cultural memory and anchor is its Judeo-Christian heritage and traditions.

THE BIBLE IS AMERICA'S ULTIMATE ANCHOR.

From a broader perspective, America's national culture is anchored in the traditional God-created, Bible-believing family. Both are stabilized by specific anchors in the past and anchors in the future.

> "For advantages so numerous and highly important it is our duty to unite in grateful acknowledgments to that *Omnipotent Being* from whom they are derived and in unceasing prayer that *He will endow us with virtue and strength to maintain and hand them down in their utmost purity to our latest* **posterity**." **President James Monroe**, 1817, First Annual Message to Congress

> "I am apt to believe that it [*Declaration of Independence*] will be celebrated by succeeding generations as the great anniversary festival. It ought to be commemorated, as the *Day of Deliverance* (parallel reference to deliverance ancient Israel), and by solemn acts of devotion to God Almighty. I am well aware of the toil and blood and treasure that it will cost to maintain this Declaration…Yet through all the gloom I can see the rays of ravishing light and glory…**Posterity** will triumph in that day's transaction, even though we may regret it, which I trust in God we shall not." **Founder John Adams** upon signing the *Declaration of Independence*, July 4, 1776

America's family culture

Figure 3: *Anchors that have stabilized the culture of America and the culture of the American family for over 400 years* demonstrate that the present stability of any family is largely due to multiple shared anchors in the past and future. The present reality arises from dynamic, complex interactions of the intellect, emotions, and spirit, as influenced by heritage anchors of the past and hoped for and expected anchors in the future.

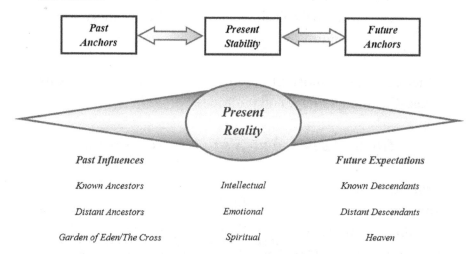

Figure 3: Anchors that have stabilized the culture of America and the culture of the American family for over 400 years.

Physical/intellectual satisfaction and comfort results from the aggregation of loving and respectful interpersonal relationships with immediate family members, known ancestors and known descendants. *Emotional well-being and a warm self-respect* is rooted in reverence for the sacrifices of ancestors from long ago generations and respect for distant future generations who may benefit from my sacrifices. Parents sometimes comment along the lines, "Don't ever forget that you are a (insert family name). Never do anything that would tarnish the family name." *Spiritual confidence* is anchored in God's love and graces from the Garden of Eden through Christ's atoning death on the cross, continuing through the present until we arrive at heaven.

Holding firmly to past and future anchors 1) stabilizes the present life (reality), 2) assures family cohesiveness, and 3) guarantees communication of godly virtues from generation to generation. However, unless jealously guarded and protected the hold on the anchors can weaken, even to the point of destroying relationships and breaking up families, leading to a chaotic, degraded, immoral national culture. Pride and materialism are the most powerful weakening agents.

We (I) MUST reach back to understand the lives, loves, and suffering of the saints and reach forward to envision our impact on future generations.

No need for an adopted son or daughter to miss out. They can claim the same anchors. After all, Jesus Christ was Himself adopted and when we repent and accept His saving grace, we are adopted into the family of God. As such, adoptees, especially young ones, grow up with the same network of anchors as naturally born children.

Contemporary families are often weakened by:

- Geographical separation in hot pursuit of materialistic goals
- Limitless ungodly temptations
- Lack of attention to spiritual priorities
- Interference from excessive time commitments outside the family
- Progressive isolation by modern technology

Both positive and negative choices are amplified through others and through time. Positive individual choices produce positive family choices leading to a culture that strengthens with time. "<u>But</u>

from everlasting to everlasting the lord's love is with those who fear him and his righteousness with their children's children with those who keep his covenant and remember to obey his precepts." [**Psalm 103:17 NIV**]

Negative individual choices produce weak, directionless families leading to a chaotic declining culture. *"...he punishes the children and their children for the sin of the fathers to the third and fourth generation."* [**Exodus 34:7b NIV**]

"Be careful to obey all these regulations I am giving you, so that it may always go well with you and your children after you, because you will be doing what is good and right in the eyes of the Lord your God." [**Deuteronomy 12:28 NIV**]

> "The contest in which the United States are engaged [War of 1812] appeals…to the sacred obligation *of transmitting…to future generations* that…which is held…. by the present from the goodness of Divine Providence." ***President James Madison***, May 25, 1813
>
> "We cannot read the history of our rise and development as a nation, without reckoning with the place the Bible has occupied in shaping the advances of the Republic…here we have been the truest and most consistent in obeying its precepts, we have attained the greatest measure of contentment and prosperity." ***President Franklin D. Roosevelt***, October 6, 1935

Without a godly time perspective, the "wisdom of age" does not make sense. Fragmented, primarily unbelieving, people dominated by intellectual influences see only the limitations of age. As people age, the importance of relationships increases and a sense of materialism decreases—that is more aligned with God's view and should be taught regularly, enthusiastically, and firmly, to the young. For the same reason, everyone living today needs routine intergenerational exposure and experience.

AFTER SALVATION, GOD ESTABLISHED THE FAMILY AS LIFE'S HIGHEST PRIORITY.

Why? The family IS the timeline between the Garden of Eden and the return of Messiah Jesus Christ. The family IS the place where children grow to become adults of strong godly character. The family IS the source of cultural stability throughout all generations. Consider God's portrait of the family.

God's Awesome Family Portrait

The traditional family is one of the most awesome, breathtaking, and vitally important of all of God's magnificent creations! Consider:

- God's portrait stabilizes and provides coherence to the family.
- The stabilized family builds stability and coherence into the culture (nation).
- A stable culture assures continuity of values across future generations.
- God's portrait facilitates growth of the God-ordained marriage partnership and family.
- Married people are happier (research supported).
- Married people are healthier (research supported).
- Family is life's boot camp for children, instilling values and guiding growth.
- Family-centered families—as opposed to career-centered "families," reduce crime.
- Family-centered families—as opposed to career-centered "families," reduce drug abuse.

- A loving family experience facilitates interpersonal relationships outside the family, enhancing the richness of career, hobby, volunteer, and recreational experiences.
- God's portrait enables family members to practice humility, forgiveness, mercy, longsuffering, and a servant's spirit in a nonthreatening environment.
- The family is an incubator for character development, for building God-ordained intellectual, emotional, and spiritual views and values.
- The positive character embedded in family members…parents and children…is carried to the outside community throughout life.
- Family members learn to overcome pride by serving other family members
- The family aligned with God's portrait ultimately leaves the greatest of all possible legacies.
- The family aligned with God's portrait is the married couple's gift back to God.

The driving passion for the family visualized in God's Portrait is the aggregate of:

1. Gratitude for the Lord's personally expressed infinite love.
2. Desire to express that gratitude by serving Him.
3. Desire to be a conduit of His love to succeeding generations by embedding His love and character in the next generation children.

Anything that erodes family culture undermines national culture, at first weakening it and ultimately annihilating it.

NO CULTURE HAS EVER SURVIVED THE BREAKDOWN OF THE FAMILY!

America's Amazing National Culture

The Founders intended to preserve the pre-existing colonial culture affirmed by the Great Awakening (~40 years; 1730s – 1770s). By the end of the Great Awakening, the Christian-based culture was nearly 170 years old. The primarily God-driven colonial culture largely exhibited godly virtues or at least people honestly striving for godly virtues. The Founders visualized a culture that:

- Was an aggregate of predominantly Christian families—recall that most descended from settlers who came to 1) escape religious persecution, 2) find, establish, and preserve religious and civil freedom, and 3) spread the message of the Bible and salvation
- Preserved God's redeemed line to provide salvation for as many people as possible. "*The Lord is not slow to fulfill his promise as some count slowness, but is patient toward you, not wishing that*

> "*If we and our posterity...live always in the fear of God and shall respect His Commandments...we may have the highest hopes of the future fortunes of our country.* But if we...neglect religious instruction and authority; violate the rules of eternal justice, trifle with the injunctions of morality and recklessly destroy the Constitution which holds us together, no man can tell how sudden a catastrophe may overwhelm us and bury all our glory in profound obscurity." **Senator Daniel Webster**, Addressing the New York Historical Society, 1852
>
> "We owe these blessings under Heaven to the Constitution and government...bequeathed to us by our fathers, and which *it is our **sacred** duty* to *transmit...to our children*." **President Millard Fillmore**, Annual Message, December 6, 1852

any should perish, but that all should reach repentance." [**2 Peter 3:9 ESV**]
- Assured <u>civil liberty</u> within which to exercise <u>religious liberty</u>, "to promote the knowledge and practice of true religion and virtue" [**President George Washington**,]
- Protected God-gifted freedom
- Proclaimed God's Word and plan of salvation

How did they do it? Answering the question requires a clarification of how to understand history.

History is what it is, the good, the bad, and the ugly. To be clearly understood by successive generations, history must be recorded and passed from generation to generation without being biased by historians, teachers, politicians, the media, or anyone else. "Those who fail to learn from history are doomed to repeat it." [**Sir Winston Churchill**, 1948 speech to the British House of Commons] Nevertheless, accurately recording and communicating history down through the ages is a virtually unattainable ideal, because of the inherent personal biases in every word, written or uttered.

The remedy is to avoid being beguiled by the experts' "interpretations of history." Otherwise, communication of the flow of history becomes a bit like the well-known party game where a story is told to the first person in a line of five. It is quietly passed through the line. By the time the fifth person tells the story, it is unrecognizable compared to the original version.

Of course, "scholarly" historians attempt to prevent such gross oral inaccuracies by performing so-called scholarly research. However, the historians tend to rely on quoting each other (often peers who know each other), creating an "official" version of groupthink, ratifying today's popular view of history.

How can people who have not devoted their lives to studying history deal with such an intellectual mess? The answer lies in forming opinions about historical figures based on exactly what they said, what they wrote, and what they did, recorded at that time, i.e. first person accounts. Avoid relying on modern interpretations. Even the original first person records must be understood in the context of the time in which they occurred.

For reference, modern sources of historical information should rely heavily on first person quotations and records with just enough background material to establish context for the quotations. Two modern historians use the quotations/minimal context approach superbly. They are David Barton, *Wallbuilders* and William Federer, *American Minute*. Both are prolific writers who have published many exciting books. Their books are easily found on the Internet.

Relying on the first person-primary source/minimal context-approach, reveals a fresh, wholesome view of the Founders that has not been taught in the public schools for a very long time. They were not "just Deists;" most were men of profound Christian faith. Of course, the Founders had faults and weaknesses like everyone else. "<u>My grace is sufficient for you, for my power is made perfect in weakness</u>." [**2 Corinthians 12:9 ESV**] However, those personal faults and weaknesses do not in any way detract from their astonishing, mind-boggling accomplishments. Overwhelming, first-person evidence confirms:

THE FOUNDERS WERE MEN OF UNCOMMON WISDOM, UNCOMMON KNOWLEDGE, UNCOMMON LOVE, UNCOMMON COURAGE, AND UNCOMMON COMMITMENT.

Such uncommon strength of character can only come from God. The Founders included many ministers and other leaders who might be called politicians today. Most were supported actively and eagerly by Christian wives with the same strength of character. They too are considered to be among the Founders. God's abundant blessings on the colonies and later the nation were readily visible and unmistakable.

Until recent decades, strength of character was prized in American culture. The wisdom of age was revered. Indeed, such character was valued and exhibited by most responsible leaders. However, the seeds of evil sown in the 19th Century sprouted in the first half of the 20th Century. The progressive influence of evil became alarmingly conspicuous in the last half of the 20th Century, continuing through the present time.

Vicious, Relentless and Aggressive Attacks on America's Culture

> *Because you did not serve the LORD your God with joyfulness and gladness of heart, because of the abundance of all things, therefore you shall serve your enemies* [external or internal] *whom the LORD will send against you, in hunger and thirst, in nakedness, and lacking everything. And he will put a yoke of iron on your neck until he has destroyed you.* [**Deuteronomy 28:47-48 ESV**]

Heritage Determines Destiny

A common view today is that religion and politics are separate, distinct, and mutually exclusive. Such a view is exactly the opposite of the view that has sustained the American culture for over 400 years. French diplomat, political scientist, and historian, Alexis de Tocqueville observed:

> On my arrival in the United States it was the religious aspect of the country that first struck my eye. As I prolonged my stay. I perceived the great political consequences that flowed from these new facts. Among us (Europeans), I had seen the spirit of religion and the spirit of freedom almost always move in contrary directions. Here, I found them united intimately with one another; they reigned together on the same soil…The Americans combine the notions of religion and liberty so intimately in their minds that it is impossible to make them conceive of one without the other… **<u>patriotism and religion</u>** *are the only two motives in the world which can permanently direct the whole of a body politic to one end.* **Alexis de Tocqueville** (1835 & 1840), *Democracy in America*

Forty years earlier, **Founder/First President George Washington** observed, "It is impossible to rightly govern a nation without God and the Bible." Further,

> *Of all the dispositions and habits which lead to political prosperity,* **Religion and Morality** *are indispensable supports.* In vain would that man claim the tribute of Patriotism who should labor to subvert these great Pillars…Let us with caution indulge

the supposition that morality can be maintained without religion. Reason and experience both forbid us to expect that national morality can prevail in exclusion of religious principle...***Morality is a necessary spring of popular government...<u>Who that is a sincere friend to it can look with indifference upon attempts to shake the foundation</u>?*** ***President George Washington***, Farewell Address, September 19, 1796

Political Parties

For most of American history, political parties championed different pathways to reaching the same or at least similar goals. Today, the two major political parties, *Republican* and *Democrat*, vigorously pursue opposite goals. The differences are so extreme that the parties have opposing definitions of good and evil. Each view themselves and their party as good and the other party as evil. Such uncompromising and mutually exclusive views render meaningful communication extremely difficult and significant compromise virtually impossible.

How did it happen? Both political parties have been seriously infected by the sin of pride and the world's "wisdom," to the extent that the terms, "Republican" and "Democrat" have largely lost their original meaning. Nevertheless, due to their prominence and significance, we must still find a way to use otherwise outdated labels.

Earthly wisdom is nothing more than man's efforts to flee from God—*slowly or quickly*—and to be "liberated" from all Biblical standards of behavior. The false liberation is achieved by denying the existence of God and trivializing the consequences of violating

God's standards. The clearest evidence, of Bible-flight, is the never ending succession of so-called liberation movements. Virtually all of them chase the mirage of painless or even supposed beneficial effects of a release from God's sacred limits.

Satan's greatest champions are those actively involved in the Humanist/liberal/progressive/ socialist/Marxist/globalist movement. All are rooted in the competition for power and control. The logic varies, but the end game is the same It is the most powerful effort to date, totally dedicated to targeting and destroying God-gifted freedom by destroying Judeo-Christian faith, the Bible, the Biblical family, the American founding documents, and the free enterprise economic system. In essence, they seek to destroy all the anchors that were designed to protect freedom.

The evil movement has taken over the media, public schools, much of higher education, the entertainment industry and virtually all of the *Democrat Party*. Until recently, the same movement had also taken over a large portion of the *Republican Party*, especially the party leadership in Washington, DC. Further development of the concept is in the chapter, *Politics is the Struggle to Protect and Promote God's Matchless Gift of Freedom*.

The diametrically opposing political views have come to be generally known as *conservatism* and *liberalism*. They are often discussed without reference to particular definitions, a practice frequently leading to confusion, misunderstanding, and conflict. For clarification, the definitions and differences are graphically displayed in Appendix III *Conservatism v. Liberalism*. Consider each, after noting this observation:

Freedom is a need of the soul, and nothing else. It is in striving toward God that the soul strives continually after a condition of freedom. God alone is the inciter and guarantor of freedom. He is the only guarantor. External freedom is only an aspect of interior freedom. Political freedom, as the Western world has known it, is only a political reading of the Bible. Religion and freedom are indivisible. Without freedom the soul dies. Without the soul there is no justification for freedom. **Whittaker Chambers**, [Journalist, author, former Communist defected to the West] (1952), *Witness*

Conservatism

Judeo-Christian believers understand that the Bible is the revealed words, desires, and commands of God. It is by far the strongest anchor for successful civilized life in the universe. Deviations from Scripture are considered as disobedience to God.

As believers, the Founders crafted the *Declaration of Independence* and the *United States Constitution* to preserve for posterity the God-gifted freedom, re-established by the Revolutionary War. Indeed, the river of God's grace flows through people. The same grace that inspired perfect Scripture substantively informed America's founding documents. Despite human weaknesses, the Founders exerted their very best efforts to align the founding documents with Biblical directives. The abundance of their own supplemental written materials and the continuity of materials written by their contemporaries and others for about two centuries clearly confirms their thought processes.

Consequently, public conservatism resists change to the founding documents except through the constitutional amendment process. In essence, the Bible and America's founding documents are rock solid anchors, because God's wisdom is much higher than man's wisdom and the Founders worked tirelessly to assure that America's founding documents were as consistent as possible with God's wisdom.

Liberalism

In the absence of God or in the weak belief of a distant, impersonal, disinterested god, or a not-always-readily-available god, liberal/progressive/socialist/Humanist/Marxist/globalists seek power—the more the better. It is the same manifestation of pride observed repeatedly throughout recorded history in virtually all cultures.

The current liberal view is that people must be "liberated" from the boundaries of Scripture and the limitations of the founding documents. The best known buzz words are "diversity," "inclusion," and "non-discrimination." Liberals seek maximum deviation from all the anchors. To do so, they must provide an alternative anchor(s). Although the word is not often heard, Humanism is the alternative, but mushy, anchor.

Humanism argues that—based on the theory of evolution—there is no god. Therefore, there is no such thing as objective truth and no universal set of values that applies to all people at all times. The result is that individuals actually or tacitly, by lifestyle, declare themselves to be their own god. In aggregate, the ultimate god becomes government or the head(s) of the federal government. Hence, they demand more and more power to control an increasing range of smaller and smaller issues. Unchecked, today's style of liberalism inevitably migrates to Socialism and eventually to total tyranny.

CONSERVATIVES STRIVE TO PRESERVE AND PROTECT INDIVIDUAL FREEDOM (DEMOCRACY/REPRESENTATIVE REPUBLIC), LIBERALS SEEK TO PRESERVE AND PROTECT THE STATE (SOCIALISM)

> Democracy (freedom) extends the sphere of individual freedom; Socialism (increasing government control) restricts it. Democracy attaches all possible value to each man; Socialism makes each man a mere agent, a mere number. Democracy and Socialism have nothing in common but one word: equality. **But notice the difference**: while <u>democracy seeks equality in liberty, socialism seeks equality in restraint and servitude</u>. **Alexis de Tocqueville**, *Democracy in America* (parenthetical clarifications added)

In short, conservatives champion and resist changes to Scriptural mandates and the founding documents, the *Declaration of Independence* and the *United States Constitution*. They are treated as sacred documents. Liberals in general seek "liberation" from all three as a means for replacing God's perfect wisdom with man's flawed "wisdom."

The political tug-of-war emerged in the 19th Century. Since people are driven by their deepest convictions, a change in spiritual attitude must precede a change in political action.

In America, early churches and church denominations tended to adhere as much as possible to Biblical authority. The first "liberation," catalyzed by the German "higher criticism" movement, exposed the Bible to human literary analysis like any other book, an activity that at least tacitly put man in the dangerous position of attempting to "judge" God. Rising doubts about the authority of Scripture encouraged, individuals, church leaders, and whole church denominations to gradually depart form the Biblical anchor. Liberal churches were born.

Perceived liberation from Biblical restraints set the stage for the second "liberation." Since Charles Darwin's theory of evolution appeared to have scientific support, it was embraced by many people. His theory spawned the idea that if life truly evolved, other areas of human thought should evolve as well. The principle triggered the evolution of sociology, psychology, philosophy, and the law. The notion of an evolving United States Constitution became inevitable.

> "Hold on, my friends, to the Constitution and to the Republic for which it stands. Miracles do not cluster, and what has happened once in 6000 years, may not happen again. Hold on to the Constitution, for *if the American Constitution should fail, there will be anarchy throughout the world.*" **Daniel Webster**

> "'*Religion-the Only Basis of Society:*' How powerless conscience would become without the belief of a God…Erase all thought and fear of God from a community, and selfishness and sensuality would absorb the whole man. Appetite, knowing no restraint…would trample in scorn on the restraints of human laws…Man would become…what the theory of atheism declares him to be-a companion for brutes.'" **William Eller Channing**, 1879, lesson in *McGuffey's 5th Eclectic Reader*

Liberal/Progressives claimed that the Constitution must evolve or change with the times. However, a "rubber" constitution is essentially no constitution at all. Today's prevailing liberal view is that the Constitution must change drastically, be summarily ignored, or entirely replaced.

Conservatives argue that any drift or "evolution" away from the Bible or away from the founding documents constitutes moving away from God and is therefore disobedience to God. The liberal argument is tantamount to raising the anchor on the ship of life, allowing the ship to drift aimlessly, directed only by competing winds of Humanistic visions.

Today, the liberal progressive movement is aggressively doing everything possible to eliminate America's cultural memory. Karl Marx has said, "Take away a people's roots, and they can easily be moved." Liberalism relentlessly strives for license rather than freedom. It works aggressively to remove all restraints from human behavior, especially moral behavior. Liberalism strives to be liberated from God's all-wise constraints expressed in His love letter, the Bible.

Liberalism, with unyielding persistence, seeks also to be liberated from the constraints of America's founding documents. Conflict would then be avoided by creating a mindless, robotic sameness masquerading as "equality." Of course, the artificial equality could only be established and maintained with a mind-numbingly, complex network of laws and regulations, vigorously and harshly enforced. Such is the very definition of tyranny which the Founders worked so fervently to avoid. "Government is not reason; it is not eloquence; it is force. Like fire, it is a dangerous servant and a fearful master." **George Washington**

All cultures need to be sustained by their heroes. Today, two major groups lead the charge to destroy America's Christian cultural memory and America's cultural heroes. The first is the liberal/progressive movement; the second is the Islamization of America.

For Islamists, destroying cultural memory is a worldwide practice with very deep historic roots, beginning with the origin of the Muslim religion. Eight types of cultural saturation jihad are detailed in Appendix IV, *What are the 8 Types of Jihad? Former Radical Muslim Explains*. The types include population jihad, media jihad, education jihad, economic jihad, physical jihad (violent force, war against infidels), legal jihad, humanitarian jihad, and political jihad.

So far, physical or violent jihad has been limited in the United States, because the pressure of political correctness is giving Muslims virtually everything they want without resorting to widespread massive violence. Unrestrained, the Sharia-dependent incremental jihad in America is a high-risk pathway leading to a tragic end.

Liberals and Islamists destroy historical artifacts, attempting to rewrite history. If Christians do not hold up Christian history for others to see, no one else will.

IF WE LOSE CHRISTIAN HISTORY OUR CULTURE WILL LOSE CHRISTIANITY AND COLLAPSE INTO CHAOS OR BE OVERTAKEN BY A TYRANNICAL LEADER.

> "The *titanic freedoms* which we once enjoyed [Bill of Rights, et.al.] have been cut loose from their Christian restraints and are becoming a force of destruction leading to chaos...*when the memory of the Christian consensus which gave us freedom within the biblical form is increasingly forgotten, a manipulating authoritarianism will tend to fill the vacuum.*" **Francis Schaeffer (1984)**

Forgiveness does not mean forgetfulness. Though, it is not

necessary to dwell on past sins—personal or cultural—we MUST learn from them.

Learning from the past, preserves the best, discards the worst, and strengthens the future, producing mature individuals and a mature culture. The American culture must learn from the past, not attempt to change or erase it. Learning from the past produces stability. Erasing the past leads to chaos. The past is an important and necessary foundation for the future. Just as an individual grows and matures—or not—a culture must grow and mature—or not. Neither can ever stand still and remain stable.

THE TRADITIONAL FAMILY IS GOD'S PLACE OF BUSINESS. AS THE FAMILY GOES, SO GOES THE INDIVIDUALS AND THE NATION

The liberal/progressive movement and Islamists seek similar goals, by attacking the traditional, American, Biblical family, attacking anyone or anything remotely tied to slavery, and attacking anything remotely related to the Bible.

"One of our great national dangers is ignorance of America's profound legacy of freedom. I firmly believe that ignorance is a threat to freedom." **Peter Lillback,** *President and Professor of Historical Theology and Church History at Westminster Theological Seminary.*

> "The most effective way to destroy people is to deny and obliterate their own understanding of their history." **George Orwell**
>
> "*Liberty* is traditional and conservative; it remembers its legends and its heroes. But *tyranny* is always young and seemingly innocent, and asks us to forget the past." **G.K. Chesterton**

Like the devil, Islamists, atheists, and liberal/progressive/Humanist/Marxist/socialist/

globalists endeavor to present themselves as enlightened "angels of light." "*And no wonder, for even Satan disguises himself as an angel of light. So it is no surprise if his servants, also, disguise themselves as servants of righteousness. Their end will correspond to their deeds.*" [**2 Corinthians 11:14-15 ESV**]

In so doing, they very professionally make anti-godliness attractive. There is no limit to the devil's disguises. He may work by negatively influencing a friend, co-worker, neighbor, spouse, or other family member. Subtle is powerful. "*Be sober, be vigilant; because our adversary the devil, as a roaring lion, walks about, seeking whom he may devour.*" [**1 Peter 5:8**]

An overemphasis on *knowledge* can actually hinder spiritual growth, because knowledge alone tends to focus on the physical world, becoming a barrier to faith. The schools have ceased teaching *wisdom* and today dwell on knowledge. The results are tragic.

By analogy, God had "chosen" America for special grace as long as Americans looked to God as the source of everything. "*How precious also are thy thoughts unto me, O God! How great is the sum of them!* [**Psalm 139:17**] As America has turned its back on God, God has increasingly withdrawn His grace. Like Nineveh turned following the preaching of Jonah, America must also turn (return). Pray for the greatest awakening ever.

Despite the extreme urgency demanded by the continuing decay of the American culture, there is still and astonishing silence among believers.

Astonishing Silence of Believers

But I have this against you that you have abandoned the love you had at first. Remember therefore from where you have fallen; repent, and do the works you did at first. If not, I will come to you and remove your lampstand from its place, unless you repent.
Revelation 2:4-5 ESV

All cultural problems have spiritual roots. No political action can ever resolve spiritual problems. Believers have and are the only solutions.

Believers ARE the conscience of the nation. The nation has no other conscience.

Believers have been enabled by the power of the Holy Spirit. They MUST NOT quench that power or that Spirit.

The three chapter-opening truths are undeniable; yet, most Christian believers continue to be astonishingly silent.

Furnace of Affliction

Isaiah, guided by the Spirit of God, said to the Israelite captives in Babylon, "*I have tried you in the furnace of affliction.*" [***Isaiah 48:10***] The contemporary American culture has declined to such an extent that the Christians find themselves in a strange land, tried in a modern furnace of affliction. But God's judgment is always tempered by mercy. His great love will prevail. Meanwhile, we MUST praise Him throughout the trial.

Today's *politically correct* culture of *tolerance* is specifically designed to tolerate all manner of sin and destroy both public liberty and Christian liberty. *Political correctness* is designed to shut down the Christian voice and message. A lie does not become the truth, wrong does not become right, and evil does not become good, just because it is accepted by a majority. *Political correctness* is intellectual terrorism. It is the children and grandchildren of the 1960s/70s hippies crying, "If it feels good, do it!"

Freedom of religion (conservative), the freedom to live an around-the-clock lifestyle of faith in God in ALL areas of life, as a way of life, is being reduced to *freedom of worship* (liberal), practice of religion limited to a very few specific times and places. *Political correctness* has effectively sequestered Christians to within the walls of their homes and inside the walls of their places of worship. Christians are being increasingly scorned and called hate groups.

Knowledge puffs pride even among the most devout believers. The puffery of knowledge is magnified in an unbelieving culture. The magnification reaches explosive thresholds when the Bible is removed from or forcefully contrasted with science. Science itself becomes a religion, especially in inexact sciences (historical geology and evolutionary biology) and pseudo-sciences (psychology and sociology). They are cloaked in scientific language but cannot satisfy the rigors of the scientific method of investigation. Perverted science becomes an excuse for a culture to abandon God.

Humanists (liberals/progressives) work tirelessly and relentlessly with a total commitment to achieving their goals, regardless of the cost. The absence of virtuous character, strong values, and objective truth facilitates any imaginable shortcut; honesty and integrity are not barriers. In the absence of truth, Humanists can only achieve their objectives by deception.

> "What is *liberty* without wisdom and without virtue? It is the greatest of all possible evils; for it is folly, vice, and madness, without restraint. Men are qualified for *civil liberty* in exact proportion to their disposition to put moral chains upon their own appetites; in proportion as they are disposed to listen to the counsels of the wise and good in preference to the flattery of knaves. *Society cannot exist unless a controlling power upon will and appetite be placed somewhere; and the less of it there is within, the more there must be without.* It is ordained in the eternal constitution of things, that men of intemperate minds cannot be free. Their passions forge their fetters." **Edmund Burke**, British Parliament, House of Commons, letter dated 1791

In contrast, *believers* are too often weak-kneed cowards who readily abandon their goals to avoid being called unkind names.

With the love of Jesus and the power of the Holy Spirit, we MUST fearlessly reclaim and proclaim His gospel, stand for all that is good and oppose all that is evil. **Abraham Lincoln** gave *political freedom* to American slaves; you and I MUST be vehicles for God's message of *spiritual freedom* from slavery to sin.

America today is reaping the painful harvest of the polluted seed sown decades ago. For centuries, America has been great, not because the people are great, but because God is great. As God is increasingly ignored or His existence rationalized away, His gracious hand of blessing is increasingly withdrawn.

ONLY GOD'S PEOPLE CAN ULTIMATELY RESTORE AMERICA'S GREATNESS.

Every great awakening began within the body of believers. "*For He said to Moses, I will have mercy on whom I will have mercy, and I will have compassion on whom I will have compassion.*" [**Romans 9:15**]

Jerry Newcombe, D.Min writes, "God is the source of our freedom—we have rights granted us by the Creator—but we forget this to our peril." (Appendix V, *The High Price of Forgetting God*). Newcombe added a series of quotations spanning American history acknowledging America's total and utter dependence upon God. Here are but two:

- **President Eisenhower** *(1955)*, "Without God, there could be no American form of Government, nor an American way of life. Recognition of the Supreme Being is the first—the most basic—expression of Americanism."

- **Ronald Reagan** *(August 23, 1974)*, "America needs God more than God needs America. If we ever forget that we are one nation under God, then we will be a nation gone under."

We are surrounded by evil. The war against evil and Satan never ends until Jesus casts Satan into the lake of fire. Whenever

Christians or the Church become spiritually slothful, evil wins by default. WE MUST NEVER slow or stop fighting the battle. Helped by the power of the Holy Spirit, we will endure. "*Michael and his angels fought against the dragon; and the dragon fought against his angels.*" [**Revelation 12:7**]

> "The *Declaration of Independence* gave *liberty* not alone to the people of this country, but *hope to all the world for all future time*. It was that which gave promise that in due time the weights would be lifted from the shoulders of all men, and that all should have an equal chance…This is the sentiment embodied in the *Declaration of Independence*…I would rather be assassinated on this sport than surrender it." **President Abraham Lincoln**, February 22, 1861 at Independence Hall, Philadelphia, Pennsylvania
>
> "In giving freedom to the slave, we assure freedom to the free…*We shall nobly save-or meanly lose-the last, best hope of earth*. Other means may succeed; this could not fail. The way is plain…a way which if followed the world will forever applaud and God must forever bless." **President Abraham Lincoln**, December 1, 1862, Second Annual Message

Terminal Apathy

As a group, Christians are being increasingly hated in America. But most fly under the radar by refusing to bear Christ's cross and take a stand. We MUST NOT be among them.

> "Beloved in the Lord, your most dangerous and formidable enemies are the kind of men who render vice mixed with apparent virtue, and clothe wickedness in the apparel of righteousness…They paint black, white; and the white they convert into black. Not content with seeming what they are not, they labor to make you what they are. Righteousness and wickedness they interweave artfully, capable of deceiving the very elect…" **George Whitehead,**

leading evangelist of the *First Great Awakening* that powered the American Revolution.

Modern examples of dangers abound:

- So-called exceptions to abortion prohibition
- Entire LGBT agenda
- Same sex "marriage"
- Multiculturalism
- Radical feminism

Worldly-mindedness is slaying the body of believers in America. *Worldly-mindedness devours the precious resource of time weakening and destroying relationships, vertical with God and horizontal with others.* Individual material things are not sinful, but their obsessive accumulation drains character.

> "Woe to those who call evil good and good evil, who put darkness for light and light for darkness, who put bitter for sweet and sweet for bitter!"
> [*Isaiah 5:20 ESV*]

Today, the church is walking the path toward its Jerusalem. The church is bearing the cross of Christ as the church is increasingly mocked, scorned, and counted as alien by the culture of unbelievers. But in the midst of persecution, "*There is a river whose streams make glad the city of God.*" [***Psalm 46:4 ESV***] As individual believers, we MUST willingly and publically bear Christ's cross.

For many today, God's love and gospel are not being handed down to subsequent generations, because in the modern American culture God's love and gospel have lost their preciousness, and lost urgency. How can today's children tell the next generation anything? To many Christian families the extent of *family religion* is having "roast preacher" on the way to Sunday lunch. Many pastors are losing relevance by not directly attacking cultural issues. If the pastors 50 years ago could have foreseen today's American culture, they would have preached on the family with far greater urgency and far more often.

The *traditional family* and *institution of marriage* are under relentless and ferocious attack. Together they are the bedrock of American culture. Yet most believers are unable to articulate, advocate, and defend them. Nor are they able to cast a godly informed vote.

Get in the Battle!

Actions speak far louder than words. *Actions, based on Scripture,*

- Scream in an amplified voice far louder than words could ever express.
- Influence many beyond our immediate awareness.

When a culture deteriorates, salacious rumors speak louder than actions, because the conscience, honesty, and integrity of the speaker and hearer have been weakened, unless one or both are believers.

"The only thing necessary for evil to triumph is for good men to do nothing." **Edmund Burke**, a member of the British Parliament who defended the rights of the American Colonies.

> "We have no government armed with power capable of contending with human passions unbridled by morality and religion. Avarice, ambition, revenge, or gallantry, would break the strongest cords of our Constitution as a whale goes through a net. *Our Constitution was made only for a moral and religious people. It is wholly inadequate to the government of any other.*" **John Adams, Founder/President**

God continually trimmed fighting forces, of the ancient Israelites, to reveal Himself and His strength (power). "*For my strength is made perfect in weakness*." [**2 Corinthians 12:9**] America's fighting forces from the earliest days through Korea prevailed, because they relied on the power of God. Military conflicts from Viet Nam forward have been reduced to political forays without clear definable endpoint objectives. Nevertheless, God still reveals Himself and His strength through individuals and small groups of individuals.

Today, the Church is in deep and severe trouble. The body of believers, for decades, has first accepted and then endorsed a series of thousands of incremental compromises and accommodations. Now, many believers are blind to the truths and the power of Scripture. Nevertheless, God always has His four carpenters:

> "Where is the clear voice speaking to the crucial issues of the day with distinctively biblical, Christian answers?...a large segment of the evangelical world has become seduced by the world spirit of this present age...we can expect the future to be a further disaster if the evangelical world does not take a stand for biblical truth and morality in the full spectrum of life. *For the evangelical accommodation to the world of our age represents the removal of the last barrier against the breakdown of our culture.*"
> *Francis Schaeffer (1984)*

- God will always find men for His work.
- He will find enough men.
- He will find the right men
- He will find them at the right time.

"*And the Lord showed me four carpenters*." [**Zechariah 1:20**] The Lord shall get the victory. We MUST be faithful to Christ. At the right time, He will raise a defense for us. We must continue praying for the greatest awakening of all time.

Do It Now!

The decline of the faithful is relentless and sure unless the faithful are intentionally and continuously girded with the WHOLE armor of God and filled with the Holy Spirit.

BELIEVERS MUST ACTIVELY FIGHT THE GODLY FIGHT OR THEY WILL PASSIVELY SUCCUMB TO SATAN'S DELUSIONS.

If believers fail to actively fight, they will become:

1. Less affected with their present and past sins
2. Less conscientious with respect to future sins
3. Less moved with warnings and cautions of God's Word or His chastisements
4. More careless of the frame of their hearts
5. Less quick sighted to discern what is sinful, and
6. Less afraid of the appearance of evil.

The gap between the natural man and the spiritual man is enormous. But the enormity of the gap becomes *less visible* and difficult to perceive when believers hide God's spectacularly wonderful grace. The gap becomes *more visible* when believers exhibit God's grace in their daily lives. A clear appreciation of the enormity of the gap attracts more souls to Christ.

God loves the humble. The world scoffs and often attempts to take unreasonable and excessive advantage of the humble, who are seen as weak. God loves the humble, because they are most open to learning, growing, and serving God and others. The opposite of humility is pride. Pride demands attention to self and is a barrier to learning virtue, growth, and service. Humility is godly; pride is satanic.

THE WAR BETWEEN GOOD AND EVIL IS FOUGHT 1) IN THE SOUL AND 2) IN THE CULTURE AS WELL AS 3) IN THE HEAVENLY PLACES.

> "*Finally, be strong in the Lord and in the strength of his might. Put on the WHOLE armor of God that you may be able to stand against the schemes of the devil. For we do not wrestle against flesh and blood, but against the rulers, against the authorities, against the cosmic powers over this present darkness, against the spiritual forces of evil in the heavenly places.*"
> [***Ephesians 6:10-12 ESV***]

We see God everywhere in the *Book of Nature* as well as in the *Book of Revelation* (Bible). His love and purity are in the rose and the snow white lily. His infinite joy and benignity are in the green trees and the song of the birds. His favor, grace, and beauty are in the crystal river and murmuring streams. His goodness and glory are in the brightness of the Sun, the golden edges of evening clouds and beautiful rainbow that spans the heavens. Wow! We have no excuse for not seeing God everywhere, in addition to His Holy Word.

An abundant Christian life manifesting readily visible spiritual fruit ["…*love, joy, peace, patience, kindness, goodness, faithfulness…*" (***Galatians 5:22 ESV***)] tends to abate the prejudice of the unbelievers toward the believer. At that point, the heart and spirit of the unbeliever may be open to the plan of salvation. A believer without readily visible fruit will be offensive to the unbeliever.

Scripture says, "*Render to Caesar the things that are Caesar's, and to God the things that are God's.*" [**Mark 13:17 KJV**] Caesar (the government) can confiscate all of my material possessions as excessive taxes, but:

§   **The institution of Marriage** was created by God millennia before man's creation of the American government. *Marriage belongs to God, not Caesar*! The government is NOT free to redefine marriage.

§   **The institution of the Family** was created by God millennia before man's creation of the American government. *The family belongs to God, not Caesar*! The government is NOT free to redefine the family.

§   **Life** was created and given by God millennia before man's creation of the American government. *Life belongs to God not Caesar*. The government is NOT free to redefine or exterminate life, except for capital punishment as prescribed by God.

§   **Freedom** was given by God millennia before man's creation of the American government. *Freedom is an incredible gift from God, not a piecemeal grant from Caesar*. The government is NOT free to restrict freedom beyond Biblical restrictions that come from God. *Freedom belong to God not Caesar*.

Believers should have no problem rendering unto Caesar that which is Caesar's, recognizing that ultimately very little belongs to Caesar. Believers must be willing to exert whatever effort is necessary to defend that which is God's and prohibit takeover by the government. We owe that much to God, to our children, to our grandchildren, and to our great grandchildren and on to posterity.

Otherwise, the iniquity (sins of omission or commission) of the fathers will be visited, "*upon the children unto the third and fourth generation*" [**Numbers 14:18 KJV**] and "*Let the iniquity of his fathers be remembered with the LORD; and let not the sin of his mother be blotted out.*" [**Psalm 109:14 KJV**] Are YOU willing to allow your **sins of neglect** to be passed on to the next three or four generations?

> "If ye love wealth greater than liberty, the tranquility of servitude greater than the animating contest for freedom, go home and leave us in peace. We seek not your council, nor your arms. Crouch down and lick the hand that feeds you; and may posterity forget that ye were our country men."
> **Samuel Adams**

I WILL NOT RENDER UNTO CAESAR THAT WHICH IS GOD'S

Jesus has already won the battle. We MUST visibly, lovingly, and frequently shout the victory. We ARE the light of the world—NOW, not someday.

The body of believers has always impacted their surrounding culture to an extent far greater than their numbers. It is unlikely that conservative believers have ever been a majority in the United States. Yet, the culture was largely driven by Judeo-Christian tradition and values for over 400 years. *Today, our light is dim and we have lost our saltiness*. In recent decades, the body of believers has negatively impacted the American culture, often by neglect. It is way past time to turn that negative impact into a lasting positive impact. The Master expects it! We owe it!

MARRIAGE, FAMILY, LIFE, AND FREEDOM ARE ALL EXTRAORDINARY GIFTS FROM GOD.

God would reasonably expect believers to respect, value, treasure, protect and defend those gifts for now and posterity (future generations).

One day, He will ask each believer, "**What did YOU do with my gifts?**" Will we be excited about sharing our love and protection of His awesome, incomparable gifts? Or will we hang our heads in shame as we feebly attempt to explain that we were so addicted to material and other self-indulgent pursuits that we allowed His precious gifts to be squandered or taken from us without a whimper?

America's founding documents, *The Declaration of Independence* and *The Constitution of the United States*, considered together, were written in their entirety to preserve, protect, and guarantee personal freedom in the broadest sense and religious freedom in a special sense. The founding package was and is unique in all of recorded history. It was designed to protect the people and their God-given gifts from a potentially runaway government. Reducing an understanding of the Founders intentions as expressed in those documents to a mere discussion of the First Amendment or even the Bill of Rights (the first ten amendments) is a monumental distortion of America's governing principles.

Today, the founding documents are continually undermined by public ignorance, apathy, and indifference enabling a government that increasingly ignores the Constitution and its strict boundaries.

> "There is no nation on earth powerful enough to accomplish our overthrow. Our destruction, should it come at all, will be from another quarter. From the inattention of the people to the concerns of their government, from their carelessness and negligence. I must confess that I do apprehend some danger. I fear that they may place too implicit a confidence in their public servants and fail properly to scrutinize their conduct; that in this way they may be made the dupes of designing men and become the instruments of their own undoing... *Hold on, my friends, to the Constitution and to the Republic for which it stands. Miracles do not cluster, and what has happened once in 6000 years, may not happen again. Hold on to the Constitution, for if the American Constitution should fail, there will be anarchy throughout the world."* **Daniel Webster**

Are YOU willing to do whatever is necessary to restore and protect our God-endowed "unalienable Rights that among these are Life, Liberty, and the Pursuit of Happiness?" Or will YOU merely slip back into your materialistic, self-indulgent slumber after reading this statement? We cannot remain silent any longer.

Cultural Impact of Liberal Churches

―――――≈―――――

But false prophets also arose among the people, just as there will be false teachers among you, who will secretly bring in destructive heresies, even denying the Master who bought them, bringing upon themselves swift destruction.

2 Peter 2:1 ESV

My salvation is secure. I was saved many years ago. But today, many people practice the protocols of religion, with a false sense of security. Those in liberal churches, especially have been "vaccinated with a small dose of Christianity." Their confidence is increased by pooling their false sense of security. Tragically, an increasing number of evangelicals are experiencing the same vaccination. We MUST speak out!

> "Destructive higher criticism of the Bible became the dominant approach among the theologians at the close of the nineteenth century and during the early twentieth century. When joined with naturalistic evolution, it produced liberalism...It [liberalism] accommodated Christianity to modern scientific naturalism...whenever objections arose on the details of the Christian religion." **Harold J. Ockenga**, in Kenneth S. Kantzer, ed., *Evangelical Roots: A Tribute to Wilbur Smith* (1978), from Francis Schaeffer's book *The Great Evangelical Disaster* (1984).

Degeneracy throughout the Christian world is wrought by men intellectually drawn to the ministry without first experiencing the new birth. A degenerate minister produces degenerate lukewarm sheep, vulnerable to all manner of evil, even appearing to put God's stamp of approval on sin. *Indeed, the sin of lukewarmness is also spreading through evangelical churches* as well. . "<u>I know your works: you are neither cold nor hot. Would that you were either cold or hot! So, because you are lukewarm, and neither hot nor cold, I will spit you out of my mouth. For you say, 'I am rich, I have prospered, and I need nothing, not realizing that you are wretched, pitiable, poor, blind, and naked.</u>'" [**Revelation 3:15-17 ESV**]

Driven by the pride of man, denominations are created over divisions of doctrine. Yet, Jesus had little to say about doctrine. Large numbers of splintered denominations become targets of the devil and all manner of atheistic movements (liberal, progressive, Humanist, Marxist, socialist, globalist) who routinely ridicule Christianity for its widespread internal dissension. *The most liberal churches are called upon to endorse sin under the guise of "tolerance" and "inclusion."*

Unconverted, mainly liberal, ministers are a treacherous bridge or segue between saints and sinners. <u>Unconverted or lapsed ministers</u> appear to sanctify Satan's causes by cloaking sin with the garb of the Bible. Such messages weaken the faith of individuals and break the cohesiveness of cultures by

> "The central theme of contemporary theology is accommodation to modernity. It is the underlying motive that unites the seemingly vast differences between existential theology, process theology, liberation theology, demythologization, and many varieties of liberal theology—all are searching for some more compatible adjustment to modernity. The spirit of accommodation has… [led to] the steady deterioration of a hundred years and the disaster of the last two decades…" ***Thomas C. Oden**, Agenda for Theology: Recovering Christian Roots* (1979), from Francis Schaeffer's book *The Great Evangelical Disaster* (1984).]

making sin acceptable, desirable, and then noble. Many liberal preachers are not saved themselves. They have an intellectual, but not soulful attraction to God. To them, religion is a discipline of study, like philosophy, psychology, or sociology, rather than a personal relationship with the Creator.

The false testimony of religious liberals is far more dangerous than the religious scorn of atheists. The mockery of atheists is clear and easily avoided or ignored by believers. However, the deceit of religious liberals and liberal-leaning evangelicals is subtle and grossly misleading. The deceit sugar coats sin. It appears to put God's stamp of approval on sin. It distracts and weakens the faith of sincere believers. It weakens or neutralized their testimony.

"Christian" liberalism and political liberalism are inextricably intertwined. Both are manifestations of racing away from God at the breakneck speed of compromise, accommodation, and outright rebellion, driven by increasingly unhindered pride.

In early centuries, the (Catholic) Church of Rome camouflaged the gospel. Today, liberal protestant denominations do the same. The outward form of religion permeates liberal churches. Sadly, it is rapidly encroaching on conservative churches. There are two types of unsaved sinners.

1. Those who outwardly ignore or mock the Lord
2. Those who wrap their sinful lifestyle in a cloak of religion.

The deception of the latter may attract greater wrath from God than the former, because the deception influences many people to follow the deceiver down the wrong path away from a personal relationship with god and away from salvation.

Many churches today attempt to teach mercy without misery. Our sin nature resulted from God's wrath, a wrath that stays with us until salvation.

Humanists and liberal/progressives are the true haters of all truth. They argue that because—in their mind—there is no god, there can be no objective truth. In bright contrast, Jesus said, "*I am…the truth*," [**John 14:6 ESV**] since many unbelievers have denied the very existence of truth, they can only achieve their objectives by deception. Regretfully, when the adversaries of Christ are *outside* the church, most <u>believers are silent</u>. When the adversaries of Christ are *inside* the church, many <u>believers are compliant</u>.

God grants mercy as a sovereign. But as a judge, justice must be satisfied. In His great mercy, He lived among us in the form of Jesus who took upon Himself God's great wrath on the cross to pay the price for my sins, your sins, and the sins of all mankind. God has extended His infinite mercy to us and He has experienced infinite pain for us. We are and MUST be His in every way. We MUST NOT be distracted by liberal platitudes.

> "The accommodate to the world spirit about us in our age is the most gross form of worldliness in the proper definition of the word…in general the evangelical establishment has been accommodating…in the most basic sense, the evangelical establishment has become deeply worldly." **Francis Schaeffer**, *The Great Evangelical Disaster (1984)*

Unbelievers are deluded by the world. "Liberal" Christians may be the most deluded of all. The late **Howard Hendricks** [Dallas Theological Seminary] was fond of saying, "One of Satan's most powerful weapons is to vaccinate people with a small dose of

Christianity." Satisfied with the occasional Sunday dose, they settle for far less than God's best and may even miss salvation altogether.

Though earthly circumstances may change, the anchors are permanent. God's country, America, is in decline. Nevertheless, God is faithful. He is with His elect people.

The Bible-driven church, beginning with you and me, must lead the way. Satan uses liberal churches to ratify ungodly liberal politics. "...*<u>Foreigners have come into the holy places of the Lord's house</u>*." **[*Jeremiah 51:51 ESV*]**

The modern conservative church is enamored by God's love but tragically neglects God's wrath. Lack of respect for God's wrath produces complacency.

Cultural Danger of "Christian" Hypocrites

For such persons do not serve our Lord Christ, but their own appetites, and by smooth talk and flattery they deceive the hearts of the naive.
ROMANS 16:18 ESV

False conversions abound among people that try to be good, give up certain vices or turn from scorners to supporters of religious activities. To a culture, false conversions can be more dangerous than atheism.

ATHEISM TYPICALLY AFFECTS ONE PERSON, BUT EACH FALSE CONVERSION LEADS MANY OTHERS DOWN THE SAME PATH.

The saved man must be visibly different than the unregenerate one. Today, much of the body of believers has been reduced to a weekly activity (church), rather than an intimate Christian lifestyle that permeates all of life.

Peace and prosperity breed large numbers of nominal Christians who enjoy the camaraderie of the Christian club (church). How pleasant it is to participate in a weekly service and perhaps a few other churchy activities. But they lack love; they have not learned to really love Jesus; they have not learned to really serve others. Why? In part because they and others around them have not had their faith challenged by severe hardship. Low key Christianity is a poor imitation of the real thing. Unchallenged believers become careless with their faith and with the condition of their souls.

Scriptural knowledge is but a beginning. Meditation drives, knowledge deep into the soul and transforms a man into the character likeness of Christ. Regretfully, many American believers today lack even rudimentary knowledge of their own faith, much less the practice of meditation.

There are many unbelievers in church who not only deceive themselves, but influence true believers to compromise. With abundant clarity, Scripture declares the difference between believers and unbelievers. ***The most dangerous people today are those who profess belief as head knowledge, but do not have Jesus in their heart (soul-deep).*** They are outwardly, "churchy," but lead individuals astray and cultures into decline, because they appear to stamp God's imprimatur on compromised or sinful behavior.

> **CULTURAL DECAY, THE DRIFT AWAY FROM GOD, IS SPREAD BY INCREMENTAL ACCOMMODATIONS AND COMPROMISES AMONG THE CLERGY, WHICH BECOME AMPLIFIED AMONG THE PEOPLE.**

That is one reason why committed national Christian leaders have so much difficulty getting support from local clergy. When

Christians compromise, the compromise—appearing to have the church's sanction—spreads rapidly throughout the culture. It becomes a self-reinforcing form of Christian groupthink.

America is filled with the "form of religion." People follow church practices but do not feel the weight of their own sins that drive them to true conversion. An overdose of *political correctness* has silenced far too many believers and severely compromised their cultural impact.

Charles Spurgeon warned of "*the iniquity of holy things*," [***Exodus 28:38***] in his day. The shallowness of public worship then was much like the *shallowness of public worship* today. It reeks with hypocrisy, formality, lukewarmness, irreverence, and wandering of heart. Our work

> "The accommodate to the world spirit about us in our age is the most gross form of worldliness in the proper definition of the word...in general the evangelical establishment has been accommodating...in the most basic sense, the evangelical establishment has become deeply worldly." ***Francis Schaeffer***, *The Great Evangelical Disaster (1984)*

for the Lord is full of carelessness, selfishness, and unbelief. Our personal devotions are lax, cold, neglected, and vain. What a mass of defilement! Fortunately, when Jesus presents fully surrendered, committed, believers before His Father, Jesus presents His own holiness, rather than their unholiness.

I MUST NOT be discouraged by the evening wolves of doubt and discouragement, especially after a hard frustrating day. "*Evening wolves.*" [***Habakkuk 1:8***]

Weak believers are most vulnerable to false teachers, especially when they masquerade as ministers, purveyors of the light.

"Christian" hypocrites are like evening wolves deceiving other believers by mixing truth with a drop of deceit or compromise.

MORE DESPERATE THAN THE HONEST UNBELIEVER IS THE ONE WHO FALSELY PROFESSES TO BE A BELIEVER IN CHURCH, BUT EMBRACES THE EVILS OF THE WORLD ELSEWHERE.

Throughout history people have tried to live both ways. They wanted to worship God at prescribed times and places and later worship all manner of false idols. Not limited to statues of false gods, today's false idols include excessive devotion to materialism, career, or anything that distracts from God's purpose or mission. "*I will cut off them that worship and that swear by the Lord, and that swear by Malcham* (and idol of Moabites and Ammonites or their king)." [***Zephaniah 1:5***]

Lord Jesus, you are my God—the only God. Protect me from any and all false gods

Today, many believers ignore heaven or at least take it for granted. Yet, heaven is our ultimate home. It is the magnet that attracts, or should attract, the heart. Heaven's great attraction must motivate believers to lead the most righteous, holy life possible.

Some things never change. Today, believers sometime lose their first love, returning to pre-salvation habits and living patterns. The ease of divorce from spouse establishes a temporal pattern that enables a relentless drift or separation from God—the divorce must be rationalized. In so doing, pride is inflated. It is impossible to divorce without also weakening one's relationship with God. Divorce, at least temporarily, stops (blocks) Christian growth.

Hypocrites who do the "church thing," attend regularly, pretend to pray to Him, sing His praises, and hear His Word are no better than Judas. Jesus was betrayed by a kiss from Judas. Similarly, the Church (bride of Jesus) is betrayed by a kiss of brief attention by the hypocrite. ***The "kiss" of slight attention marks the Church for ridicule by unbelievers (neighborhood, co-workers, media, politicians, and entertainment figures).*** The scoffers themselves may well be on their way to hell, while doing their best to destroy the Church. Lord, help me to never be a hypocrite in thought or in deed.

Moment of self-reflection: If I serve God only when I am in good company or when religion is profitable and respectable, I am a hypocrite. If I "love the Lord" only when His blessings are tangible, and comfortable, I am a hypocrite. However, if I truly love the Lord during adverse circumstances, my love is true. Lord, help me to love you always because you are love. What begins in hypocrisy ends in apostasy! "*Can the rush grow up without mire?*" [***Job 8:11***]

The modern *multiculturalism* movement became possible only after the American culture was weakened, i.e. drifted from faith in God. Every culture is driven by its deepest religious (spiritual) convictions. Mixing cultures inevitably commingles religions and produces individual conflict just as historically it has produced conflict among nations. The superficial politically correct imposition of un-bounded "tolerance" simply allows conflict to fester and erupt at a later time. Consider that Christianity and Islam are diametrically opposed. The unholy alliance between Islam and the liberal/progressive movement is temporary, for a time holding a major eruption of Islam at arm's length.

Remember that ancient Israel accepted "strangers" in their midst only when they agreed to worship the God of Abraham, Isaac, and Jacob. Widespread deviations commingled cultures, promoted the worship of false idols, and resulted in common interfaith marriages. The price was high. The children of Israel engaged in their own civil war, splitting into the kingdoms of Judah and Israel. Both were eventually carried into captivity. Lasting peace and blessedness only comes after accepting Christ's offer of a personal relationship with Him.

Assimilators, immigrants, must seek a common identity with a new culture. The common identity begins with God. Everything else in the culture flows from God. Many contemporary immigrants to the United States reject assimilation, at least tacitly, thereby rejecting order which leads to increasing chaos. Immigrating Muslims are one of the most visible groups who reject assimilation. Consider Appendix IV, <u>What are the 8 Typed of Jihad? Former Radical Muslim Explains.</u>

The Israelites survived 40 years in God's *natural wilderness*. Today's Baby Boomers chose their *spiritual wilderness* in which they have wandered for 40 years. They have produced the tragic "fruit" of disobedience (rebellion against God), including high crime rates, commonplace abortion, sharp increase in drug abuse, mainstreamed unwed motherhood and single parent "families," endorsed easy divorce, spawned effectively feral children raised by "strangers" (endless round of day care and baby sitters), substantially increased cultural anxiety and incivility, produced many broken relationships, and continually seek for partial fulfillment of spiritual needs by anything other than God (meaning in career, affinity groups or pagan religions).

By the power of the Holy Spirit, Judeo-Christian believers MUST recover God's precious gifts. They must become much more aware of their own relationship with God and increasingly aware of the politics in which they—like it or not—are immersed. They must talk about politics frequently and cast their precious and sacred vote wisely.

Politics is the Struggle to Protect & Promote God's Matchless Gift of Freedom

But he who looks into the perfect law of liberty and continues in it, and is not a forgetful hearer but a doer of the work, this one will be blessed in what he does.
JAMES 1:25 NKJV

Thomas Jefferson codified the "pursuit of happiness" in the American Declaration of Independence as an unalienable right (truth), "endowed by our Creator." That Declaration honored and proclaimed to the world an ironclad commitment to the original announcement of the gospel, "peace on earth" and "good will toward men"

> *"I regard it (U.S. Constitution) as the work of the purest patriots and wisest statesmen that ever existed, aided by the smiles of a benignant Providence;* for when we regard it as a system of government growing out of discordant opinions and conflicting interests of thirteen independent States, it almost appears a Divine interposition in our behalf...*The hand that destroys the Constitution rends our Union asunder forever."* Danial Webster, U.S. Senator

"Can two walk together, except they be agreed?" [**Amos 3:3**]—Applies to all relationships including political ones.

They (believers) shall:

- All be near to Christ,
- All ravished with His love,
- All eating and drinking at the table with Him,
- All equally beloved as His favorites and friends even if not all equally rewarded as servants.

Such is the spiritual root of American free enterprise and culture: equal opportunity (love), unequal outcomes (rewards). Here the free market rewards. There (heaven), Jesus rewards (crowns).

Believers have been adopted into the family of God and have become part of the bride of Christ. Heaven is their home. The anticipation is the foundation of their deep-seated joy now in good times and bad. The "pursuit of happiness" cited in the *Declaration of Independence* is the pursuit of God; it is the pursuit of holiness; it is the pursuit of godly character, utterly free from any government interference. It is a gift from God. *"Happy are you, O Israel; who is like unto thee, O people saved by the Lord!"* [**Deuteronomy 33:29**]

> "If religious books are not widely circulated among the masses in this country, I do not know what is going to become of us as a nation. ***If truth be not diffused, error will be***; if God and His Word are not known and received, the devil and his works will gain the ascendancy; If the evangelical volume does not reach every hamlet, the pages of a corrupt and licentious literature will; if the power of the Gospel is not felt throughout the length and breadth of the land, anarchy and misrule, degradation and misery, corruption and darkness will reign without mitigation or end." ***Danial Webster***

> "The known propensity of a democracy is to licentiousness which the...ignorant believe to be *liberty*." ***Fisher Ames***, January 1788"

THE NUCLEUS OF CIVILIZATION AND ANY CULTURE IS THE FAMILY.

Therefore, politics begins with the family. The family is strong and stable to the extent that it is the MOST LOCAL church. Our families MUST always be a church. It is the most visible and powerful evidence of God's love and the ultimate forgiveness provided by the ultimate sacrifice of Jesus Christ. "<u>The Church in your house</u>." [***Philemon 1:2 ESV***] More is expected of a Church than of an ordinary household:

- *Family worship* MUST, in such a case, be more devout and hearty;
- *Internal love* MUST be more warm and unbroken, and
- *External conduct* MUST me more sanctified and Christlike.

THE FAMILY MUST PRODUCE VOTERS OF GOOD CHARACTER TO VOTE FOR GOVERNMENT LEADERS OF GOOD CHARACTER.

The British fought for religious liberty (1605—The papists plotted to destroy the Houses of Parliament.) as did the Americans. The papacy had become a source of religious tyranny. The American Thanksgiving should be a time of pleading to Jesus for the "overturning of false doctrines and the extension of divine truth." [***Charles Spurgeon***].

SHORT OF THE GREATEST AWAKENING OF ALL TIME, THE RESTORATION OF THE AMERICAN CULTURE IS THE RESPONSIBILITY OF BELIEVERS.

America's national motto, *E Pluribus Unum*, out of many one, is rooted in **Romans 12:5 ESV**, "...*though many are one body, in Christ and individually members one of another*." Such was reaffirmed by **George Whitefield** saying, "The Spirit of God is the center of unity." and "Christianity [and America] will never flourish until we are all of one heart and one mind." Such was the case until about 1960. Since then the devil's wedge has been allowed to split America due to the twin acceptance of the theory of evolution and the perceived flexibility of the Constitution. Identity politics has Balkanized America into competing groups sorted by race, ethnicity, and gender.

Knowing that Adam's sin affected all his posterity causes, or should cause, all Christians to be very concerned about their own posterity. The concern for posterity begins with the families. The American Founders did their best in the *Declaration of Independence* and the *United States Constitution* to protect their posterity from future cultural evil. Regretfully, posterity is seldom discussed today. *It is up to Christians to restore God's long-term view to the American culture.*

Believers' days MUST NOT be idle. Like Jesus, their conversation—lifestyle and verbal conversation— MUST continually point

> "We must seek revival of our strength in the spiritual foundations which are the bedrock of our republic. *Democracy is the outgrowth of the religious conviction of the sacredness of every human life.* On the religious side, its highest embodiment is the **Bible**; on the political side, the **Constitution**. Former **President Herbert Hoover** during WWII (Joint statement with 5 Presidential widows)

heavenwards. The *"pursuit of happiness"* is the *pursuit of holiness* (godly character).

Only God can satisfy a man's soul. The *Declaration of Independence* guaranteed the earthly right, i.e. the freedom to enjoy God's gifts without any hindrance from government whatsoever.

Political leaders can stimulate unity among the people by promoting virtue. Situational "ethics" is essentially no ethics; it causes disorder, conflict, chaos, and the breakdown of the culture and the country. However, the influence of honorable leaders has a tendency to:

- Promote wealth and prosperity
- Continually reinforce virtue as well as moral and ethical standards
- Unite people one to another in peace and mutual benevolence, and
- Make them happy in society; each one the instrument of his neighbors' quietness, comfort, and prosperity.

GOD'S GIFT UNPROTECTED, IS GOD'S GIFT SQUANDERED. FREEDOM UNPROTECTED IS FREEDOM SQUANDERED.

What will you say when you stand before God (Jesus) one day, when He asks, "What did YOU do with my precious gift of freedom that cost me my life?"

Unbelievers desire freedom from all manner of restraint

> "Atheism is unknown there [America]; Infidelity rare and secret; so that persons may live to a great age in that country without having their piety shocked by meeting with either an Atheist or an Infidel." ***Benjamin Franklin*** *(pamphlet for Europeans considering migrating to America)*

Politics is the Struggle to Protect & Promote God's Matchless Gift of Freedom

which is license to sin in all forms. Such is not true freedom because the lack of any restraints inevitably produces confusion, conflict, chaos, cultural breakdown, and anarchy. True freedom is God's freedom. It is freedom within the restraints established by the omniscient, omnipotent, omnipresent God of the universe. His restraints are an expression of His infinite love. God's restraints provide:

1) comfort
2) stable relationships
3) stable families
4) stable cultures.

These benefits can be passed on from generation to generation and on to *posterity*.

> "I'm being accused of being controversial and political. I'm not political. But moral issues that become political, I still fight. It isn't my fault that they've made these moral issues political. But because they have doesn't stop the preachers of the Gospel from addressing them..."
>
> "*What then is wrong*? I say the problem, first of all, is in the pulpits of America. We preachers must take the blame. For too long we have fearfully stood back and failed to address the issues that are corrupting the republic. I repeat *Proverbs 14:34*: '*Righteousness exalteth a nation.*' Not military might, though that's important. Not financial resources, though that has been the enjoyment of this nation above all nations in the last 200 years. But <u>*spiritual power is the backbone, the strength, of a nation*</u>."
>
> *Rev. Jerry Falwell*

Sixty to seventy years ago, the Republican and Democrat parties often advocated different paths to reaching similar goals. In recent decades, because the liberal/progressive movement has totally taken control of the Democrat party, the party's goals themselves have become socialist or worse.

Today, the goals of the major political parties are diametrically opposed and mutually exclusive. "Reaching across the aisle" to forge a compromise is no longer possible, in most cases. The ultimate political conflict is God-given freedom (self-government) versus tyranny (socialist pathway to total government control—little to no freedom).

Virtually any alleged compromise forfeits freedom, moving America a notch closer to tyranny. Each successive compromise ratchets the culture a bit further away from God and a bit closer to amoral chaos. Consider Jerry Newcombe's *10 Reasons Why the Church Should Not Abandon Politics*, Appendix VI. For convenience, the reasons are listed here; the supporting arguments are in the appendix:

1) *The Word of God has something to say about all of life, beyond just the spiritual.*
2) *The Bible itself addresses the issue of governing in different texts.*
3) *The Scriptures also teach that on occasion, there may be a need for civil disobedience.*
4) *Jesus said, "Render to Caesar the things that are Caesar's, and to God the things that are God's."*
5) *When the Church does not speak out, evil can fill that void.*
6) *The Church is called to be salt and light. Salt preserves and prevents decay.*
7) *We pray, "Thy kingdom come, Thy will be done, on earth as it is in heaven."*
8) *Christians bless everybody when we properly apply our faith to politics.*
9) *Politics may be the calling of some in the congregation. Therefore, ministers should encourage political involvement that is motivated by the desire to serve.*
10) *Religion and morality are "indispensable supports to our political prosperity."*

Politics is the Struggle to Protect & Promote God's Matchless Gift of Freedom

"*As for me and my house, we will serve the Lord.*"
[*Joshua 24:15*]

In the new millennium, reaching across to aisle to reach a compromise, is the political equivalent of the highly controversial *Half-Way Covenant* (HWC) adopted by the New England Congregational churches in the 1660s. The HWC allowed people to join the churches without a specific profession of faith that evidenced a personal conversion experience and allowed children of unconverted parents to be baptized. The inevitable but unforeseen outcomes were tragic.

Jonathan Edwards was one of the best known leaders of the *Great Awakening* that later spurred the War for Independence (better known today as the American Revolution). During that time, he pastored a Congregational church in Northampton, Massachusetts, for about 20 years. Ultimately, the church members voted to oust Jonathan Edwards from the church. Why? The number of non-professing Half-Way Covenantors had grown to exceed the number of true believers. Eventually, liberal-leaning Congregational churches became Unitarian churches, championing a form of spiritual chaos. Spiritual chaos leads directly to political chaos.

SPIRITUAL SEPARATION FROM GOD'S WORD (BIBLE) MUST PRECEDE POLITICAL SEPARATION FROM THE DECLARATION OF INDEPENDENCE AND THE U.S. CONSTITUTION

United States history has been punctuated by two great separations or splits:

1. In the late 19th Century, *German "higher criticism"* invaded America in a provocative way. The invasion triggered a major

split, separating Bible-believing conservative churches and denominations from emerging religious liberal churches and denominations. The point of the movement was the idea that the Bible could be intellectually analyzed just like any other book. Effectively, man became the judge of God, a fearsome place to be. The infallible, inerrant, direct inspiration of Scripture was challenged, because direct inspiration did not seem compatible with man's wisdom. Instead, some church denominations attempted to re-interpret Scripture to accommodate Charles Darwin's rapidly growing theory of evolution. God's wisdom took a major hit from man's "wisdom," especially in the liberal churches.

Conservative churches/denominations understand the Bible as the perfect, inspired, infallible, Word of God revealing Himself through the writers by the direct inspiration of the Holy Spirit. *Liberal churches/denominations* have compromised Scripture from God's Word, to less than total inspiration, some reducing the Bible to little more than a religious history book. Still others claim that the Bible "contains God's word." However, that position places man in the dangerous position of deciding which part of the Bible is God's word and which is not, effectively putting man in the position of judging God.

> "I hope that you have re-read the Constitution of the United States in these past few weeks. Like the Bible it ought to be read again and again." **President Franklin D. Roosevelt**, March 9, 1937, Fireside Chat

2. A compromised view of Scripture combined with virtually unquestioned adherence to the theory of evolution have facilitated a political separation, introducing the idea that the U.S. Constitution

must be "flexible" to keep up with the times. Such a view elevates man's "wisdom" above God's perfect wisdom.

The *first great separation* challenged the authority of **America's spiritual anchor, the Bible**, creating an ever-widening gap between conservative and liberal Christian believers. Conservatives holding fast to the anchor; liberals seeking creative ways of reinterpreting the anchor to accommodate "modern ways," including ever-increasing and creative forms of deviant behavior.

Since all behavior is ultimately driven by a person's deepest spiritual convictions. The spiritual split had to precede the political bifurcation.

The *second great separation*, growing out of the first, challenged the authority of **America's cultural anchor, the United States Constitution**. The adherents argued that the Constitution must be flexible and continually re-interpreted accommodate a changing culture. The argument conveniently sidesteps the Constitution's amendment process and the voters, first by recognizing and later awarding to judges de facto authority to alter, expand, or contract the Constitution's authority at will, with little or no accountability to the people.

The combined loss of both America's spiritual and cultural anchors is accelerating her slide into the abyss of cultural chaos. **Dr. Francis A. Schaffer** reported in, *The Great Evangelical Disaster*, "We are not only losing the

> "Religion and liberty are the meat and drink of the body politic. Withdraw one of them and it dies…Without religion we may possible retain the freedom of savages, but not the freedom of New England…If our religion were gone, our state of society would perish with it and nothing would be left worth defending." **Timothy Dwight**, President, Yale College (1798)

> "They that would give up essential liberty for a little temporary safety deserve neither liberty nor safety." **Benjamin Franklin**

church, but our entire culture as well." In *The Brothers Karamazov*, novelist **Fyodor Dostoevsky** explained the ultimate end. "If there is no God everything is permitted." The pain and suffering that follows is unthinkable.

Politics and Religion are Intimately Linked

Have you ever heard someone say, "I never talk about politics or religion?" Good heavens, why not? Those two define who you are, what you think, choices you make and how you act. If those discussions are off limits, what is left to talk about—the weather, sports scores, latest fashions, and what's for dinner? How boring is that?

Conservatives are often Christians who are beneficiaries of God's infinite mercy, love, and hope. There is joy in their hearts. *Liberals* are often humanists, driven to sin and covetousness. Since they have no hope, despair and anger are common among them.

The concept of *separation of church and state* was understood for about 150 years to mean that the Federal government was prohibited from interfering in the affairs of the church in any way. Beginning with the case *Elverson v. Board of Education*, 330 U.S. 1 (1947), the original understanding was turned on its head.

> "The First Amendment, however, does not say that in every and all respects there shall be a separation of Church and State...Otherwise the state and religion would be aliens to each other-hostile, suspicious, and even unfriendly. *We are a religious people whose institutions presuppose a Supreme Being...when the state encourages religious instruction...it follows the best of our traditions.* For it then respects the religious nature of our people and accommodates the public service to their spiritual needs. To hold that it may not would be to find in the Constitution a requirement that the government show a callous indifference to religious groups. That would be preferring those who believe in no religion over those who do believe. We find no constitutional requirement which makes it necessary for government to be hostile to religion...We cannot read into the Bill of rights such a philosophy of hostility to religion."
> **William Orville Douglas**, Supreme Court Justice, *Zorach v. Clauson* (1952)

From that time on the Supreme Court began striking down virtually all direct or indirect vestiges of religion in public life. The high Court began aggressively asserting its will over state and local governments as well. From time to time federal and state legislatures countered by passing laws intended to protect religious freedom. Typically, they have been struck down by the federal courts.

Where are we today? Understandably, opposing views and political controversies have created considerable misunderstanding regarding the separation of church and state. The bottom line, quite simply, is that while there is a First Amendment separation of the church organization and the government organization, there is no separation between religion and public life. In this context, "public life" means individual lifestyle, individual public expressions of religious views and public expressions of political views. Specifically, the First Amendment was written to protect the individual from any form of federal government coercion regarding religious views and to prevent the establishment of an official religion for the country.

OUTWARD POLITICAL VIEWS ARE SIMPLY EXPRESSIONS OF INWARD RELIGIOUS VIEWS (OR LACK OF THEM).

Christianity totally transforms a life in a manner which should and must be visible to others all day, every day; it is a lifestyle of love that cannot be compartmentalized. To do so would be 1) antagonistic to Scripture, 2) offensive to God, 3) insulting to Jesus Christ, 4) grievous to the Holy Spirit, and 5) extremely damaging to others by effectively hiding the greatest gift in the universe.

A Christian has no choice. He/she is and MUST be the *"light of the world"* [**Matthew 5:13 KJV**] and the *"salt of the earth."* [**Matthew 5:14 KJV**] Every compromise nails Jesus to the Cross again—and again—and again!

POLITICS IS SIMPLY THE EARTHLY MANIFESTATION OF WHAT IS IN THE SOULS OF THE AGGREGATE PUBLIC.

Beginning in the 19th Century, German conceived "higher criticism" of the Bible elevated *man's wisdom* above *God's wisdom*, a fearful thing to do. Higher criticism also elevated the intellect over the emotions and the spirit. God intended all three to work in concert.

> "Statesmen, my dear Sir, may plan and speculate for *liberty*, but it is Religion and Morality alone, which can establish the Principles upon which Freedom can securely stand...The only foundation of a free Constitution is pure Virtue, and if this cannot be inspired into our People in a greater Measure, than they have it now, they may change their Rulers and the forms of Government, but they will not obtain a lasting liberty." ***John Adams***, June 21, 1776

Unbelievers ridicule God's Word, expressed in the Holy Bible even though it has all the answers for their needs, wants, and desires. They ridicule the Word to justify sin. God's revelation in Scripture is perfect in every way. It is the ultimate treasure. Satan's deception manifested through the liberal/progressive movement is destroying America.

The self-imposed boundary is particularly egregious for Judeo-Christian believers. "I never talk about politics or religion" is something a Judeo-Christian believer must never say. It is a betrayal of God, faith, and other believers. Capitulation to *political correctness*—which always sugar coats the poison pill of sin—substantially interferes with the believer's relationship and obligations to

God. *Political correctness* is simply the Humanist's tool designed to shut down the Judeo-Christian worldview. Consider God's <u>commands</u> in Deuteronomy:

> <u>Fix these words of mine in your hearts and minds... Teach them to your children, talking about them when you sit at home and when you walk along the road, when you lie down and when you get up. Write them on the door frames of our houses and on your gates, so that your days and the days of your children may be many...</u> [**Deuteronomy 11:18-21 NIV**]

We are required to talk about scripture virtually all the time, teach it to our children, and advertise it outside our home. It is not possible for a believer to be completely saturated with God's words and His love, without that love spilling out in every area of life.

> "The known propensity of a democracy is to licentiousness which the...ignorant believe to be *liberty*." **Fisher Ames,** January 1788"

Just to make sure, God warns anyone suppressing His love, because of *political correctness*. "<u>Be careful, or you will be enticed to turn away and worship other gods and bow down to them. Then the Lord's anger will burn against you...and you will soon perish from the good land the Lord is giving you.</u>" [**Deuteronomy 11: 16-17 NIV**]

To have an impact on our surrounding culture, we must be able to freely, enthusiastically, and lovingly discuss politics and religion. When *political correctness* silences the Judeo-Christian worldview, the Humanist worldview aggressively fills the vacuum with little opposition or hindrance.

ALL POLITICAL ISSUES HAVE SPIRITUAL ROOTS.

Politics is an outward expression of a world view which emerges from deep inward religious convictions. Our religious and political views emerge from one of just two worldviews that are an earthly manifestation of the eternal battle between good and evil, God and Satan or in earthly terms believers and non-believers. Consider the graphic below. It qualitatively displays the conservative to liberal religious spectrum horizontally and the conservative to liberal political spectrum vertically.

Conservative religion and conservative politics at the lower left visually exhibit the Judeo-Christian worldview. Why? Because the believer relies on God (not government). Government is sharply restrained by the U.S. Constitution. It is the only worldview that assures a sustainable American culture, where the family reigns supreme, the freedom gifted by God is treasured, and the passions of men are voluntarily restrained by their faith in God.

In contrast, liberal religion and liberal politics at the upper right visually display the ultimate Humanist worldview that God does not exist. Man either tacitly or actually has declared himself to be his own god. The Humanist relies on government (not God). Growth of government is largely unrestrained, because of the belief that the "best and brightest," whoever they are, should be vested with whatever authority and resources are necessary for them to make decisions for the rest of us.

The elite Humanist decision-makers are convinced that the rest of us are not capable of making basic life decisions. Some of the self-proclaimed best and brightest simply consider themselves more highly evolved than the rest of us. Remember, "*For the foolishness of God is wiser than men, and the weakness of God is stronger than men."* [**1 Corinthians 1:24 ESV**] and *"For my thoughts are not your thoughts, neither are your ways my ways, declares the LORD. For as the heavens are higher than the earth, so are my ways higher than your ways and my thoughts than your thoughts."* [**Isaiah 55:8-9 ESV**]

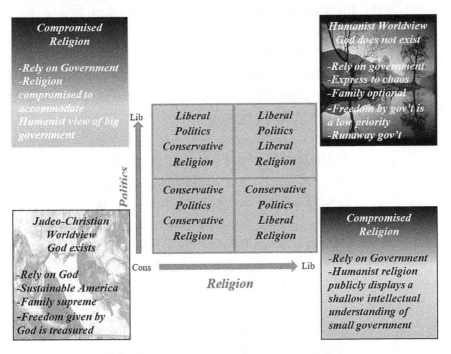

The Humanist road is a pathway to cancerous government growth, eventual self-destruction, and chaos. The family is optional and has a structure that defies definition. A fictitious or imagined freedom arises from the "grace" of government and is strategically dribbled out as a means of controlling the people.

Occasionally, a Humanist with a liberal mindset, perhaps cultivated in a liberal church or by childhood memories of religious training will remind the rest of us that scripture tells us to be merciful and feed the poor, clothe the naked, care for the sick, and visit those in prison. However, those admonitions were directed at individuals and small groups that later became known as churches. When the government co-opts those important tasks, its actions are both inefficient and deficient.

When the government does anything, it is, by design, financially inefficient (therefore wasteful) and an inefficient use of the labor of the employees. More importantly, government actions are emotionally and spiritually deficient. For example, the essence and quality of mercy is elegantly explained by Portia during her famous courtroom speech in Shakespeare's *The Merchant of Venice*:

> The quality of **mercy** is not strained;
> It drops as the gentle rain from heaven
> Upon the place beneath<u>: it is twice bless'd;</u>
> <u>It blesses him that gives, and him that takes:</u>
> 'Tis mightiest in the mightiest: it becomes'
> The thronéd monarch better than his crown;
> His scepter shows the force of temporal power,
> The attribute to awe and majesty,
> Wherein does sit the dread and fear of kings;
> <u>But mercy is above this sceptered sway</u>;
> It is enthroned in the hearts of kings,
> **It is an attribute to God himself;**
> <u>And earthly power does then show like God's</u>
> <u>When mercy seasons justice.</u>

Portia proclaims that the "quality of mercy…is twice bless'd; It blesses him that gives and him that takes" and is "above this sceptered sway" (above the physical or brute power government). Finally, "It is an attribute to God himself…When mercy seasons justice."

When God directly instructs us in scripture to feed the poor, clothe the naked, care for the sick, and visit those in prison each effort is intended to bless the benefactor as well as those who benefit. When the government undertakes the same activities, the people and churches are robbed of the blessings and character building opportunities that result from giving. (Author's personal note: I've never been blessed by paying taxes.).

Most schools, including Ivy League universities, were started by churches to enable people to read the Bible for themselves and build strong character. The early Ivy League universities were established to prepare young men for the ministry. Most hospitals were created by the churches. Later, the schools and health care were commandeered by the government, with honorable intentions and still later commanded by the government sometimes with less than honorable intentions.

When people claim to hold conservative religious views and liberal political views or vice versa, their faith has been compromised to accept and support some degree of Humanism. The claim to be "moderate" is even worse.

> *I know your deeds, that you are neither cold nor hot; I wish that you were either one or the other. So because you are lukewarm, and neither hot nor cold, I will spit you out of my mouth. You say, "I am rich, I have acquired wealth, and do not need a thing. But you do not realize that you are wretched, pitiful, poor, blind and naked...* **[Revelation 3:15-17 NIV]**

Now that you understand, take a stand—for the Lord. Express your religious and political views whenever they naturally arise in conversation. Along the way, be sure to live a life that others will envy, because of your strength of character, love, and calm assurance that God still has everything under control. That way your views will be respected even if not agreed upon.

> *Always be prepared to give an answer to everyone who asks you to give the reason for the hope that you have. But do this with gentleness and respect, keeping a clear conscience so that those who speak maliciously against your good behavior in Christ may be ashamed of their slander. It is better, if it is God's will, to suffer for doing good than for doing evil.* **[1 Peter 3:15-17 NIV]**

Presidential Election 2020

As of this writing, 2020 is shaping up to be the most important election year ever. The titanic forces of good and evil, freedom and Socialism (constantly increasing government control), are visibly and mightily clashing in a way seldom seen. Literally, the future of America is at stake. **Conservatism** *preserves the America which has been God blessed for 400 years and a recognized world leader since the formation and founding of the United States of America.* **Liberalism** *relentlessly steals freedom from the people eventually and inevitably leading to chaos, tyranny or both.*

In a rapidly declining American culture the most visible presidential candidate is President Donald J. Trump, running for re-election. Many people seem to have formed rather inflexible opinions of him, pro or con. Supporters need no encouragement.

Those who are skeptical or even dislike the President tend to hurl negative epithets generally using politically correct terms to condemn actual or perceived behavior in his life preceding the presidency. For Judeo-Christian skeptics there are important considerations that cannot be avoided. One of them is forgiveness.

The Lord's Prayer (called by some, The Model Prayer), says in part, "...*forgive us our debts as we also have forgiven our debtors.*" [**Matthew 6:12 ESV**] The principle is clarified in the two verses, following the prayer, "*For if you forgive others their trespasses, your heavenly Father will also forgive you, but if you do not forgive others their trespasses, neither will your Father forgive your trespasses.*" [**v. 14**] It is as if the Lord said, "Just in case you didn't get the forgiveness thing the first time around, here it is again." His message is plain, abundantly clear, and non-negotiable. Except for salvation, God's forgiveness for us is tied to our actively forgiving others.

On October 6, 2006, the Pennsylvania Amish gave the world a powerful lesson in forgiveness. Charles Carl Roberts IV walked into West Nickel Mines Amish (elementary) School shot 10 young girls, killing five, before committing suicide. *The Amish immediately forgave the shooter!* Within hours, the Amish leadership approached the home of the shooter's now widow and fatherless children. They nervously imagined all sorts of repercussions from the Amish. Instead, the Amish leaders said they understood the horrific impact on the shooter's own family and offered to comfort and help them in any way. Later, the Amish attended the shooter's funeral to support the family and invited the family to attend the funerals of the slain girls. Such forgiveness is seldom seen even though it is scripturally commanded.

Lack of forgiveness embitters the one refusing to forgive. In the case of President Trump, any lack of forgiveness by the voters, especially Christian voters, seriously clouds their judgment with respect to forming a meaningful opinion of the President, either positive or negative.

Any Christian insisting on clinging to a negative, unforgiving opinion of the President has a compelling moral obligation to identify an alternative candidate who is 1) better than President Trump, 2) electable, 3) has an abundantly clear lifetime record of tangible and sustainable achievements, 4) provided positive evidence that he/she will be more productive than the President, and 5) will work tirelessly to advance and protect Biblical principles and values. To date, no other candidate of either party can come even close to these criteria.

Sidestepping all the rhetoric on both sides, lengthy lists of President Trump's accomplishments can easily be found on the Internet. The items listed number in the several hundreds. Any reasonable person may disagree with a few of them. The ones you choose to disagree with may be different than the ones with which this author disagrees. Nevertheless, the vast majority of explicit accomplishments are very positive and widely appealing.

From a Christian perspective, despite a few personal flaws President Trump's views and values are far more closely aligned with scriptural standards than any other candidate. He is pro-America, pro-freedom, pro-life, pro-Israel, pro-Judeo/Christian values, pro-family, pro-free market (free enterprise), pro-U. S. Constitution, and pro-Democracy (Representative Republic). Refreshingly, and unlike many other public figures, President Trump actually does—insofar as possible—what he says he intends to do. Finally, he actively opposes anything which would compromise the anchors that protect American freedom or the God-gifted rights of ALL Americans.

President Trump gave up a billionaire's lifestyle to work, far more than full time, for the public without pay; allow his personal mistakes, including moral ones to be trumpeted to the world; and voluntarily expose himself to the fiercest, vilest, most relentless and savage personal attacks ever experienced by any American. Why? He loves America! Would you be willing to do the same?

On Election Day, it's up to YOU!

Socialism Destroys

Socialism is evil! It is evil, because as the State increasingly reigns supreme, Socialism increasingly sacrifices the freedom and rights of individuals, until the State becomes tyrannical and the individual become expendable. In Scriptural terms, Socialism is Satan's tool for depriving people of God's priceless gift of freedom. "They who can give up essential liberty to obtain a little temporary safety, deserve neither liberty nor safety." ***Benjamin Franklin***, (1775), during a negotiation with Britain

Despite claims to the contrary, by some political figures, **there is no such thing as a Democratic Socialist in the United States**. The descriptors are mutually exclusive. Adding "Democratic" ahead of the word "Socialist" is an attempt to soften the reality and harshness of real Socialism. Let the experts speak for themselves.

Vladimir Lenin, founder of Communism, proclaimed that the object of Socialism is to get to Communism. Decades later,

British Prime Minister, **Margaret Thatcher** said that, "Socialism is Communism on the installment plan." **Lenin** and **Joseph Goebbels**, Reich Minister of Propaganda of Nazi Germany, both advocated the principle that a lie told enough time becomes the truth. Today, the idea has been truncated to "perception is reality." It is hard to conceive of any two people more opposite than Lenin and Thatcher or more similar than Lenin and Goebbels. There is no way to soften or disguise it: Socialism is a pathway to Communism or tyranny/dictatorship.

Democracy (actually a representative republic) is based on freedom and the rights of the individual. *Socialism*, and all other deviations from Democracy, focuses on the primacy of the state. *The difference is God*. When the state is regarded as more important than the individual, the state inevitably gravitates towards violence which increases in intensity as spiritual, emotional, and moral and ethical barriers are cast aside.

- ***Democracy (representative republic) works*** *when people understand that they were made in the image of God and that human life is precious and sacred, from beginning to end*.

- ***Democracy works*** *when people understand that they are loved by the God who created them*. As an expression of gratitude and their love of God and His son, Jesus Christ, the people, for the most part voluntarily live within the Biblical lifestyle limits. Living within the limits is freeing, rather than confining.

- ***Democracy works*** *when people understand that freedom is a gift from God, not a grant from government*. Governments can only take away freedom. The United States government is chained to the Constitution and the Bill of Rights, specifically to prevent significant loss of freedom. A gift from God is to be cherished and protected at any cost.

God's wonderful gift of freedom was restored by the *Declaration of Independence*, firmly established and confirmed by the *War for Independence* (Revolutionary War) and codified by the *Unites States Constitution*. Freedom was bolstered by the free enterprise economic system, a.k.a. capitalism, spiritually supported by Judeo-Christian values, and civilly/practically buttressed by the God-created family. The family is the ONLY way to pass on a stable culture from generation to generation.

When people widely understand the sacredness and great value of freedom as well as the numerous anchors designed to protect our freedom, the cultural foundation is nearly impregnable.

However, as a culture drifts away from God, fewer people voluntarily abide by the established limits and the anchors weaken. In recent decades, America's previously rock solid foundation has been breached with increasing frequency and severity, producing all of today's cultural challenges. The challenges are great, but not impossible to resolve.

The solution is to right the wrongs by frequent conversation about the role of all people in government, at the ballot box, and by various courses of direct action, as lead by the Lord. The solution is NOT destroying the anchors that have protected American freedom for centuries and replacing democracy with socialism.

Socialism and any other "...isms" deny God, consider man the highest evolved animal, and the self-proclaimed leaders the highest evolved among the people. Beware, "_Do not be deceived: God is not mocked, for whatever one sows, that will he also reap._" [*Galatians 6:7 ESV*]

Socialism, because of the sin of pride takes away freedom, slowly at first and accelerating later. America is at the acceleration stage now. The erosion of freedom is softened by promises of free "stuff." The ancient Romans promised the citizens "bread and circuses." Today's Socialists promise long lists of unattainable freebies.

> **THE INDIVIDUAL RIGHTS TO LIFE, LIBERTY, AND THE PURSUIT OF HAPPINESS, ENSHRINED IN THE DECLARATION OF INDEPENDENCE, VANISH UNDER SOCIALISM, WHEN THE STATE REIGNS SUPREME.**

Socialism has always failed worldwide, throughout all recorded history. Although estimates vary, Socialism/Communism cost the lives of nearly 100,000,000 people in just the 20th Century. One can only imagine that perhaps ten times that number were seriously injured or mentally tormented during the same period.

No Socialist Government has ever achieved its widely touted utopia. Instead, the monumental failures are legion and infamous. Governments such as the National SOCIALIST German Workers Party (Nazi German government), Union of Soviet SOCIALIST Republics (Soviet Union), DEMOCRAT Peoples Republic of Korea (North Korea), DEMOCRATIC Kampuchea (Cambodia under Pol Pot, Khmer Rouge), and the Peoples Republic of China were among those that lead mass killings.

Modern Socialist countries include Cuba and Venezuela. Both were at one time very prosperous. Today, under socialist rule, both are undeniable examples of abject poverty, even though Venezuela has large oil resources. **Socialism has NEVER worked, anywhere.**

The perennial struggle rages between *power deliberately limited* and *power forcefully concentrated*. Often the struggle generates disputes over what constitutes individual "rights." All true freedom and rights are intangible, unalienable, and gifts from God Consider two conditions:

- Anything the government gives, the government can take away in the future.
- You and I have no right to another person's time, talent, or treasure.

Thoughtfully consider a scenario where you and other committed Christians were the only occupants of a particular region, perhaps an island. What kind of government would you establish? Would you want to protect your freedom or give it away to the government you create? If protecting freedom is a high priority, you are thinking like the Unites states Founders.

Remember, the Great American Experiment in self-government can only succeed when much of the population is devoted to high standards of morals and virtues.

> "What is *liberty* without wisdom and without virtue? It is the greatest of all possible evils; for it is folly, vice, and madness, without restraint. Men are qualified for *civil liberty* in exact proportion to their disposition to put moral chains upon their own appetites; in proportion as they are disposed to listen to the counsels of the wise and good in

preference to the flattery of knaves. *Society cannot exist unless a controlling power upon will and appetite be placed somewhere; and the less of it there is within, the more there must be without.* It is ordained in the eternal constitution of things, that men of intemperate minds cannot be free. Their passions forge their fetters." **Edmund Burke**, British Parliament, House of Commons, letter dated 1791

"Men, in a word, must be controlled either by a power within them, or a power without them; either by the word of God, or by the strong arm of man; either by the Bible or by the bayonet." **Robert Winthrop**, U.S. Speaker of the House, 1849

Posterity is depending on YOU, me, and all of America.

"If we and our *posterity*...live always in the fear of God and shall respect His Commandments...we may have the highest hopes of the future fortunes of our country. But if we...neglect religious instruction and authority; violate the rules of eternal justice, trifle with the injunctions of morality and recklessly destroy the constitution which holds us together, no man can tell how sudden a catastrophe may overwhelm us and bury all our glory in profound obscurity." **Senator Daniel Webster**, Addressing the New York Historical Society, 1852

"Hold on, my friends, to the Constitution and to the Republic for which it stands. Miracles do not cluster, and what has happened once in 6000 years, may not happen again. Hold on to the Constitution, for *if the American Constitution should fail, there will be anarchy throughout the world."* **Senator Daniel Webster**

HOLY SPIRIT-EMPOWERED CHRISTIANS MUST ACT NOW!

...and for me, that utterance may be given to me, that I may open my mouth boldly to make known the mystery of the gospel,
EPHESIANS 6:19 NKJV

Breathtaking Obstacles

In a fallen world, hate is an easy default. It requires little thought and no action. True unconditional love requires both 1) *unyielding commitment* and 2) *deliberate action*. Such is possible and sustainable only through the power of the Holy Spirit, because "God is love." [*1 John 4:8 ESV*]

Based on the intellect alone, which relies primarily on the physical senses, some have erroneously concluded that there is no god. They do so at their own peril. In addition, the short-term delight of sin

> "I ... call upon America to be more careful with its trust ... **Prevent** those ... who are attempting to establish even finer ... legal shades of **equality** — because of their distorted outlook ... short-sightedness and ... self-interest –from falsely using the struggle for peace and for **social justice** to lead you down a false road ... They are trying to weaken you; they are trying to disarm your strong and magnificent country in the face of this fearful threat ..."
> *Alexander Solzhenitsyn*, Russian author and Nobel Prize Winner, June 30, 1975

that meets selfish physical needs becomes a huge barrier between the unbeliever and God.

Faith is rational, but it requires more. The "more" is the gentle tug of the Holy Spirit who raises the consciousness of the spirit to needs that can only be satisfied by Jesus. The believer's sense of discernment is wholly intellectual, emotional, and spiritual.

Satan has facilitated the Christian split into many denominations by fueling man's pride which initially severed the Jewish roots of the church. Then he scattered beliefs based on externals. Often a new denomination was spawned when the focus on Jesus was gradually replaced with a focus on the denomination's founder. Thus the focus on the founder became more important than the focus on the founder of Grace. All Christians MUST unite to fight the greatest battle of all that originates in the heavenlies and increasingly manifests in this life.

Satan and unbelievers laugh at the multitude of Christian denominations. His divide and conquer strategy has been spectacularly successful. He has lured people (groups) to focus on foolish questions, fertile ground for tempting man's wisdom to replace God's wisdom to varying degrees. Combined with an overdose of materialism, the modern church has declined to marginal effectiveness. Today, we MUST raise the banner of Love high. We MUST restore Jesus to the prominence that made America the lighthouse of the world.

Most self-help books/plans leave out God. Yet, many believers have a voracious appetite for them. "Self-help" can be a major distraction from God. We must be utterly dependent upon God with my every breath, thought, and deed. "*For he knows our frame; he remembers that we are dust.*" [**Psalm 103:14**]

Today, many clergy fail to preach the fullness of God's Word. Some even endorse obvious sins such as LGBT relationships. But Paul exhorts all believers to "*stir up one another to love and good works.*" [**Hebrews 10:24-25 ESV**] When they are faithful to do so, most will love truth and cry out against the rampant public sins of the day. Much conservative thought and principles have Biblical roots, firing the unbelieving fury of "The Swamp."

> "We cannot read the history of our rise and development as a nation, without reckoning with the place the Bible has occupied in shaping the advances of the Republic ...where we have been the truest and most consistent in obeying its precepts, we have attained the greatest measure of contentment and prosperity." ***President Franklin D. Roosevelt***, October 6, 1935
>
> "The Almighty...did prepare this American continent to be a place of the second chance...Millions have ...found...freedom of opportunity, freedom of thought, freedom to worship God." ***President Franklin D. Roosevelt***, 1936 (50th Anniversary of the Statue of Liberty)

George Whitefield, *leader of the Great Awakening that fueled the American Revolutionary War*, rued the lack of family-religion in the 18th Century. His concern was great during the rising culture of the day, which may have been the most Christian culture in the history of America.

Whitefield's family religion was an urgent action-oriented around-the-clock mindset, which clearly pervades all of life, launched twice daily in family gatherings. Continually emphasizing that Biblical virtues, among life's highest priorities, stabilizes the family and the culture for generations to come and ultimately to posterity.

Sadly, since Whitefield's time *family religion* in America has eroded first to

- morning and evening family devotions, then sequentially to
- once a day family devotions;
- once a day personal devotions;
- occasional personal devotions;
- weekly worship service attendance, without personal devotions;
- periodic worship service attendance; and
- eventually, some walk away from their faith altogether.

Fortunately, there are some glorious exceptions to the tragic trend. God always has a remnant!

How much greater is the need for family religion in the falling culture of our day! Lord, help me to follow and live according to Joshua's dictum, "...<u>*as for me and my house,*</u> **<u>*we will serve the Lord*</u>**." [***Joshua*** **24:15**]

Today, most people worship the golden calf of materialism and the shrine of pride. With rare exceptions, we have all been guilty of both. Lord, help us to devote the remainder of our lives to you, routinely casting pride aside and ignoring the lure of materialism.

As long as the Bible was only in Latin, it was not available to ordinary people. Priests controlled the Word and therefore controlled the people. Secrecy fostered abuses. Today, the Bible is available to everyone, but it is not being read regularly and much of the clergy is not teaching it in a practical way.

The world's temptations are Satan's distractions. One of today's greatest temptations is the misuse of time for things and technology, rather than relationships (vertical with God and horizontal with family and others). However, with an enthusiastic love for Jesus and others:

- Difficulties are surmounted
- Sacrifices become pleasures, and
- Sufferings are honors.

A SILENT CHURCH AND HOSTS OF SILENT BELIEVERS BEG FOR CALAMITY.

Whether ordered by God or simply allowed by God as a natural result of individual and collective sin, catastrophe is inevitable. *It can only be avoided by 1) the greatest awakening of all time or 2) a body of believers willing to stand up, stand out, and speak out in support of all things good and in opposition to all things evil.* Perhaps the former is the prerequisite for the latter. Only Jesus and His gracious loving Holy Spirit can awaken the body of believers and their leaders from an apparent spirit of terminal apathy. "<u>Even so, come, Lord Jesus</u>." [**Revelation 22:20**]

Sin (mine and others) MUST horrify each of us and make us tremble. Sin crucified Christ. We MUST see the nails and the spear in every sin. If we laugh at sin today, it may become a temptation tomorrow. It is alarming to see so many believers flying like moths into the blaze of sin. *Incremental and aggregate sin is destroying America.* Growing up, it never occurred, to many of us that such a colossal disaster was even remotely possible. The greatest shock today is that few believers seem to care. Even fewer are sufficiently alarmed to take action.

The American culture has largely lost an understanding and appreciation of the beauty of virtue. Only Christians can restore that beauty in word and deed (by example).

One of the greatest shortcomings, perhaps THE greatest shortcoming, within the body of believers today is the lack of soul-deep unconditional love. Why:

- The love and commitment to God and Jesus is not as rich as it should be. Modern believers tend to "love" God with limits or conditions.
- Modern believers are over-committed. Time is scarce and grossly misdirected.
- Modern believers are poor listeners. The needs of others cannot be identified without active listening.
- While material needs are obvious, modern believers have not been taught to identify emotional and spiritual needs.
- Deep within, many modern believers continue to value themselves more than others. Pride too often trumps humility.

Satan seeks *eternal captivity* of the souls he already owns by right of original sin. Jesus seeks and offers the soul *eternal freedom* from sin's captivity. Jesus is the ultimate and infinite escape artist. He designed the perfect and eternal escape from Satan and hell. "<u>For the Son of man is come to seek and to save that which was lost</u>." [**Luke 19:10**]

<u>God's Family is His Greatest Army</u>

God's greatest army in this life is His network of godly families. We must not be dissuaded from building a spiritual temple within (the family) and the church without. No matter how great the problems in the church, it remains a bright light against a rapidly darkening background culture. The church MUST be preserved, nourished, and committed to a continual expression of God's infinite love.

> "Good government generally begins in the family and if the moral character of a people once degenerate, their political character must soon follow...." **Elias Boudinot,** *President of Continental Congress, Founder of American Bible Society, July 4, 1793*

Immigrants (new members) into the church must assimilate just as immigrants into the country must assimilate, and as Ruth the Moabite assimilated into Israel adopting both their culture and their religion. *"But Ruth said, "Do not urge me to leave you or to return from following you. For where you go I will go, and where you lodge I will lodge. Your people shall be my people, and your God my God."* [***Ruth 1:16 ESV***].

Today, incremental liberalism within the Bible-believing conservative churches is destroying the church, Christian universities and Christian schools. **Dr. Francis A. Schaefer** commented extensively on incremental liberalism in his last and perhaps most important book, *The Great Evangelical Disaster*, (1984), Crossway, Wheaton, Illinois.

God's universal family includes all believers in heaven and on earth. *"Of whom the whole family in heaven and earth is named..."* [***Ephesians 3:15 KJV***] In this life, God's family operates as an aggregation of individual family units that provide stability to the larger culture, to the nation, and assures that the stability can be passed from generation to generation and on to posterity.

Holy Spirit-Empowered Christians Must Act Now!

THE INDIVIDUAL FAMILY UNIT IS GOD'S PLACE OF BUSINESS.

Strong faith and families have been the source of America's strength for over 400 years. Strong families are also strong evidence of the existence of God, the nearness of God, the love of God, and the flow of God's love through believers.

Yet, in recent decades, **heavy artillery has been aimed at YOUR family by powerful enemies of God. They include**:

- radical feminists
- multiculturalists
- Planned Parenthood
- American Civil Liberties Union (ACLU)
- LGBT organizations,
- abortion activists
- pornographers
- Humanists/ liberals/ progressives/Socialists/ Marx-ists/globalists
- Southern Poverty Law Center (SPLC).

Their **targets for destruction** include the:

- traditional biblical family (INCLUDING YOURS)
- patriotism—an outgrowth of Judeo/Christian tradition
- United States Constitution
- democracy (representative republic)
- free enterprise system (capitalism)
- Founding Fathers
- sanctity of marriage
- sanctity of life
- God-given sovereignty of the family.

The **heavy artillery** used by the enemies of God to destroy traditional America and the family includes:

- Political correctness, a means of protecting man's "wisdom," while eliminating God's wisdom from the marketplace of ideas
- Unconditional abortion often paid for by the government
- Universal use of pornography, by children and adults
- No-fault divorce
- Encourage/subsidize single-parent families
- K-12 Kinsean sex education that teaches sexual anarchy
- Social approval of out-of-wedlock births
- Malignant welfare state establishing permanent dependence on government
- Effectively banning religion from public discourse by abusive interpretation of the First Amendment to the U.S. Constitution
- Legal recognition of same-sex "marriage."
- Theory of evolution
- Child adoption by same-sex couples
- Surrogate births for same-sex couples
- Unlimited regulations in every life area
- Easy student loans which create dependence on the government
- Massive changes using the judicial system to bypass the voting public
- Career assigned a higher priority over family, withdrawing women and love from the home
- Legal recognition of transgendered individuals.
- "Tolerance" of all manner of perverse

behavior followed by legal recognition of "equality" of practitioners (establishes the moral equivalence of good and evil; lack of tolerance for sinful behavior is proclaimed "evil"
- Government takeover of parental responsibilities

To date, **the leading attackers** have included:

- Highest level politicians
- Mainstream press
- Outspoken entertainment celebrities
- Poor behavior of sports celebrities
- Peer pressure of a rapidly collapsing American culture
- Corrupt public school systems
- Arrogance in traditional universities
- Brute force of the federal government facilitated by a runaway judiciary

The lists simply capsulize the formidable nature and power of the enemy and his relentless determination to defeat the people of God. Do NOT fear! "..._you are from God and have overcome them, for he who is in you is greater than he who is in the world_." [*1 John 4:4 ESV*] Clearly, the big guns have become a prominent part of modern American culture. It is abundantly clear that one of their objectives is the destruction of the traditional Biblical American family.

NO CIVILIZATION HAS EVER SURVIVED THE BREAKDOWN OF THE FAMILY!

The numerous anti-family groups and movements are large and well-funded. They have identified specific targets, including your family, are armed with heavy artillery, and possess fearsome power. The situation may seem intimidating, but is no match for the power of God. "*It is he who made the earth by his power, who established the world by his wisdom, and by his understanding stretched out the heavens.*" [*Jeremiah 10:12 ESV*] "*The LORD your God is in your midst, a mighty one who will save; he will rejoice over you with gladness; he will quiet you by his love; he will exult over you with loud singing.*" [*Zephaniah 3:17 ESV*] "*But Jesus looked at them and said, 'With man this is impossible, but with God **all** things are possible.*'" [*Matthew 19:26 ESV*]

The Judeo-Christian family has been severely damaged by the heavy and continuous bombardment of the growing array of anti-Biblical forces. The ONLY way to recover America is to trumpet and recover the traditional Biblical family, created by God. As a bright beacon of light, God's restored families will chase away the rapidly approaching darkness in America.

An earthly father is absolutely essential and MUST model the attributes of the heavenly Father. The father provides the tangible example. The mother provides the vision and value. She places value on the father's example. Together they seal the family, pass godly character to subsequent generations, stabilize the culture, and stabilize the nation. Obedience to the heavenly Father begins with obedience to the earthly father. There is no substitute for the godly example provided by the earthly father for his children.

Anything, anyone, or any group that destabilizes the family necessarily destabilizes the culture and the nation.

The only way for America to survive the ruthless and relentless attacks on the family is for Judeo-Christian believers to deliberately and substantially restore God's family structure, preserved with a loving and ironclad 'til-death-do-us-part commitment. Loving home relationships are made possible by God and provide the most visible and profound example of God's love to the world. How tragic it is that the American homes including the homes of many believers have been splintered by the forces of Satan, evidenced by the high divorce rate among Christians.

Our homes on earth MUST once again become a picture of our future home with God in heaven. After all, He does dwell in both places. "*The eternal God is your refuge.*" [**Deuteronomy 33:27**] God is our abode:

- Home is where we feel safe.
- Home is where we rest.
- Home is where we let our hearts loose.
- Home is the place of our truest and purest happiness.
- Home is the benefit and motivation of our work and labor.
- Home is where we prepare for battle.
- Home is where we are armed to fight the war between good and evil.
- Home is the boot camp for life.

Physical (materialistic) pleasures can never satisfy spiritual needs. Culturally, temporary government or political "solutions" can never resolve spiritually-rooted social problems.

Whether individually or culturally, this life is a network of interpersonal relationships that can ONLY thrive with a godly transformation of takers into givers. The transformation is called love. The ultimate individual transformation is by God's love at the point of salvation, a transformation that allows God's love to continually flow through the individual for the rest of this life.

THE ULTIMATE CULTURAL INFLUENCE IS GOD'S LOVE SPREAD BY GOD'S FAMILY.

The body of believers, beginning with family, must become one just as the Trinity is three in one. ***Unity is a powerful witness!*** My enjoyment of and nearness to God becomes greater when those around me, family, friends, church, and denominations are one and wholly devoted to God.

Regardless of whether God bestows on you or me a lot or a little (materially, intellectually, emotionally, and spiritually), His blessings must be exposed and visible to others as tangible evidence of God's existence, love, provision, protection, forgiveness, mercy, and salvation. In short, people MUST see God in and through you, me, your family, and my family. Ultimately, they cannot know the source of God's blessings unless we visibly model the blessings and tell them the source.

God's Word Fueling the Witness of God's Family is God's Chosen Weapon

Regardless of circumstances, God protects the elect, from the darkness of their own trials and the darkness of the culture. Love shines brightest against a background of darkness.

The magnificent Holy Trinity is three persons in one. We tend to overanalyze the three at the expense of the one. The oneness of the Trinity is represented in this life by:

1. The oneness of the Church
2. The oneness of marriage and family, and
3. The oneness of the three coequal branches of the American government (Executive, Legislative, and Judicial).

The three members of the Trinity are coequal with differing and overlapping roles. The same is true regarding the roles in marriage, family, and of government. Anything that weakens or destroys the unity of marriage, family, or government creates a barrier to understanding the other two and understanding God's amazing Trinity.

We MUST step out in faith. God will hold us up in the face of many foes. Today, as the American culture crumbles, the foes are legion, but God is greater than them all. I MUST trust and lean on God to help me resist sin as well as live for and proclaim Jesus. "<u>Able to keep you from falling</u>." [**Jude 24**]

Salvation in and through Christ is the ONLY escape from God's ultimate judgment. Today, folly has duped America, including the most malignant of follies—doubting or denying the true God. Unless checked, the folly of doubting or denying God will continue weakening the foundation of America, inevitably destroying the country. It is OUR responsibility to wave God's banner, because "…<u>his banner over me is love</u>." [**Song of Solomon 2:5 ESV**] We MUST continually share God's love in word and deed. It is life's highest priority.

The glories of heaven, the ignominies of hell, and the infinite distance between the two are seldom preached today. Yet, it is the stark contrast that, in part, propels *witnessing* of any kind. Christians desire to share the love of Jesus, but occasionally need a swift kick, by the realities of hell.

Witnessing often requires both the attractive pull of heaven and the flight away from hell. Common grace, at least occasionally, opens the hearts of men, otherwise on the road to hell. We MUST be alert and find those openings. They are the greatest opportunities to share the wonderful saving news about Jesus.

When the concept of sin is continuously eroded and diluted, there comes a time when few actions are regarded as sinful or wrong. Any residual guilt is seemingly washed away by blaming others for even minor discomforts. The culture creates the appearance that there is no need for repentance or forgiveness. Yet, very few people are truly happy, because all that is left is pride, which can never be satisfied. The lack of satisfaction breeds increasing conflict. At the same time, cultural camouflage hinders understanding the eternal nature of the soul.

As always, Christ still protects believers from the evils that surround us, IF we ask for His protection. If we fail to ask, we become vulnerable to all manner of temptations. In heaven, there will be no temptations, only an endless ocean of God's eternal love. For now, we must lean on Jesus to avoid succumbing to temptations.

God has graciously made all the provisions for His reconciliation with every man. Justice has been satisfied by the voluntary crucifixion of Jesus. Death and hell have been conquered. Righteousness is available through the power of the Holy Spirit.

Yet, God will rarely overrule our precious, God-given, gift of free will. He beckons, "<u>Come to me</u>...." [**Matthew 11:28 ESV**] The only remaining requirement, for reconciliation with God, is an individual's desire for forgiveness from sin and a desire for reconciliation with God and eternal residency with Him in heaven. God's complete preparation and the freely given consent of an individual, offered in prayer, is called salvation. That is how, "Jesus Saves!"

The more we seek the Lord, the more He reveals Himself to us. The greater the longing, the greater and more vibrant the reveal. "<u>This is the generation of them that seek him</u>." [**Psalm 24:6**] The greater the reveal, the greater the desire to witness, the greater the fruit of the witness.

<u>Prayer is the Warrior's Greatest Power</u>

In ancient Israel,

> the prophet (Zephaniah) calls to national repentance, as the only way to prevent national ruin. A nation not desiring, that has no desires toward God, is not desirous of his favor and grace, has no mind to repent and reform...Let the poor, despised, and afflicted, seek the Lord, and seek to understand and keep his commandments better, that they may be more humbled for their sins. **The chief hope of deliverance from national judgments rests upon prayer.** Those that are ever so good must still strive to be better; those that have ever so much grace must be still be praying and laboring for more. Nay, those that excel in any particular grace must still

seek to excel yet more in that… [***Matthew Henry—*** Bible commentary on ***Zephaniah 2:1-3 ESV***]

"<u>*The love of Christ constrains us*</u>." [***2 Corinthians 5:14***] The *Great American Experiment* in self-rule cannot survive when spiritual principles are separated from American public policies (government). If so, America fails. While continuing to ***pray*** for the greatest awakening of all time, we MUST do everything we can to assure the integration of spiritual principles into the American culture. These spiritual principles stabilized and drove the American culture for nearly 400 years. Increasing abandonment of biblical principles has created a slide towards Gomorrah.

In good times, we are easily distracted from God. Good times may be the greatest of all temptations. The body of believers in America slumbers. It has been anesthetized by the good times of the world of materialism and easy virtue. "<u>*Why do you sleep? Rise and **pray**, lest you enter into temptation*</u>." [***Luke 22:46***]

America needs prayer; you need prayer; I need prayer. There is no shortage of prayer needs, just a shortage of believers and churches willing to devote significant amount of time to prayer. You and I MUST do our part. Prayer is a primary mission of the church and individual believers like us. "<u>*Men ought **always** to pray*</u>." [***Luke 18:1 KJV***] "<u>*Rejoice ALWAYS, pray without ceasing*</u>…" [***1 Thessalonians 5:16-17 ESV***]

Our prayers MUST become more fervent and more earnest. Regardless of how or when God answers prayers, our fervency and earnestness will draw us closer to Him. We MUST regularly pray for everyone in our family, especially our children and their families.

Any *goodness* we may have is by God's grace.
Any *worthiness* we may possess is by Christ's sacrifice.
Any *good works* we have or may accomplish are enabled by the Holy Spirit.

On our own, we are and can do nothing. By His grace, we are saved; on a prayerful foundation, we can do all things consistent with His plan for our lives.

Voting is the Warrior's Greatest Political Weapon

Civil or personal freedom, including freedom to practice lifestyle religion, cannot be separated from spiritual freedom from sin. Freedom from bondage to government and freedom from bondage to sin must not be separated.

CIVIL FREEDOM MUST BE AVAILABLE TO FREELY PRACTICE SPIRITUAL FREEDOM.

Spiritual freedom from bondage to sin is a gift from God. His great gift became universally available to anyone who repents and accepts the atoning death of Jesus Christ on the cross. Christ's resurrection is incontrovertible proof of His standing to offer forgiveness and eternal salvation.

God also gifted *civil freedom* to certain historic peoples. The greatest example is the deliverance of the ancient Israelites from bondage to Egypt. Throughout recent centuries, America has been commonly viewed as an analog of the ancient Israelites. Early colonists were delivered from the oppressive bondage of various European governments.

Later colonists (early Americans) were delivered from the oppressive bondage to England as a result of the Revolutionary War. Common wartime rallying cries were, "No king, but King Jesus!" and "Resistance to tyranny is obedience to God!" Resistance to tyranny was justified when the government acts to hinder, block, or confiscate things which belong to God. *"Render to Caesar the things that are Caesar's and to God the things that are God's."* [**Mark 12:17 ESV**]

Remember:

- Freedom both civil and spiritual are God-gifted.
- America's Founders protected both civil and spiritual freedom for posterity.
- We are their posterity; we are obligated, with God's help, to continue the Founders' protections for our posterity.

The political process is merely the manifestation, the evidence, or the picture of what is in the hearts of the people. The only good in this world or in citizens of the United States of America is what God imputes to the hearts of believers. The remainder of the world is full of evil. Consequently,

IF JUDEO-CHRISTIAN BELIEVERS SIT OUT THE POLITICAL PROCESS, OR PARTICIPATE CARELESSLY, EVIL REIGNS AND EVENTUALLY AMERICA FALLS.

Throughout history everywhere, pride has always caused power to concentrate. As power continues to concentrate, tyranny emerges and grows. Ultimately, tyranny becomes a radioactive fire-breathing Godzilla (represented fictionally as king of the monsters). The beast feeds on vast amounts of money, resources and pompous ceremonies. ***It demands obedience and devours freedom.*** The antidote is a soul-deep understanding that God prizes humility over pride and power.

The Founders knew the story of the pride monster, because they understood history. They worked tirelessly to confine the prideful federal government to the box defined by the *Declaration of Independence* and the *Unites States Constitution*. They put chains, called the *Bill of Rights*, around the box. The overarching reason for abundant caution was to protect God's amazing gift of freedom for all citizens.

God's freedom was expressed by Washington as the sacred fire of liberty. "The preservation of the **sacred fire of liberty** and the destiny of the republican model of government are justly considered as deeply, perhaps as finally, staked on the experiment entrusted to the hands of the American people," **President George Washington**, *First Inaugural Address*, April 30, 1789. Notice that President Washington (and many others) considered liberty to be sacred. He also sounded an extremely serious cautionary warning about preventing or resisting a runaway government, "Government is not reason; it is not eloquence; it is force! Like fire, it is a dangerous servant and a fearful master." **George Washington**

In a fallen world, there is a constant tension, a battle between freedom and captivity. In ancient times, when the Israelites became "stiff-necked," abusers of God's precious gift of freedom, disobedient to God, and worshippers of false idols, the people of the Southern Kingdom of Judah were eventually carried into captivity by the Babylonians; the people of Northern Kingdom of Israel were eventually held in captivity by the Assyrians. Today, as the American culture drifts away from God, taking on the characteristics of the rebellious ancient Israelites, Americans are racing toward captivity by their own government.

As Creator and much, much more, God has moral and absolute standing to demand obedience from His people. In contrast, the government has no moral standing to demand obedience; it does have limited legal standing to require obedience to the U.S. Constitution. However, it does have the ability to apply all manner of force to coerce obedience from its citizens to ever increasing demands. Every new law (passed by Congress, a state legislature, or a local city council) or regulation (adopted by an executive branch agency) is at the expense of freedom.

Do not be careless with freedom. Giving away freedom is surrendering permanently to government. Once lost, freedom is nearly impossible to regain. "God grants liberty only to those who love it, and are always ready to guard and defend it." ***Senator Daniel Webster***, June 3, 1834

The American Culture is in very serious trouble. Many people have been wandering in a spiritual wilderness for 40 years. Judeo-Christian believers are the only ones who have the answers. They must act; they must act <u>*now*</u>! The future of the *Great American Experiment* in self-government and the centuries-long hope of the world is at stake.

The situation is critical; the urgency has never been greater. The ACTION PLAN has just four parts, but each one must be pursued vigorously:

- <u>*Pray fervently*</u>—Nothing worthwhile happens without specific, fervent prayer. Pray for America. Pray for America's leaders. Pray for the widespread opening of the eyes of the people to the overwhelming importance of cultural and public affairs.

- <u>Speak often about our beloved American culture</u>—Stay informed! Speak often about public and cultural issues. Every issue has spiritual roots and scriptural answers. Public and cultural issues will never be resolved by surface political "solutions" alone, because—in most cases—political "solutions" elevate man's flawed wisdom above God's perfect wisdom and either neglect or ignore the spiritual roots. Any farmer knows that a crop is grown to the fullest by fertilizing the roots. Weeds are destroyed permanently by poisoning the roots. Do not ever say to yourself anything like, "I keep my politics and my religion separate." If you have read this far, you already know that such a separation cannot be rationally or spiritually supported.

- <u>Witness enthusiastically</u>—Good heavens! Share your faith. Conversations about public and cultural issues, especially controversial ones and their spiritual roots, offer an abundance of opportunities to tell others about God's love and His impact on your life as well as His guidance and impact on America's spectacularly beautiful and exciting story (history).

- <u>Vote with sacred conviction</u>—Voting is the single most important action of any citizen. The *Great American Experiment* in freedom and self-government depends on citizens voting with conviction. Historically, it has been referred to as *casting a **sacred vote*** or *casting a **solemn vote***.

Consider several examples from Appendix VII, *Importance of Thoughtful Planned Voting*:

"We electors have an important constitutional power placed in our hands; we have a check upon two branches of the legislature . . . the power I mean of electing at stated periods [each] branch. . . . <u>It becomes necessary to every [citizen] then, to be in some degree a statesman, and to examine and judge for himself of the tendency of political principles and measures.</u> Let us examine, then, with a sober, a manly . . . and a Christian spirit; let us neglect all party [loyalty] and advert to facts; let us believe no man to be infallible or impeccable in government any more than in religion; take no man's word against evidence, nor implicitly adopt the sentiments of others who may be deceived themselves, or may be interested in deceiving us." **John Adams**, Founder and 6th President

"<u>Let each citizen remember at the moment he is offering his vote</u> that he is not making a present or a compliment to please an individual–or at least that he ought not so to do; but <u>that he is executing one of the most **solemn** trusts in human society for which he is accountable to God and his country.</u> Nothing is more essential to the establishment of manners in a State than that all persons employed in places of power and trust be men of unexceptionable characters. The public cannot be too curious concerning the character of public men." **Samuel Adams**, Founder

Holy Spirit-Empowered Christians Must Act Now!

"*<u>Impress upon children the truth that the exercise of the elective franchise is a social duty of as **solemn** a nature as man can be called to perform; that a man may not innocently trifle with his vote; that every elector is a trustee as well for others as himself and that every measure he supports has an important bearing on the interests of others as well as on his own.</u>*" *Senator Daniel Webster*

"Consider well the important trust . . . which God . . . [has] put into your hands. . . . To God and posterity you are accountable for [your rights and your rulers]. . . . <u>Let not your children have reason to curse you for giving up those rights and prostrating those institutions which your fathers delivered to you.</u> . . . [L]ook well to the characters and qualifications of those you elect and raise to office and places of trust. . . . Think not that your interests will be safe in the hands of the weak and ignorant; or faithfully managed by the impious, the dissolute and the immoral. Think not that men who acknowledge not the providence of God nor regard His laws will be uncorrupt in office, firm in defense of the righteous cause against the oppressor, or resolutely oppose the torrent of iniquity. . . . <u>Watch over your liberties and privileges - **civil and religious** - with a careful eye.</u>" ***Matthias Burnett***

When choosing to vote for anyone for any office from local dog catcher to President of the United States, several questions demand your thoughtful attention:

- <u>Will the candidate work vigorously to protect your God-gifted freedom as the highest priority</u>? God's gift is perfect and precious; we must treasure and protect it at all cost.

- <u>Is the candidate a visibly outspoken Christian</u>? Virtually all American presidents, except one, have stressed the importance of Christian character.

- <u>Is the candidate a person of known strong character</u>? Everyone has weaknesses. Candidates for public office simply have their weaknesses exposed to the real and technological universe.

- <u>Does the candidate have an abundantly clear record of positive achievement</u>? Governors move into the Oval Office more often that legislators, because governors have clear executive experience and visible documented achievement records. Legislators are generally part of a crowd; any of their achievement tend to be heavily camouflaged.

Your vote is precious; your vote is sacred. Casting your vote is the most solemn civic act any citizen can perform. There is no perfect candidate this side of heaven. Vote for the candidate that allows you to say "yes" to more of the above questions than any other candidate.

Pray, then vote. Remember, once your vote is cast it is irrevocable. Cast your vote solemnly; cast it wisely, then pray again, thankfully. Never miss an opportunity to vote. You are not done yet. Teach your children and grandchildren how to vote with the same tenacity, integrity and caution.

<u>God's Non-Negotiable Challenge</u>

> **"The fear of the Lord is the beginning of wisdom..."**
> **[Proverbs 9:10 ESV]**

Godly fear produces a drive to do the right thing according to the Bible and to live the right thing according to the laws of the government. Therein resides cultural stability. True liberty (freedom) can only exist to the extent there is godly fear (ultimate accountability). *Ungodly fear* is a <u>spirit of bondage</u>; it drives people away from the Lord. *Godly fear* is a <u>spirit of liberty</u>; it magnetically attracts people toward the Lord. Clearly, the distinction is extremely important.

A holy fear of God (overwhelming reverential awe) sharply reduces the frequency of sin in a believer's life and weakens the temptation to sin. However, to be life-changing, Scripture must become a spiritual passion (beautiful soul-deep conviction), rather than merely an intellectual or emotional passion (temporary fascination). Sadly, America, including many believers, has largely become emotionally fascinated with sin, rather than becoming a vehicle for spreading God's infinite love.

In the 21st Century, many believers have lost the sense of fearing God. We must fear god's wrath as much as we embrace God's love. The fear of wrath must be coupled with attraction of love. My soul must flee sin as well as purpose to do good. The repulsion of the negative adds spiritual energy to the attraction of the positive (God's love).

THE GULF BETWEEN HEAVEN AND HELL IS INFINITE; THE CONTRAST IS BREATHTAKING.

Today, the glories of our future in heaven and the easily avoided torments of hell are seldom discussed or preached. Why not? There could not be any greater contrast between the beauty and desirability of GOOD and the repulsion and disgust of EVIL. "<u>And there was no more sea</u>." [**Revelation 21:1**]

Hell is so easily avoided. "<u>Pride goes before destruction, and a haughty spirit before a fall</u>." [**Proverbs 16:18 ESV**] Pride is the nearly insurmountable barrier that prevents so many from embracing Christ. We MUST live our lives in a way that elicits envy from some amidst the background of cultural scorn. *"...salvation is come unto the Gentiles, for to provoke them to jealousy...If by any means I may provoke to emulation them which are my flesh, and might save some of them."* [**Romans 11:11-14 KJV**] We MUST endure the world's hatred to attract God's elect. "*Know you not that it will be bitterness in the latter end?*" [**2 Samuel 2:26 KJV**]

CHRISTIAN HOLINESS IS A BEAUTY GREATER THAN ANY OTHER; IT IS FAR ABOVE ALL UNBELIEVING "VIRTUE."

Believers, genuinely living for the Lord are the happiest people on earth. "*The glory of the Lord shall be revealed, and all flesh shall see it together.*" [**Isaiah 40:5**] Unbelievers are plagued with incessant unhappiness, perhaps most visible in the public utterances of liberal/progressives and in social media.

Many people devote endless hours to studying philosophy, various sciences, and humanities. Such studies have limited temporal value and no long-term impact. However, the study of divine truths in Scripture have eternal impact on everyone who pursues the study. We MUST devote significantly more time to studying and implementing divine truths than temporal ones.

Christian holiness is far above all the heathen virtue. Christian holiness is beautiful to behold. True Christians regard others better than self and will provoke others to ask the reason for the Christian's peace, serenity, and sweet spirit. What a great opportunity to share Jesus!

Despite persecution, the Christian life is the most pleasurable life available. Why? The Christian enjoys the pleasures of knowing his glorious God, the unconditional love of Jesus, and communion with the beloved Spirit of God. The result is true peace and true liberty.

Acquiring the beauty of Christian holiness begins with salvation

We cannot love the world and love Christ simultaneously. The objectives are diametrically opposed. For us, the true test is where we devote our time. As a young Christian, despite the appearance of piety and churchiness, the author's life emphasis was career (the world). Today, his life emphasis is the Lord. Thank you Jesus for the conversion.

The principle of salvation is abundantly clear to the believer, but abundantly fanciful to the unbeliever. What could be clearer than the abundance of eternal light in heaven and the relentless eternal darkness in hell; eternal bliss or eternal pain. However, understanding the contrast requires first an understanding that God exists, and that Jesus was sacrificed and resurrected. The resurrection proves the credibility of Christ and the scriptures. Combined with the promptings of the Holy Spirit, everything else becomes inescapably clear.

Jesus knocks at the door of every soul. He knocks continually; He may keep knocking for many years. Opening the door is entirely voluntary. Eternal freedom is readily available. It is available by God's love and mercy through Jesus. It must only be accepted.

Salvation requires both faith and repentance. *Faith* is the unshakable belief in the unseen God induced by the Holy Spirit. *Repentance* acknowledges, respects, and remorsefully rejects evil, especially the evil in one's own life. Repentance is both sorrow for sins and an utter dependence on Jesus for deliverance from sin. As part of salvation, God's Holy Spirit indwells the repentant believer, replacing the believer's dark old nature with a bright new nature. Sin and the Holy Spirit cannot coexist. Faith and repentance produce absolute trust in Jesus for salvation and everything else that follows.

Salvation has made it possible for me to talk with God now, and to live with Him hereafter.

These thoughts are thrilling! You can prayerfully ask Him for salvation right now.

After salvation, we all MUST be outspoken bearers of the Truth.

> "To be really Bible-believing Christians we need to practice simultaneously, at each step of the way, two biblical principles. *One principle is that of the purity of the visible church*...we must actually practice it, even when it is costly. *The second principle is that of an observable love among all true Christians*...Spirituality begins to have real meaning in our lives as we begin to exhibit simultaneously the *holiness of God* and the *love of God*." **Francis Schaeffer *(1984)*** [emphasis added]

We are born into sin (virtually in the arms of Satan). We have been saved, from the otherwise unbreakable shackles of sin and the default passage to hell, and now belong to the army of God. Satan fights with lies. God loves with truth. The truth goes marching on! ***All believers, MUST be outspoken bearers of the Truth***. Today, progressives in all major institutions are bearers of lies. They cannot do otherwise, because they are convinced that there is no such thing as objective, unalterable truth. The Truth cannot and must not be hidden by intimidated believers.

The Holy Spirit enabled us to seek Jesus before we discerned Him as a suitable object for love. He is infinitely lovely and excellent; His matchless love is directed towards His children and He has a storehouse of graces for us. God's love passes through us to bless and serve others to the extent that our pride barrier is set aside. That barrier is nearly impenetrable in the hearts of unbelievers, rendering true *agape* (unconditional) love virtually impossible for them.

There will be trials along the way, because hardship builds character. Trials must make His light burn ever brighter in the lives of believers. All believers—like John the Baptist—must point the way toward Jesus. "*He must increase, but I must decrease.*" **[John 3:30 KJV]**

The benefits of salvation are vast; they include eternal life in heaven and a tender heart now. A tender heart is a sign of a pardoned state. We MUST love God and abhor sin as much as He does. In today's American culture it is far too easy to become numbed to the sin that saturates the culture and is relentlessly promoted as "good." We MUST enthusiastically and resolutely guard against sin that grows in slight increments.

A true Christian has the tender heart of a child. For the Christian, it is a heart that:

1) moves easily in spiritual things,
2) weeps freely when others are in distress,
3) is readily won by kindness,
4) melts and weeps at the evils of sin, and
5) is alarmed by the appearance of moral evil and anything that threatens to hurt the soul.

A tender heart is not a sign of weakness; instead, it is a sign of openness to the needs of others, producing a personal desire to help.

The time for action is now, beginning with our own family.

From experience, we know that we dwell on whom we love. Distraction is virtually impossible. Since the divorce rate among American Christians is about 50%, virtually the same as background secular marriages, it is clear that the distractions have overtaken the original wedding vows. The early emotions have given way to today's harsh realities. Sadly, the original emotional foundation of sand was too weak to withstand the relentless assaults of life. Instead, marriage MUST be supported on a spiritual foundation of rock; it must be a rock-solid, soul-deep, 'til death-do-us-part conviction. Marriage must shift from a Hollywood-style emotional love to a godly spiritual love that renders the lifetime commitment appealing and beautiful, despite all manner of earthly assaults.

Christians must be noticeably different from others, 1) to the eye, 2) to the ear, and 3) to the spirit.

- Eye—modest dress, smile, joyful
- Ear—avoid profane language; speak the truth; Jesus said, "I am the…truth…" [**John 14:6 ESV**]
- Spirit—Love for God; love for others

The *Spirit of God* is the **author** of sanctification. The *Word of God* is the **instrument** of sanctification. "*Thy word is a lamp unto my feet and a light unto my path.*" [**Psalm 119:105 KJV**] Do not say of any error or sin, "It is a mere matter of opinion." No one indulges an *error of judgment* without sooner or later tolerating and *error in* *practice*. Hold fast the truth, for by so holding the truth shall you be sanctified by the Spirit of God.

The Church is inwardly tranquil, facilitating personal growth, and is victorious because of God's infinite grace. But—as modeled by Jesus and the Apostles—outwardly the Church must proclaim Christ Jesus and His great love. <u>The proclamation MUST come from the Holy Spirit-lead **pastors** to invigorate and motivate the body of believers</u>.

Charles G. Finney, the famous 19th Century evangelist and minister, during the *Second Great Awakening* had powerful and prophetic words for <u>leaders in the ministry</u>. During a sermon in 1873 Finney proclaimed:

> "**Brethren, our preaching will bear its legitimate fruits.**
>
> - *If <u>immorality</u> prevails in the land,* **the fault is ours in a great degree.**
>
> - *If there is a <u>decay of conscience</u>,* **the pulpit is responsible for it.**
>
> - *If the public press lacks moral discrimination,* **the pulpit is responsible for it.**
>
> - *If the <u>church is degenerate and worldly</u>,* **the pulpit is responsible for it.**
>
> - *If the <u>world loses its interest in religion</u>,* **the pulpit is responsible for it.**

- *If <u>Satan rules in our halls of legislation,</u> **the pulpit is responsible for it.***

- *If our <u>politics become so corrupt that the very foundations of our government are ready to fall away,</u> **the pulpit is responsible for it.***

Let us not ignore this fact, my dear brethren; but let us lay it to heart, and be thoroughly awake to our responsibility in respect to the morals of this nation."

"The time has come for Christians to vote for honest men, and take consistent ground in politics or the Lord will curse them…<u>Politics are a part of a religion in such a country as this, and Christians must do their duty to their country as a part of their duty to God</u>…**<u>God will bless or curse this nation according to the course Christians take in politics</u>**."

As a Christian, we MUST be continually active as long as we have breath. The graces bestowed on us MUST be in constant motion. God's love MUST overflow through us. The Holy Spirit will provide direction; the Holy Spirit will provide the fruit. "<u>The trees of the Lord are full of sap</u>." [**Psalm 104:16**]

Our light, i.e. God's light shining through us, MUST ALWAYS be conspicuously bright. Unbelievers will persistently try to quench our fire, but the flame of God must be and is eternal. Our pride MUST be continually cast aside, never hindering God's light so that some may be drawn to Christ. Our fire MUST burn brighter than could ever be quenched or diminished by the water of a multitude of unbelievers.

Remember, Jesus said to Peter and the multitudes, "*...to whom much was given, of him much will be required.*" [**Luke 12:48 ESV**] We have been blessed beyond belief. What could be greater than salvation? What could ever be greater than all the blessings and graces that flow from salvation? Lord, help us to share those blessings with as many people as possible. ALL praise to God!

Contemporary Christian Education

Regretfully, many Christian universities have become hooked on government aid or financial aid for students. They have encouraged students to become dependent on government. The universities themselves have incrementally compromised their Christian teaching. The public schools at all levels have almost entirely surrendered to secular anti-God forces.

All higher education tends to fan the flames of pride leading to all manner of sin, unless by the power of the Holy Spirit, *pride* is knowingly and deliberately replaced by *humility*. For example, an <u>*unbeliever* holding a doctoral degree</u> often has "an ego the size of Texas," based on the vast knowledge he/she has apparently accumulated. In contrast, a <u>*believer* holding a Ph.D.</u> is more often impressed by an increasing awareness of how much he/she does not know, rather than being puffed by how much he/she does know. "*Who of God is made unto us wisdom?*" [**1 Corinthians 1:30**]

Nevertheless, **without learning religion, any education is woefully incomplete**, because of the comprehensive influence Christianity has had on world and American history. The compelling need for religion in education has been reinforced many times. Consider a few examples:

"[The] Bible...should be read in our schools in preference to all other books." **Dr. Benjamin Rush**, Founder, signer of the *Declaration of Independence*, and founder of Dickenson College

"The only foundation for useful education in a republic is to be laid in religion." **President Thomas Jefferson**

"Religion is the only solid basis of good morals; therefore education should teach the precepts of religion, and the duties of man toward God." **Gouverneur Morris**, Founder, wrote the preamble to the United States Constitution

"Education is useless without the Bible." **Noah Webster**, writer, best known work is the first complete dictionary of American English

"Education without values, as useful as it is, seems rather to make man a more clever devil." **C.S. Lewis**, British writer and theologian

"Education without religion is in danger of substituting wild theories for the simple common sense rules of Christianity." **Samuel Morse**, painter, inventor

"I would advise no one to send his child where the Holy Scriptures are not supreme. Every institution that does not unceasingly pursue the study of God's Word becomes corrupt...I greatly fear that the [schools], unless they teach the Holy Scriptures diligently and impress them on the young students, are wide gates to Hell." **Martin Luther**, protestant reformer

Consider the potential impact of conspicuously loving, enthusiastic, proactive Christians on America.

AMERICA MAY BE IN THE WINTER OF ITS CAPTIVITY TO MATERIALISM AND HEDONISM, BUT A GREAT AWAKENING IS COMING!

Earthly wrongdoing and cultural chaos are the visible manifestations of the extraordinary battle between good and evil in the heavens. <u>For we do not wrestle against flesh and blood, but against the rulers, against the authorities, against the cosmic powers over this present darkness, against the spiritual forces of evil in the heavenly places.</u> [**Ephesians 6:12**] It is the Holy Spirit's work to turn your eyes and my eyes toward Jesus at all times. It is Satan's work to lure our focus to our pride. When we choose to look toward Jesus, the Holy Spirit will give us the power to keep it there.

God grants freedom, Christianity protects it. God gifts freedom as an expression of His infinite love. Christians protect freedom to the extent that they love God and love others as the highest priority of their lives. Are YOU willing to sacrifice your life for freedom, either literally or figuratively? Either the breath of life or the day-to-day practice of life? **God called the United States to be a witness to the world.** Our nation can be God's witness only to the extent that His people are willing to stand up, stand out, and speak out in support of all things good—God's perfect wisdom—and in opposition to all things evil—man's flawed "wisdom."

Prior to and during *America's War for Independence* (Revolutionary War), the clergy played a particularly powerful role. Even as they grappled with [**Romans 13:1 ESV**], "<u>Let every person be subject to the governing authorities. For there is no authority except from God, and those that exist have been instituted by God</u>," they often concluded that resistance to tyranny is obedience to God. Jesus said, "<u>Render to Caesar the things that are Caesar's, and to God the things that are God's</u>." [**Mark 12:17 ESV**] The tipping point occurs when a government commandeers "the things that are God's." The arguments are expressed with abundant clarity in the *Declaration of Independence*:

> We hold these truths to be self-evident, that all men are created equal, that they are endowed by their Creator with certain unalienable Rights, that among these are Life, Liberty and the pursuit of Happiness.— That to secure these rights, Governments are instituted among Men, deriving their just powers from the consent of the governed, —**That whenever any Form of Government becomes destructive of these ends, it is the Right of the People to alter or to abolish it, and to institute new Government**, laying its foundation on such principles and organizing its powers in such form, as to them shall seem most likely to effect their Safety and Happiness.

Many of the clergy became military chaplains, actively engaging in combat. Numerous clergy delivered fiery pro-freedom sermons and then lead the men in their church to war with the British. The influence of the clergy was so feared by the British that they referred to the clergy as, "The Black Regiment," referring to the robes they wore while preaching.

The clergy often had a bounty on their head; some were martyred. Their stories are legion. An excellent source is *The Chaplains and Clergy of the Revolution* (1864), by Joel Tyler Headley. Read just one excerpt, a discussion of a sermon preached by **Rev. George Duffield** :

> *The patriots of the first (Continental) Congress flocked to his church, and* **John Adams** *and his compeers were often his hearers, for he preached as Jonas Clarke had before preached at Lexington.*
>
> *In a discourse delivered before several companies of Pennsylvania militia and members of Congress, four months before the Declaration of Independence, he took bold and decided ground in favor of that step, and plead his cause with sublime eloquence, which afterwards made him so obnoxious to the British that they offered a reward of fifty pounds for his capture.*
>
> *He declared that Heaven designed this western world as the asylum for* <u>liberty</u>, *and that to raise its banner here their forefathers had sundered the dearest ties of home, friends and native land, and braved the tempests of the ocean and the terrors of the wilderness.*

"Providence has place you where you must stand the first shock...If we submit to these regulations, all is gone. Our forefathers passed the vast Atlantic, spent their blood and treasure, that *they might enjoy their liberties* **both civil and religious** *and transmit them to their* **posterity**...Now if we should give them up, can our children rise up and call us blessed?" **Colonel William Prescott**, commanded at the **Battle of Bunker Hill** ordering, "Do not fire until you see the whites of their eyes!"

*Not through the fostering care of Britain, he said, had they grown and flourished, but her "tyranny and oppression, **both civil AND ecclesiastical**," had driven noble souls hither "to enjoy in peace the fair possessions of <u>freedom</u>." "Tis this," he exclaimed, "has reared our cities, and turned the wilderness, so far and wide, into a fruitful field.*

And can it be supposed that the Lord has so far forgotten to be gracious, and shut up His tender mercies in His wrath, and so favored the arms of oppression, as to deliver up their asylum to slavery and bondage? Can it be supposed that that God who made man free, and engraved in indefaceable characters the love of <u>liberty</u> in his mind, should forbid freedom already exiled from Asia and Africa, and under sentence of banishment from Europe—that He should forbid her to erect her banners here, and constrain her to abandon the earth? As soon shall He subvert creation, and forbid the sun to shine.

He preserved to the Jews their cities of refuge, and whilst sun and moon endure America shall remain a city of refuge for the whole earth, until she herself shall play the tyrant, forget her destiny, disgrace her freedom, and provoke her God.

When that day shall—if ever come—then, and not till then, shall she also fall, slain with them that go down to the pit." In such strains of impassioned eloquence did he sustain his high argument for <u>liberty</u>, and pour his own brave, glowing soul into his excited *listeners, till they were ready, when he ceased, to shout, "To arms: to arms!"*

The love of God, and the love, courage, strength, and determination of our Founders, the clergy, and their compatriots echo to us through the last couple centuries.

Can we do any less?
Can you do any less?
Can I do any less?

THE GREATEST AWAKENING OF ALL TIME MUST BEGIN WITH ME

---

*... let him know that whoever brings back a sinner
from his wandering will save his soul from death
and will cover a multitude of sins.*
JAMES 5:20 ESV

AUTHOR'S NOTE: Any real and lasting change must begin with you and me allowing God to touch others through us. God's flow of love and his graces through us happens to the extent that we set aside the barrier of our personal pride. As such, the message of this last chapter comes to life and is best understood when you, the reader, apply the personal pronouns to yourself.

I am deeply concerned about our rapidly collapsing modern American culture. Increasing numbers of people are denying God in word or actions. The responsibility lies largely within the church. My responsibilities are at least sevenfold:

The Greatest Awakening of All Time Must Begin With Me

- Express those concerns often at appropriate times and places.
- Pray frequently and consistently.
- Set a godly example for others.
- Act directly to firmly stabilize and protect my family and to assist other families in doing the same.
- Vote at every opportunity.
- Participate in public affairs as lead by the Lord.
- Leave the results to God. He is a far better burden-bearer than I am.

> "Providence has place you where you must stand the first shock…If we submit to these regulations, all is gone. Our forefathers passed the vast Atlantic, spent their blood and treasure, that *they might enjoy their liberties **both civil and religious** and transmit them to their **posterity**…*Now if we should give them up, can our children rise up and call us blessed?" **Colonel William Prescott**, commanded at the **Battle of Bunker Hill** ordering, "Do not fire until you see the whites of their eyes!"

The church is full of almost Christians. An almost Christian, who likes the religious idea and the comfort and joy of a worship service, may have been "vaccinated" by Satan with a small dose of Christianity. With the power of the Holy Spirit I MUST strive to pierce the vaccination shield, leading the almost Christian to a genuine saving faith in Jesus. Still, too many saved Christians continue to live the pride-driven life of an almost Christian.

Despite my own best efforts, I know my sin nature will cause me to default to sin (evil) if my soul is not constantly re-nourished with God's love and graces. There is no substitute for the re-nourishment provided by the Bible, prayer, and other committed believers.

THERE HAS NEVER BEEN A MORE URGENT TIME.

<u>Time is short; our time is even shorter. It MUST NOT be wasted. We are here to serve God and serve others</u>. Even my leisure diversions MUST become opportunities to serve. Time is a human idea marking progress between birth and death. Heaven has no time. There is no need for time. When the saints are perfected, no further change is necessary and no progress to be measured. The destination of bliss is eternal (timeless). God lives outside of time and so will we after we arrive in heaven.

Meanwhile, spiritual growth and spiritual warfare are both lifelong endeavors. They never end in this life. There is no retirement from either. **Lord, *give me the grace to stay the course of spiritual growth and with your help to aggressively fight the battles of spiritual warfare.***

> "...with the promises of God before our eyes and the grace that they offer, *our unbelief grievously wrongs God, if we do not with unshrinking courage boldly set him against all our enemies.*" **John Calvin, Reformer** commentary on: "*The Lord is my light and my salvation; whom shall I fear? The Lord is the strength of my life; of whom shall I be afraid?*" [**Psalm 27:1 KJV**]
>
> "Plead my cause, Oh, Lord, with them that strive with me...Let those be turned back and humiliated who devise evil against me." Prayer by **Rev. Jacob Duche** before the first session of the Continental Congress, September 7, 1774

The fuel and ammunition for the battle is God's love. After all, "<u>God is love</u>." [**1 John 4:8 ESV**] What an awesome thought! God is **not just** the **creator** *of love*, the **sponsor** *of love*, the **purveyor** *of love*, or the **promoter** *of love*. <u>He IS love</u>. He is the source and fountain of ALL love. The Christian life is God's love flowing through us. **Lord, *let God's magnificent love flow through me at ALL times; let not my pride hinder the flow in any way.***

Even suffering is a fruit of love. When we express God's love directly or exhibit the fruit of the Spirit indirectly as a lifestyle, some unbelievers will dislike or even hate us. The reason is that the direct or indirect expressions of God's love:

1) Set a standard to which unbelievers do not want to conform,
2) Set a standard to which unbelievers cannot conform, because of their sin nature, and
3) Hinder the "fun" of their sinful lifestyle. Their false perception of freedom masks the true freedom of the Christian life.

If people dislike or hate us because we love God, how much more will they hate God whose Holy Spirit seeks to convict them daily. "*If the world hates you, know that it has hated me before it hated you. If you were of the world, the world would love you as its own; but because you are not of the world, but I chose you out of the world, therefore the world hates you. Remember the word that I said to you: 'A servant is not greater than his master.' If they persecuted me, they will also persecute you.*" [**John 15:18-20 ESV**]

Unbelievers fear that accepting Christ will restrict their freedom. The fear becomes a huge barrier. The reality is that accepting Christ frees a man from the captivity of sin, producing the ultimate freedom of an unhindered free will. A Christian simply chooses to avoid sinful behaviors. He does not want to abuse God's extraordinary gift of a free will.

The unbelieving background culture, including many political and religious leaders, hated Jesus because the fallen world is evil. If we express God's love and our love for Jesus visibly, the world will hate us also. If the world does not hate us, our ambassadorship for Christ is not visible.

The battle between good and evil in heavenly places is also continuously fought in the American culture and in the depth of my soul. Ultimately, God wins the battle in the heavenly places. He also wins the battle in the American culture and in my soul. The least we can do is be committed and available to cooperate with Him.

WE MUST SERVE GOD AND OTHERS, BY EXHIBITING GODLY CHARACTER

God's graces to us and for us abound. They are beyond measure. We can do no less than our very best to exhibit godly character, at all times, in all that we think and do. When others become envious, they will ask about the hope that is within us.

We MUST *avoid* foolish questions "*Avoid foolish controversies.*" [***Titus 3:9 ESV***] Topics include:

> *Because I fear the Lord and have accepted His infinite love,* I know that His eye is on me, He has delivered me from death and keeps me alive in a culture of (spiritual) famine. [***Psalms 33:18, 19*** *personal paraphrase*]
>
> Because I fear God, the armies of heaven look after me, take charge of me, encamp about me, and deliver me. [***Psalms 34:7; Hebrews 1:14*** *personal paraphrase*]
>
> The Lord blesses me because I fear Him. [***Psalms 115:13*** *personal paraphrase*]
>
> When strangers greet me, I MUST respond like Jonah, "I am a Hebrew (analog Christian today) and I fear the Lord, the God of heaven, who made the sea and the dry land." [***Jonah 1:8-9 ESV***]

- Points where Scripture is silent
- Mysteries belonging to God alone
- Prophecies of doubtful interpretation
- Modes of observing human ceremonies

We MUST _daily_ tackle wise and important questions:

- Do I believe in the Lord Jesus Christ?
- Am I renewed in the spirit of my mind?
- Am I walking not after the flesh, but after the Spirit?
- Am I growing in grace?
- Does my conversation and behavior adorn the doctrine of God my Savior?
- Am I looking for the coming of the Lord?
- What more can I do for Jesus?

We MUST constantly beware of Humanist and hypocritical spider webs (attractive distractions called "snares" in Scripture) remembering that our greatest debt is to the sovereign grace of God. "_...they weave the spider's web._" [**Isaiah 59:5 ESV**]

> "I call upon all Americans to pray to Almighty God and to perform acts of service...Across our Nation, many selfless deeds reflect the promise of the Scripture: '_For I was hungry and you gave Me food; I was thirsty and you gave Me drink; I was a stranger and you took Me in._'" **President George W. Bush**, declared a Day of Prayer and Remembrance, 2005¶

We MUST be a burning and shining light, revealing the mind and will of God to the world in darkness. Jesus is THE Way, THE Truth, and THE Life. He cannot be the explosive secret carefully hidden in the hearts of believers. As with the Apostles, Jesus MUST be readily visible as the overflowing delight and joy in us regardless of external circumstances.

CAUTION: Satan is real despite widespread cultural denial. He is vigilant to hinder me every moment of every day. "_...Satan *hindered us.*" [**1 Thessalonians 2:18 ESV**] His hindering evokes a greater appreciation of God's perfect love

Since we are known by many to be a Christian, we MUST conduct our life carefully:

1) *Unbelievers and almost believers* watch us warily hoping to discredit our influence by attaching the label, "hypocrite" to us.
2) *Believers* watch us carefully hoping to see a model of strong character.

We MUST NOT give any unbelievers or believers an opportunity to discredit our life example.

> "Those of you who feel that the church has no responsibility in the cultural area...What if it were 1943 and you were in Nazi Germany and you knew what Hitler was doing to the Jews...Would you say, 'We're not political-that's somebody else's problem?' I thank God <u>Dietrich Bonhoeffer</u> did not give that answer, and he was arrested by the Nazis and hanged in 1945, naked and alone because he said, 'This is not right.'" **Dr. James Dobson** to National Religious Broadcasters, February 16, 2002
>
> "The same Holy Spirit...that gave (Dietrich) Bonhoeffer the strength to stand up against Nazi tyranny is available to us today." **President Jimmy Carter**, *Sources of Strength*
>
> "We can't have it both ways. We can't expect God to protect us in a crisis and just leave Him over there on the shelf in our day-to-day living." **President Ronald Reagan**, Alfred M. Landon Lecture Series, 1982

WE MUST SERVE BY PROCLAIMING GOD IN ALL AREAS OF LIFE

"Forgive me Jesus for failing to be the best possible example to my family and others. Restore to me the power and eagerness to proclaim your glory. Make my life a clear testimony:"

- I need not say, "I am true." I must be true.

- I must not boast of integrity; I must BE upright, so my life will be that people cannot help seeing it.
- I must not restrain my example or witness for fear of feeble man.
- In season and out of season I must witness for the Savior."

WE *MUST* SERVE BY ENTHUSIASTICALLY SHARING GOD'S PLAN OF SALVATION

The witnessing of 21st Century American believers is shameful. "<u>*... and you will be my witnesses.*</u>" [***Acts 1:8 ESV***] They have allowed themselves to become sequestered by political correctness to within the four walls of their house and the four walls of their place of worship. Tragically, believers have allowed political correctness to rob them of their freedom of speech and sap their motivation to witness for Jesus. Sadly, our own witness has been negatively affected as well.

Sharing the incredible news of salvation in Jesus Christ is our greatest honor and privilege. We MUST NEVER shrink from it or succumb to the silence of <u>political correctness</u>. The <u>spiritual correctness</u> of God's glorious salvation message is far more important and powerful.

"Many who profess the gospel fail to endure when trouble comes, and alas! Their hearts fail them. O how many depart from Christ at this crossroads! Do not say you have royal blood running in your veins, and you are born of God, except you can prove your pedigree by this heroic spirit; to dare to be holy in spite of men and devils. How uncomely a sight it is to see a bold sinner and a fearful saint: one resolved to be wicked, and a Christian wavering in his holy course; to see hell keep the field while the saints hide their colours for shame. Take heart, O ye saints, and be strong; your cause is good. God himself adopts your quarrel. He shall lead you on with courage, and bring you off with honour. He lived and died for you. For mercy and tenderness to his soldiers, there is none like him." ***William Gurnall*** *The Christian in complete Armour, 1:15-17, circa 1662*

God help us to freely and routinely to stand up, stand out, and speak out about your wonderful and incredibly awesome salvation. "*<u>I have become all things to all people that by all means I might save some</u>*." [***1 Corinthians 9:22 ESV***]

I would much rather have the *mark of Christ*, than the *mark of the beast*. The mark of Christ is the infallible mark of regeneration and adoption. "*<u>The spot of His children</u>*." [***Deuteronomy 32:5 KJV***] The mark is a hearty faith in my Redeemer. The unseen mark of the Redeemer becomes visible only through the love of the elect and service to others. The visible mark of the Beast identifies a target for persecution or destruction, like the yellow star identified Jews in World War II.

Salvation in Christ is powerful; it is exciting. It MUST be shared. We MUST share it. All history is the story of redemption. It is His story! Remove Jesus and history collapses into chaotic clusters of facts, without significance or meaning. Include Jesus and history reveals infinite beauty and harmony as an expression of His infinite love. All the tragic moments of history are rebellion against God.

Like the flood of Noah, the flood of God's wrath is fast approaching. We MUST warn as many others as possible that our Savior's love and sacrifice is the only remedy for sin and the only escape from God's wrath. Heaven is a far better destination than hell.

Instead of "raising awareness" for the cause of the day, it is our duty and profound privilege as a Christian to actively and regularly raise awareness of the Bible and proclaim the saving work of Jesus. We MUST do so as an ongoing way of life.

Conversations about freedom as God's great gift and the powerful groups working mightily and incessantly to take away that freedom create opportunities to discuss God, the Bible, and the salvation message.

NOW, THE NEXT GREAT AWAKENING IS UP TO YOU AND ME. WITH GOD'S HELP, WE WILL BE THE TRIGGERS, THE PROMOTERS, AND THE SUPPORTERS.

Appendix I

FALL OF ROME: ARE THERE LESSONS WE CAN LEARN?

Posted By *Bill Federer* 09/03/2019

The fall of Rome was a culmination of external and internal factors. By 220 A.D., the Later Eastern Han Dynasty had extended sections of the Great Wall of China along its Mongolian border. This resulted in the Northern Huns attacking west instead of east. This caused a domino effect of displaced tribes migrating west across Central Asia, and overrunning the Western Roman Empire.

OPEN BORDERS

Illegal immigrants poured across the Roman borders: Visigoths, Ostrogoths, Franks, Anglos, Saxons, Alemanni, Thuringians, Rugians, Jutes, Picts, Burgundians, Lombards, Alans, Vandals, as well as African Berbers and Arab raiders.

Will and Ariel Durant wrote in "The Story of Civilization" (Vol. 3 – Caesar and Christ, Simon & Schuster, 1944, p. 366): "*If Rome* *had not engulfed so many men of alien blood in so brief a time, if she had passed all these newcomers through her schools instead of her slums, if she had treated them as men with a hundred potential excellences, if she had occasionally closed her gates to let assimilation catch up with infiltration, she might have gained new racial and literary vitality from the infusion, and might have remained a Roman Rome, the voice and citadel of the West."*

LOSS OF COMMON LANGUAGE

At first immigrants assimilated and learned the Latin language. They worked as servants with many rising to leadership. But then they came so fast they did not learn Latin, but instead created a mix of Latin with their own Frankish, Spanish, Portuguese, Italian, Romanian, Germanic and Anglo tribal tongues (Romance Languages). The unity of the Roman Empire began to dissolve.

WELFARE STATE

"Bread and the Circus!" Starting in 123 B.C., the immensely powerful Roman politician, **Gaius Gracchus** began appeasing citizens with welfare, a free monthly dole (hand out) of grain. Roman poet **Juvenal** (circa 100 A.D.) described how Roman emperors controlled the masses by keeping them ignorant and obsessed with self-indulgence. This way, they would be distracted and not throw them out of office, which they might have done if they had realized the true dire condition of the Empire: *"Already long ago, from when we sold our vote to no man, the People have abdicated our duties; for the People who once upon a time handed out military command, high civil office, legions everything, now restrains itself and anxiously hopes for just two things: bread and circuses."*

Juvenal continued: "*Tyrants would distribute largess, a bushel of wheat, a gallon of wine, and a sesterce; and everyone would shamelessly cry, 'Long live the King.' ... The fools did not realize that they were merely recovering a portion of their own property, and that their ruler could not have given them what they were receiving without having first taken it from them.*"

Marcus Tullius Cicero wrote: "*The evil was not in bread and circuses, per se, but in the willingness of the people to sell their rights as free men for full bellies and the excitement of games which would serve to distract them from the other human hungers which bread and circuses can never appease.*"

John Stossel, host of "Stossel" on the Fox Business Network and author of "No They Can't: Why Government Fails, but Individuals Succeed," wrote in his article "Are We Rome Yet?" (7/11/13, www.johnstossel.com): "*The president the Foundation for Economic Education, Lawrence Reed, warned that Rome, like America, had an expanding welfare state. It started with 'subsidized grain.' The government gave it away at half price. But the problem was that they couldn't stop there – a man named Claudius ran for Tribune on a platform of free wheat for the masses. And won. It was downhill from there. ... Soon, to appease angry voters, emperors gave away or subsidized olive oil, salt and pork. People lined up to get free stuff.*"

Will and Ariel Durant wrote in "The Lessons of History" (1968, p. 92): "*The concentration of population and poverty in great cities may compel a government to choose between enfeebling the economy with a dole (government handout of bread) or running the risk of riot and revolution.*"

In "***The Great Ages of Man – Barbarian Europe***" (NY: Time-Life Books, 1968, p. 39), one Roman is recorded as stating: "*Those who live at the expense of the public funds are more numerous than those who provide them.*"

Violent, sensual entertainment

The **Circus Maximus and Coliseum** were packed with crowds of Romans engrossed with violent entertainment, games, chariot races, and until 404 A.D., gladiators fighting to the death.

John Stossel wrote: "*Nero traveled with 1,000 carriages. Tiberius established an 'office of imperial pleasures,' which gathered 'beautiful boys and girls from all corners of the world' so, as Tacitus put it, the emperor 'could defile them.' Emperor Commodus held a show in the Colosseum at which he personally killed five hippos, two elephants, a rhinoceros and a giraffe.*"

The value of human life was low. Slavery and sex-trafficking abounded, especially of captured peoples from Eastern Europe. "Slavs," which meant "glorious" came to have the inglorious meaning of a permanent servant or "slave." (Great Ages, p. 18).

Gerald Simons wrote in "Great Ages of Man – Barbarian Europe" (NY: Time-Life Books, 1968, p. 20): "*In the causal brutality of its public spectacles, in a rampant immorality that **even Christianity could not check**.*"

Church withdrawal from involvement

A hyper-pietism movement swept the church, teaching that the way to truly follow Christ was to withdraw from public involvement, give away all one's money and live as a poor beggar or join a monastery. It was an early version of separation of church and state.

Richard A. Todd wrote in "The Fall of the Roman Empire" (Eerdmans' Handbook to the History of Christianity, Grand Rapids, MI: Wm. B. Eerdmans Co., 1977, p. 184): "<u>The church, while preaching against abuses, contributed to the decline by discouraging good Christians from holding public office</u>."

<u>Birth control, Planned Parenthood, fewer children</u>

Roman families had fewer children. Up until 374 A.D., when a Roman mother bore a child, she would lay it at the father's feet. If he picked it up, they would keep it. If he did not pick it up, feeling it was a financial burden or looked unhealthy, the mother would have to put the baby in a box and leave it outside, exposed to the weather to die. Early Christians condemned this inhumane practice with the same pro-life arguments used today against the abortion industry.

Some Romans sold unwanted children into slavery. The **Durants** wrote in "The Story of Civilization," Vol. 3 – Caesar and Christ (Simon & Schuster, 1944, p. 134): "<u>Children were now luxuries which only the poor could afford</u>."

The **Durants** observed <u>that as Roman culture advanced, women waited longer to have children and had fewer of them</u>, yet in less-advanced cultures women began having children sooner and had more of them. Thus, inevitably, the less advanced cultures overrun the more advanced ones.

Julius Caesar noticed this and tried to counter it, as the **Durants** wrote: "Family limitation played some part in the history of Greece and Rome. It is amusing to find Julius Caesar offering (59 B.C.) rewards to Romans who had many children, and forbidding childless women to ride in litters (chairs on poles carried by porters) or wear jewelry. **Augustus** renewed this campaign some forty years later, with like futility. Birth control continued to spread in the upper classes while immigrant stocks from the Germanic North and the Greek or Semitic East replenished and altered the population of Italy."

One of the lessons the Durants observed was biological: "The ... biological lesson of history is that life must breed. Nature has no use for organisms ... that cannot reproduce. ... She does not care that a high birth rate has usually accompanied a culturally low civilization, and a low birth rate a civilization culturally high; and she (here meaning Nature) sees to it that a nation with _a low birth rate shall be periodically chastened by some more virile and fertile group._"

IMMORALITY, INFIDELITY, LOSS OF VIRTUE

There was court favoritism, the patronage system, injustice in the legal system, infidelity, bathhouses rampant with homosexuality, sexual immorality, gluttony and gymnasiums ("gym" being the Greek word for naked).

Fifth-century historian **Salvian** wrote: "_For all the lurid Roman tales of their atrocities ... the barbarians displayed ... a good deal more fidelity to their wives._" (Great Ages, p. 13.) "O Roman people be ashamed; be ashamed of your lives. Almost no cities are free of evil dens, are altogether free of impurities, except the cities in which the barbarians have begun to live. ... _Let nobody think otherwise, the vices of our bad lives have alone conquered us._ ... The

Goths lie, but are chaste, the Franks lie, but are generous, the Saxons are savage in cruelty ... but are admirable in chastity. ... What hope can there be for the Romans when the barbarians are more pure than they?"

Samuel Adams wrote to **John Scollay** of Boston, April 30, 1776: "*The diminution of public virtue is usually attended with that of public happiness, and the public liberty will not long survive the total extinction of morals. 'The Roman Empire,' says the historian, 'must have sunk, though the Goths had not invaded it. Why? Because the Roman virtue was sunk.'*"

As Roman virtue declined, the number of laws increased. Cornelius Tacitus wrote: "*The more corrupt the state, the more numerous the laws.*"

CLASS WARFARE

City centers were abandoned by the upper class, who bought up farms from rural landowners and transformed them into palatial estates.

The **Durants** wrote in "The Story of Civilization" (Vol. 3 – Caesar and Christ, Simon & Schuster, 1944, p.90): "*The Roman landowner disappeared now that ownership was concentrated in a few families, and a proletariat (working class) without stake in the country filled the slums of Rome.*" Inner cities were destabilized, being also plagued with lead poisoning, as the plumbing that brought water into the city was made out of lead pipes ("plumb" is the Latin word for "lead").

HIGH TAXES

Welfare and government jobs exploded, especially with emperors wanting to honor themselves by leaving legacies of massive public building projects, such as bath houses, coliseums, parade grounds, etc. Taxes became unbearable, as "collectors became greedy functionaries in a bureaucracy so huge and corrupt." Tax collectors were described by the historian ***Salvian*** as "more terrible than the enemy." (Great Ages, p. 20).

Arther Ferrill wrote in "The Fall of the Roman Empire: The Military Explanation" (New York: Thames and Hudson Ltd., 1986): "<u>The chief cause of the agricultural decline was high taxation on the marginal land, driving it out of cultivation</u>." **Wealth began to flee the Empire, and with it, the spirit of liberty and patriotism.**

President William Henry Harrison warned in his inaugural address, 1841: "<u>It was the beautiful remark of a distinguished English writer that 'in the Roman senate Octavius had a party and Antony a party, but the Commonwealth had none.' ... The spirit of liberty had fled, and, avoiding the abodes of civilized man, had sought protection in the wilds of Scythia or Scandinavia; and so under the operation of the same causes and influences it will fly from our Capitol and our forums.</u>" More recently, ***John F. Kennedy*** observed, Jan. 6, 1961: "<u>Present tax laws may be stimulating in undue amounts the flow of American capital to industrial countries abroad</u>."

OURSOURCING

Rome's economy stagnated from a large trade deficit, as grain production was outsourced to North Africa. ***Gerald Simons*** wrote in "Great Ages of Man – Barbarian Europe" (NY: Time-Life Books,

1968, p. 39): "As conquerors of North Africa, the Vandals cut off the Empire's grain supply at will. This created critical food shortages, which in turn curtailed Roman counterattacks."

EXPLODING DEBT, COINAGE DEBASEMENT

As the Roman economy declined, those unable to pay their mortgages abandoned their properties, renounced their Roman citizenship, and went off to live with the barbarians. As a result, **Emperor Diocletian** decreed that people could never run away from their debts, thus tying them and their children to the land in perpetuity, *creating the feudal system.*

Rome was crippled by huge government bureaucracies and enormous public debt. Rather than curb out-of-control government spending, Roman emperors decided to debase coins by mixing them with cheaper base metals. This devalued their monetary system and caused exponential inflation.

The **Durants** wrote in "The Lessons of History" (p. 92): "<u>Huge bureaucratic machinery was unable to govern the empire effectively with the enormous, out-of-control debt</u>."

John Stossel wrote: "<u>To pay for their excesses, emperors devalued the currency. Nero reduced the silver content of coins to 95 percent. Then Trajan reduced it to 85 percent and so on. By the year 300, wheat that once cost eight Roman dollars cost 120,000 Roman dollars</u>."

In "Great Ages of Man – Barbarian Europe" (NY: Time-Life Books, 1968, p. 20), **Gerald Simons** wrote: "<u>The Western Roman economy, already undermined by falling production of the great Roman estates</u>

and an unfavorable balance of trade that siphoned off gold to the East, had now run out of money."

Rolf Nef of Global Research, wrote in "Falling Empires and their Currencies" (1/5/07, www.globalresearch.ca): *"When empires fall, their currencies fall first. Even clearer is the rising debt of empires in decline, because in most cases their physical expansion is financed with debt.* …

The common thing is that the currencies of each and every one of these falling empires lost dramatically in value. … The Roman Empire existed from 400 B.C. to 400 A.D. Its history is the history of physical expansion, like the history of almost all empires. Its expansion was driven by a citizen soldier army, paid in silver coins, land and slaves from occupied territories. If there was not enough silver in the treasury to conduct a war, base metals were added to coin more money. That is to say, the authorities debased their currency which presaged the fall of the Empire. There was a limit to the expansion. The empire became over-stretched, running out of silver money, and eventually went under, overrun by barbarian hordes."

The noted astronomer **Nicolaus Copernicus** observed: *"Nations are not ruined by one act of violence, but gradually and in an almost imperceptible manner by the depreciation of their circulating currency, through its excessive quantity."*

Richard W. Fisher, President and CEO of the Federal Reserve Bank of Dallas, remarked before the Commonwealth Club of California, San Francisco, California, May 28, 2008: *"We know from centuries of evidence in countless economies, from ancient Rome to today's Zimbabwe, that running the printing press to pay off today's bills* *leads to much worse problems later on. The inflation that results from the flood of money into the economy turns out to be far worse than the fiscal pain those countries hoped to avoid."*

John Stossel added: *"Rome's government, much like ours, wasn't good at making sure subsidies flowed only to the poor, said Reed: 'Anybody could line up to get these goods, which contributed to the ultimate bankruptcy of the Roman state.' As inflation increased, Rome ... imposed wage and price controls. When people objected, Emperor Diocletian denounced their 'greed,' saying, 'Shared humanity urges us to set a limit.' Doesn't that sound like today's anti-capitalist politicians? ... Rome enforced controls with the death penalty – and forbid people to change professions. Emperor Constantine decreed that those who broke such rules 'be bound with chains and reduced to servile condition."*

DEEP **S**TATE ESTABLISHMENT POLITICIANS

The Roman emperor usurped so much power, that the Roman Senate, instead of ruling Rome and defending the rights of the people, existed only to maintain their own positions. Common people were discourage from getting involved in politics.

The **Durants** wrote in "The Lessons of History" (p. 92): "***The educated and skilled pursued business and financial success to the neglect of their involvement in politics.***"

John Stossel wrote in his article "Are We Rome Yet?": "**Historian Carl Richard said that today's America resembles Rome. The Roman Republic had a constitution, but Roman leaders often ignored it. 'Marius was elected consul six years in a row, even though under the constitution (he) was term-limited to one year.'"**

Fall of Rome: Are There Lessons We Can Learn?

Ben Franklin addressed the Constitutional Convention, June 2, 1787: "*There are two passions which have a powerful influence in the affairs of men ... ambition and avarice – the love of power and the love of money. ... Place before the eyes of such men a post of honor, that shall, at the same time, be a place of profit, and they will move heaven and earth to obtain it. ...*" "*What kind are the men that will strive for this profitable preeminence, through all the bustle of cabal, the heat of contention, the infinite mutual abuse of parties, tearing to pieces the best of characters? It will not be the wise and moderate, the lovers of peace and good order, the men fittest for the trust. It will be the bold and the violent, the men of strong passions and indefatigable activity in their selfish pursuits. These will thrust themselves into your government and be your rulers.*"

Harry S Truman stated April 3, 1951: "**Without a firm moral foundation, freedom degenerates quickly ... into anarchy. Then there will be freedom only for ... those who are stronger and more unscrupulous than the rank and file of the people.**"

DEFENSE CUTS, OVER-EXTENDED MILITARY

Emperors realized that if they kept citizens preoccupied with endless external wars, the citizens would be distracted from complaining about internal problems and political strife. Though the Roman military was superior and marched with speed on a system of highly advanced Roman roads, the Roman Legions were over-extended and strained fighting continual conflicts from the Rhine River to the Sassanid Persian Empire. Roman borders were over-extended and border patrol troop strength was cut back to dangerously low ranks.

Stossel wrote: "*Eventually, Rome's empire was so large – and people so resentful of centralized control – that generals in outlying regions began declaring independence from Rome.*"

LOSS OF PATRIOTISM

Will and Ariel Durant noted in "The Lessons of History" that Rome's rapid demographic change threatened the patriotic impulse to defend it: "*Very probably this ethnic change reduced the ability or willingness of the inhabitants to resist governmental incompetence and external attack.*"

Non-Roman citizens were enlisted into the Roman military, being offered citizenship in exchange for their military service. This carried a risk, for how could they be expected to defend Roman borders from invading Germanic tribes, when, in many cases, those tribes were their relatives? Non-Roman soldiers who defected carried their military training with them to the enemy.

The **Durants** wrote in "The Story of Civilization" (Vol. 3 – Caesar and Christ, Simon & Schuster, 1944, p.90): "*The new generation, having inherited world mastery, had no time or inclination to defend it; that readiness for war which had characterized the Roman landowner disappeared.*" With the increase of invading hordes, Roman legions had to be recalled from the frontiers to protect the city of Rome itself. It was at this time that young **Saint Patrick** was kidnapped from Roman Britain and sold as a slave in Druid Ireland, which he later evangelized.

Fall of Rome: Are There Lessons We Can Learn?

Terrorist attacks

The law of nature demonstrates that weakness invites attack. As Rome exhibited weakness, **Attila the Hun**, "The Scourge of God," attacked with an army of a half-million soldiers. Christians thought Attila was the anti-christ as he <u>killed, by some estimates, 20 million people</u>.

After attacking cities in Persia, North Africa, and Eastern Europe, Attila took his army with battering rams and siege towers and sacked the European cities of: Strasbourg, Worms, Mainz, Cologne, Trier, Metz, Reims, Tournai, Cambrai, Amiens, and Beauvais.

When **Attila** headed toward Paris in 451, young **Saint Genevieve** convinced the inhabitants not to flee but instead to pray. She began a "<u>***prayer marathon***</u>," after which Attila inexplicably bypassed Paris and instead attacked Orleans. Aquileia was an Italian city on the coast of the Adriatic Sea. It was the ninth-largest city in the world, with over 100,000 people. Attila so completely decimated Aquileia that the inhabitants fled into marshy lagoons, hammered logs into the sand, and built platforms to live on. This grew into the city of Venice.

When **Attila** headed toward Italy in 452, **Pope Leo** rode out to persuade him to spare Rome. The Pope's mission was successful, but it only delayed the fall of Rome by a few decades. Finally, in 476, barbarian **Chieftain Odoacer** attacked. This is considered the date of the fall of Rome, Sept. 4, 476 A.D.

LESSONS FROM THE FALL OF ROME

Future generations can learn from the *factors that led to the fall of Rome*:

- open borders
- loss of common language
- welfare state
- violent, sensual entertainment and sex-trafficking
- *church* withdrawal from involvement
- birth control, planned parenthood and fewer children
- immorality, infidelity and loss of virtue
- class warfare
- high taxes
- out-sourcing
- exploding debt and coinage debasement
- deep state, establishment politicians
- defense cuts and over-extended military
- loss of patriotism
- terrorist attacks

The **Durants** wrote in "The Lessons of History" (p. 89-90): "<u>Oswald Spengler (1880-1936) … divided history into … two periods: – one of centripetal organization, unifying a culture in all its phases into a unique coherent, and artistic form; – the other a period of centrifugal disorganization, in which creed and culture decompose in division and criticism, and end in chaos.</u>"

John Stossel wrote: "<u>At FreedomFest, Matt Kibbe, president of FreedomWorks, also argued that America could soon collapse like Rome did. 'The parallels are quite ominous – the debt, the expansionist foreign policy, the arrogance of executive power taking over our country,' says Kibbe. '**But I do think we have a chance to stop it**. …'</u>" "<u>The **triumph of liberty** is not inevitable. … Empires do</u>

crumble. Rome's lasted the longest. The Ottoman Empire lasted 623 years. China's Song, Qing and Ming dynasties each lasted about 300 years. We've lasted just 237 years so far. ..." **"We've accomplished amazing things, but we shouldn't take our continued success for granted. Freedom and prosperity are not natural. In human history, they're rare."** https://www.wnd.com/2019/09/fall-rome-lessons-can-learn/

Appendix II

AMERICA'S SPIRITUAL HERITAGE

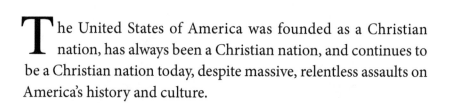

The United States of America was founded as a Christian nation, has always been a Christian nation, and continues to be a Christian nation today, despite massive, relentless assaults on America's history and culture.

The evidence is overwhelming. America has far deeper roots than the original founding. In reverse chronological order, America's spiritual roots extend beyond the Declaration of Independence, beyond the arrival of the early settlers, through several waves of the Protestant Reformation in Europe, all the way to the origin of the first Protestant Reformation itself.

Near the turn of the 20th Century, United States Supreme Court Justice David J. Brewer wrote one of the most remarkable opinions in the history of the Supreme Court, *Church of the Holy Trinity v. United States, 143 U.D. 457 (1892) No. 143*. The entire second half of the ruling chronicles the inescapable evidence that the United States of America is and always has been a Christian nation. After reviewing 80 exhibits, the ruling of the Supreme Court was unanimous. The unanimity of justices' view that the United States is a

Christian nation supported ruling in favor of the Church of the Holy Trinity with regard to the specific, disputed legal issue.

Since the United States Constitution was ratified on June 21, 1788:

Every United States President has been a visibly devoted, outspoken Christian, except Barak Obama (For details regarding Barak Obama, refer to, *America's Most Biblically-Hostile U.S. President*, https://wallbuilders.com/americas-biblically-hostile-u-s-president/).

- Every President has enjoyed a stellar career ahead of the Presidency.
- Every President was an outstanding role model, despite occasional personal failures
- Every President was confident and proud to publically proclaim their faith in God and uncompromising belief in Jesus Christ as savior.
- Since virtually all presidents have been visible outspoken Christians, they had to be elected by a predominantly Christian electorate that desired a Christian President and a culture-wide promotion of the stable Christian values represented by the President.
- The U.S. Senate has always had a chaplain. All chaplains from the nation's founding to the present have been Christians.
- The U.S. House of Representatives has always had a chaplain. All chaplains from the nation's founding to the present have been Christians.
- All military branches have chaplains. Until recently, they have been Christian or Jewish. Today, there are some Muslim Chaplains.

- About 93% of all U.S. Supreme Court justices have been Christian; about 7% have been Jewish.

Historians have recognized four great spiritual awakenings, beginning with the first one that immediately preceded and propelled the Revolutionary War. In this context, a spiritual awakening is a profound reconnection with God that visibly transforms the lives of individuals and spreads rapidly throughout the American culture. Altogether, the four great spiritual awakenings total 170 years, much of the life-to-date of this country.

Many presidents have issued proclamations for days of humiliation, prayer, fasting, or any combination thereof. In addition, there have always been enormous numbers of churches, missionary organizations, para-church organizations. The famous circuit riders took the gospel message westward. Christian holidays are the most celebrated holidays of all. Most early universities were founded as Christian universities, schools at all levels were founded as Christian schools, and hospitals were founded as Christian institutions.

What is the evidence for these bold statements? Let the historic leaders speak for themselves. The following 35 pages of direct quotations provide undeniable proof of the veracity of the truths above. No other commentary is necessary.

Since the quotations span the lives of the leaders, titles such as "President" are not used until a leader actually achieves that position. After leaving office, the title is retained as is commonplace in the American Culture.

"I would advise no one to send his child where the Holy Scriptures are not supreme. Every institution that does not unceasingly pursue the study of God's Word becomes corrupt…I am much afraid that schools will prove to be the great gates of hell unless they diligently labor in explaining the Holy Scriptures, engraving them in the hearts of youth." *Martin Luther* circa 1520

"A man with God is always in the majority." *John Knox*, Reformer, November 24, 1572

1730s First Great Awakening Begins (Lasted 40 years ~ 1730s/1770s) Spiritual Leaders: Samuel Davies; Jonathan Edwards; George Whitefield

"It was wonderful to see…From being thoughtless or indifferent…it seemed as if all the world were growing religious, so that one could not walk thro' the town in an evening without hearing psalms sung in every street." *Benjamin Franklin* on the Great Awakening, circa 1750

"Proclaim Liberty throughout the land unto all the inhabitants thereof." [*Leviticus 25:10*] Inscribed on the **Liberty Bell**, August, 1752

"The Bible…[is] a necessary part of a polite education." ***Founding Father Henry Laurens***, a President of Congress, 1772

1754-1763 French and Indian Wars

"Atheism is unknown there; Infidelity rare and secret; so that person may live to a great age in that country without having their piety shocked by meeting with either an Atheist or an Infidel.

And the Divine Being seems…please to favor the whole country." **Benjamin Franklin**, *Information to Those Who Would Remove to America*, 1754

April 19, 1775 Revolutionary War Begins

"A patriot without religion in my estimation is as great a paradox as an honest Man without the fear of God. Is it possible that he whom no moral obligations bind, can have any real Good Will towards Men? Can he be a patriot who, by an openly vicious conduct, is undermining the very bonds of Society, corrupting the Morals of Youth, and by his bad example injuring the very Country he professes to patronize more than he can possibly compensate by intrepidity, generosity and honour?" **Abigail Adams**, wife of John Adams and mother of John Quincy Adams, November 5, 1775 (Letter to Mercy Otis Warren)

"In the language of the Holy Writ, there is a time for all things. There is a time to preach and a time to fight." **Rev. John Peter Muhlenberg**, [paraphrase of Ecclesiastes Chapter 3] 1775

"He is the best friend to American liberty, who is most…active in promoting true and undefiled religion….to bear down profanity and immorality of every kind. Whoever is an avowed enemy of God, I scruple not to call him an enemy of his country. It is in the man of piety and inward principle that we may…find the uncorrupted patriot, the useful citizen, and the invincible soldier. God grant that in America true religion and civil liberty may be inseparable." **Rev. John Witherspoon**, [descendent of John Knox] President of Princeton-taught nine writers of the U.S. Constitution (many of his other students became the highest level officials), May 17, 1776, when the Continental Congress declared a Day of Fasting

"Statesmen, my dear Sir, may plan and speculate for liberty, but it is Religion and Morality alone, which can establish the Principles upon which Freedom can securely stand...The only foundation of a free Constitution is pure Virtue, and if this cannot be inspired into our People in a greater Measure, than they have it now, they may change their Rulers and the forms of Government, but they will not obtain a lasting liberty." *John Adams*, June 21, 1776

"Let them revere nothing but Religion, Morality and Liberty. *John Adams* (expressing concern to his wife Abigail for their sons.

JULY 4, 1776 DECLARATION OF INDEPENDENCE

"We have this day restored the Sovereign to whom all men ought to be obedient. He reigns in heaven and from the rising to the setting of the sun, let His kingdom come." *Founder Samuel Adams* upon signing the Declaration of Independence, July 4, 1776

"I am apt to believe that it will be celebrated by succeeding generations as the great anniversary festival. It ought to be commemorated, as the Day of Deliverance [reference to ancient Israel], and by solemn acts of devotion to God Almighty. I am well aware of the toil and blood and treasure that it will cost to maintain this Declaration...Yet through all the gloom I can see the rays of ravishing light and glory...Posterity will triumph in that day's transaction, even though we may regret it, which I trust in God we shall not." *Founder John Adams* upon signing the Declaration of Independence, July 4, 1776

"We must hang together or most assuredly we shall hang separately." *Founder Benjamin Franklin* upon signing the Declaration of Independence, July 4, 1776

"The General hopes and trusts, that every officer and man, will endeavor so to live, and act, as becomes a Christian Soldier, defending the dearest Rights and Liberties of his country." **General George Washington**, July 9, 1776

"When you have done all things, then rely upon the good Providence of Almighty God for success, in full confidence that without his blessings, all our efforts will inevitably fail…The Holy Gospels are yet to be preached to these western regions, and we have the highest reason to believe that the Almighty will not suffer slavery and the gospel to go hand in hand. It cannot, it will not be." **John Jay, First Chief Justice, U.S. Supreme Court** to New York Convention, December 23, 1776

"These are the times that try men's souls. The summer soldier and the sunshine patriot will, in this crisis, shrink from the service of his country…Tyranny, like hell, is not easily conquered; yet we have this consolation with us that the harder the conflict, the more glorious the triumph. What we obtain too cheaply, we esteem too lightly…Heaven knows how to put a price upon its goods; and it would be strange indeed if so celestial an article as freedom should not be highly rated…God Almighty will not give up a people to military destruction…who have so earnestly…sought to avoid the calamities of war…'Show your faith by your works,' that God may bless you…I thank God, that I fear not." **Thomas Paine**, December 23, 1776, in the Pennsylvania Journal (General Washington ordered the article read to his troops.)

"The use of the Bible is so universal and its importance so great…it was resolved accordingly to direct said Committee of Commerce to import 20,000 copies of the Bible." **Order of Continental Congress**, September 11, 1777

"The Hand of Providence has been so conspicuous in all this-the course of the war-that he must be worse than an infidel that lacks faith, and more wicked that has not gratitude to acknowledge his obligations; but it will be time enough for me to turn Preacher when my present appointment ceases." **General George Washington**, August 20, 1778

"Law...communicated to us by reason and conscience...has been called natural; as promulgated by the Holy Scriptures, it has been called revealed...But it should always be remembered, that this law, natural or revealed...flows from the same divine source; it is the law of God. Human law must rest its authority, ultimately, upon the authority of that law, which is divine." **Justice James Wilson**, Original U.S. Supreme Court; signer of both the Declaration of Independence and the U.S. Constitution, *Lectures on Law*, 1789-1791

"A general dissolution of the principles and manners will more surely overthrow the liberties of America than the whole force of the common enemy. While the people are virtuous they cannot be subdued; but once they lose their virtue, they will be ready to surrender their liberties to the first external or internal invader. If we would enjoy this gift of Heaven, let us become a virtuous people." **Founder, Samuel Adams**, Letter to James Warren, February, 12, 1779

1770s FIRST GREAT AWAKENING ENDS

Print "a neat edition of the Holy Scriptures for the use of schools. Resolved, That the United States in Congress assembled highly approve the undertaking of Mr. Aitken...and...recommend this edition of the Bible to the inhabitants of the United States, and hereby authorize him to publish this recommendation." ***Continental Congress***, Authorization to print America's first English language Bible, September 10, 1782

September 3, 1783 Treaty of Paris Ends Revolutionary War

"In our lowest and most dangerous state, in 1776 and 1777, we sustained ourselves against the British Army of 60,000 troops, commanded by...the ablest generals Britain could procure throughout Europe, with a naval force of 22,000 seamen in above 80 men-of-war. Who but a Washington, inspired by Heaven, could have conceived the surprise move upon the enemy at Princeton-or that Christmas Eve when Washington and his army crossed the Delaware? The United States are under peculiar obligations to become a holy people unto the Lord our God." ***Ezra Stiles***, President, Yale University, May 8, 1783

"Religion [is] the basis and Foundation of Government. ***James Madison***, June 20, 1785

"Almighty God hath created the mind free...All attempts to influence it by temporal punishments...tend only to begat habits of hypocrisy...and are a departure from the plan of the Holy Author of religion, who being Lord both of body and mind, yet chose not to propagate it by coercions on either, as was in His almighty power to do, but to extend it by its influence on reason alone." ***Virginia Statute of Religious Freedom***, authored by ***Thomas Jefferson***, 1786

"[T]here is the most knowledge in those countries where there is the most Christianity...[and] those....parents or school-masters who neglect the religious instruction of their children and pupils, reject and neglect the most effectual means of promoting knowledge in our country." **Dr. Benjamin Rush**, 1787

JUNE 21, 1788 UNITED STATES CONSTITUTION RATIFIED

"The known propensity of a democracy is to licentiousness which the...ignorant believe to be liberty." **Fisher Ames**, January 1788"

"Select passages of Scripture...may be read in schools, to great advantage. In some countries the common people are not permitted to read the Bible at all. In ours, it is as common as a newspaper and in schools is read with nearly the same degree of respect. My wish is not to see the Bible excluded from schools but to see it used as a system of religion and morality." **Noah Webster**, 1788, essay "*On the Education of Youth in America*," printed in <u>American Magazine</u>.

"It would be peculiarly improper to omit, in this first official act, my fervent supplications to that Almighty Being who rules over the universe...No people can be bound to acknowledge and adore the Invisible Hand which conducts the affairs of men more than the people of the United States. Every step by which they have advanced to the character of an independent nation seems to have been distinguished by some token of Providential agency." **President George Washington**, Inaugural Address, April 30, 1789

"If I could have entertained the slightest apprehension that the Constitution framed by the Convention, where I had the honor to preside, might possibly endanger the religious rights of any ecclesiastical Society, certainly I would never

George Washington 1789-1797

have place my signature to it." ***President George Washington***, Letter to United Baptist Churches of Virginia, May 10, 1789

"All men have an equal, natural and unalienable right to the free exercise of religion, according to the dictates of conscience; and that no particular sect or society of Christians ought to be favored or established by law in preference to others." Draft of First Amendment to the U.S. Constitution submitted by ***George Mason***, "Father of the Bill of Rights," 1789

"...no man who is profligate in his morals...can possible by a true Christian." ***President George Washington***, 1789

"We have a dangerous trend beginning to take place in our education. We're starting to put more textbooks into our schools...containing fables and moral lessons...We are spending less time in the classroom on the Bible which should be the principal text in our schools. The Bible states these great moral lessons better than any other manmade book." ***Fisher Ames***, September 20, 1789, *Palladium Magazine*

1790s Second Great Awakening Begins (Lasted 40 Years ~ 1790s/1840s) Spiritual Leaders: Lyman Beecher; Timothy Dwight; Charles Finney; Asahel Nettleton; Nathaniel Taylor

"Christianity is part of the common law." ***James Wilson***, Original U.S. Supreme Court; signer of both the Declaration of Independence and the U.S. Constitution, *Course of Lectures* (3rd Vol. Of his *Works*, 122), circa 1790

"God who gave us life gave us liberty. Can the liberties of a nation be secure when we have removed a conviction that these liberties are the gift of God? Indeed I tremble for my country when I reflect that God is just, that his justice cannot sleep forever." ***Inscription on the Jefferson Memorial***

December 15, 1791 Bill of Rights Ratified

"What is liberty without wisdom and without virtue? It is the greatest of all possible evils; for it is folly, vice, and madness, without restraint. Men are qualified for civil liberty in exact proportion to their disposition to put moral chains upon their own appetites; in proportion as they are disposed to listen to counsels of the wise and good in preference to the flattery of knaves. Society cannot exist unless a controlling power upon will and appetite be placed somewhere; and the less of it there is within, the more there must be without. It is ordained in the eternal constitution of things, that men of intemperate minds cannot be free. Their passions forge their fetters." **Edmund Burke**, British Statesman and member of Parliament, (defender of the rights of the American colonies), 1791

"Before I state my arguments in favor of teaching children to read by means of the Bible, I shall assume the five following propositions: I.—That Christianity is the only true and perfect religion, and that in proportion as mankind adopts its principles and obeys its precepts, they will be wise and happy; II.—That a better knowledge of this religion is to be acquired by reading the Bible than in any other way; III.—That the Bible contains more knowledge necessary to man in his present state than any other book in the world; IV.—that knowledge is most durable and religious instruction most useful when imparted in early life; and V.—That the Bible, when not read in schools, is seldom read in any subsequent period of life." **Dr. Benjamin Rush**, 1791, signer of the Declaration of Independence in *A Defense of the Use of the Bible in Schools*

"The Bible...should be read in our schools in preference to all other books." **Dr. Benjamin Rush**, 1791, signer of the Declaration of Independence in *A Defense of the Use of the Bible in Schools*

"Religion is the only solid basis of good morals; therefore, education should teach the precepts of religion and the duties of man towards God." **Gouverneur Morris**, circa 1792, Signer of the U.S. Constitution

"Of all the dispositions and habits which lead to political prosperity, Religion and Morality are indispensable supports. In vain would that man claim the tribute of Patriotism who should labor to subvert these great Pillars...Let us with caution indulge the supposition that morality can be maintained without religion. Reason and experience both forbid us to expect that national morality can prevail in exclusion of religious principle...Morality is a necessary spring of popular government...Who that is a sincere friend to it can look with indifference upon attempts to shake the foundation?" **President George Washington**, *Farewell Address*, September 19, 1796

"It has been the error of the schools to teach...sciences and subjects of natural philosophy as accomplishments only whereas they should be taught...with reference to the Being who is the author of them: for all the principles of science are of Divine origin... When we examine an extraordinary piece of machinery, an astonishing pile of architecture, a well-executed statue or a highly finished painting...our ideas are natural led to think of the extensive genius and talents of the artist. When we study the elements of geometry, we think of Euclid. When we speak of gravitation, we think of Newton. How then is it, that when we study the works of God in the creation, we stop short and do not think of God? It is from the error of the schools…The evil that has resulted…has been that of generating in the pupils a species of atheism. Instead of looking through the works of the creation to the Creator Himself, they stop short and employ the knowledge they acquire to create doubts of His existence." *Thomas Paine*, speech delivered in Paris, January 16, 1797

"Religion and liberty are the meat and drink of the body politic. Withdraw one of them and it dies…Without religion we may possibly retain the freedom of savages, but not the freedom of New England…If our religion were gone, our state of society would perish with it an nothing would be left worth defending." *Timothy Dwight, President of Yale University*, 1798

"To destroy us therefore…our enemies must first…seduce us from the house of God." *Timothy Dwight, President Yale University*, 1798

John Adams
1797-1801

"As no truth is more clearly taught in the Volume of Inspiration, nor any more fully demonstrated by the experience of all ages, than that a deep sense and a due acknowledgement of the growing providence of a Supreme Being and of the accountableness of men to Him as the searcher of hearts and righteous distributer of rewards and punishments are conducive equally to the happiness of individuals and to the well-being of communities…

"I have thought proper to recommend, and I hereby recommend accordingly, that Thursday, the twenty-fifth day of April next, be observed throughout the United States of America as a day of solemn humiliation, fasting and prayer; that the citizens on that day abstain, as far as may be, from their secular occupation, and devote the time to the sacred duties of religion, in public and in private; that they call to mind our numerous offenses against the most high God, confess them before Him with the sincerest penitence, implore his pardoning mercy, through the Great Mediator and Redeemer, for our past transgressions, and that through the grace of His Holy Spirit, we may be disposed and enabled to yield a more suitable obedience to his righteous requisitions in time to come; that He would interpose to arrest the progress of that impiety and licentiousness in principle and practice so offensive to Himself and so ruinous to mankind; that He would make us deeply sensible that "righteousness exalteth a nation but sin is a reproach to any people" (Proverbs 14:34)" **President John Adams**, March 6, 1799, Declaration of a National Day of Humiliation, Fasting, and Prayer.

"Without morals a republic cannot subsist any length of time. They therefore who are decrying the Christian religion, whose morality is so sublime and pure and which insures to the good eternal happiness, are undermining the solid foundation of morals, the best security for the duration of free governments." **Charles Carroll**, November 4, 1800, signer of the Declaration of Independence and the U.S. Constitution

"Whenever the pillars of Christianity shall be overthrown, our present republican forms of government, and all the blessings which flow from them, must fall with them…The nearer I approach to the end of my pilgrimage, the clearer is the evidence of the divine origin of the Bible, the grandeur and sublimity of God's remedy for fallen man are more appreciated, and the future is illumined with hope and joy." ***Jedediah Morse***, (father of Samuel Morse, inventor of Morse code) circa 1800

"The education of youth should be watched with the most scrupulous attention…[I]t is much easier to introduce and establish an effectual system…than to correct by penal statutes the ill effects of a bad system…The education of youth…lays the foundations on which both law and gospel rest for success." ***Noah Webster***, circa 1800

"Nothing that imagination can paint can make a stronger impression…Sinners dropping down on every hand, professors praying, others in raptures of Joy!…There can be no question but it is of God, as the subjects…can give a clear and rational account of their conversion." ***Rev. Moses Hodge***, Second Great Awakening, 1801

"In matters of religion I have considered that its free exercise is placed by the Constitution independent of the powers of the General government." ***President Thomas Jefferson***, March 4, 1805, *Second Inaugural Address*

Thomas Jefferson 1801-1809

"I consider the government of the United States as prohibited by the Constitution from intermeddling with religious institutions, their doctrines, discipline, or exercises… This results not only from the provision that no law shall be made respecting the establishment of free exercise of religion, but from that also which reserves to the states the powers not delegated to the U.S. [government]. Every religious society has a right to determine for itself the times for these exercises, and the objects proper for them, according to their own particular tenets… " ***President Thomas Jefferson***, January 23, 1808, letter to Samuel Miller

"My dear son…You mentioned that you read to your aunt a chapter in the Bible …every evening. This information gave me real pleasure…" "So great is my veneration for the Bible, and so strong my belief, that when duly read and meditated on, it is of all books in the world, that which contributes most to make men good, wise, and happy that the earlier my children begin to read it…the more lively and confident will be my hopes that they will prove useful citizens of their country." **President John Quincy Adams**, Letter to son, 1811

1812-1814 WAR OF *1812*

"The contest in which the United States are engaged appeals…to the sacred obligation of transmitting…to future generations that…which is held…. by the present from the goodness of Divine Providence." **President James Madison**, May 25, 1813

James Madison 1809-1817

"The religion I have is to love and fear God, believe in Jesus Christ, do all the good to my neighbor, and myself that I can, do as little harm as I can help, and trust on God's mercy for the rest." **Daniel Boone**, Letter to his sister-in-law Sara Boone, October 17, 1816

"For advantages so numerous and highly important it is our duty to unite in grateful acknowledgments to that Omnipotent Being from whom they are derived, and in unceasing prayer that He will endow us with virtue and strength to maintain and hand them down in their utmost purity to our latest posterity." **President James Monroe**, 1817, First Annual Message to Congress

James Monroe 1817-1825

"Have you ever found in history, one single example of a Nation thoroughly corrupted that was after wards restored to virtue?... And without virtue, there can be no political liberty. Will you tell me how to prevent luxury from producing effeminacy, intoxication, extravagance, vice and folly"...I believe no effort in favour of virtue is lost." Former **President John Adams** letter to Thomas Jefferson, 1819

"The liberty, prosperity, and happiness of our country will always be the object of my most fervent prayers to the Supreme Author of All Good." *President James Monroe*, March 5, 1821, Second Inaugural Address

"Since your last meeting at this place, the fiftieth anniversary of the day when our independence was declared...two of the principal actors in that solemn scene, the hand that penned the ever-memorable Declaration [Thomas Jefferson] and the voice that sustained it in debate [John Adams]-were by one summons, at the distance of 700 miles from each other, called before the Judge of All to account for their deeds done upon earth." **President John Quincy Adams**, Second Annual Message to Congress, 1826 continuing, "A coincidence...so wonderful gives confidence....that the patriotic efforts of these...men were Heaven directed, and furnishes a new...hope that the prosperity of these States is under the special protection of a kind Providence." **President John Quincy Adams**, Executive Order, 1826

John Quincy Adams 1825-1829

"In my view, the Christian religion is the most important and one of the first things in which all children, under a free government ought to be instructed...No truth is more evident to my mind than that the Christian religion must be the basis of any government intended to secure the rights and privileges of a free people. To that great and benevolent Being…who has borne me and my manuscripts in safety across the Atlantic, and given me strength and resolution to bring the work to a close, I would present the tribute of my most grateful acknowledgements." **Noah Webster**, April 14, 1828, preface to Webster's first Dictionary

"It is my fervent prayer to that Almighty Being before whom I now stand, and who has kept us in His hands from the infancy of our Republic to the present day…that He will…inspire the hearts of my fellow-citizens that we may be preserved from danger." **President Andrew Jackson**, 2nd Inaugural Address, 1828

Andrew Jackson 1829-1837

"The Government of God is the only government which will hold society against depravity within and temptation without." **Rev. Lyman Beecher**, Second Great Awakening, 1831

"Religion in America…must be regarded as the foremost of the political institutions of that country; for if it does not impart a taste for freedom it facilitates the use of it…This opinion is not peculiar to a class of citizens or a party, but it belongs to the whole nation. The sects that exist in the United States are innumerable. They all differ in respect to the worship which is due to the Creator; but they all agree in respect to the duties which are due from man to man. Each sect adores the Deity in its own peculiar manner, but all sects preach the same moral law in the name of God…Moreover, all the sects of the United States are comprised within the great unity of Christianity, and Christian morality is everywhere the same. There is no country in the whole world where the Christian religion retains a greater influence than in America…and nothing better demonstrates how useful it is to man, since the country where it now has the widest sway is both the most enlightened and the freest." **Alexis de Tocqueville**, French social scientist, 1831

"All the miseries and evils which men suffer from vice, crime, ambition, injustice, oppression, slavery and war, proceed from their despising or neglecting the precepts contained in the Bible." **Noah Webster**, 1832, *The History of the United States*

"The American population is entirely Christian, and with us Christianity and Religion are identified. It would be strange indeed, if with such a people, our institutions did not presuppose Christianity and did not often refer to it and exhibit relations with it." **Chief Justice John Marshall**, Letter to Jasper Adams, May 9, 1833

"Upon my arrival in the United States, the religious aspect of the country was the first thing that struck my attention…In France I had almost always seen the spirit of religion and the spirit of freedom marching in opposite directions. But in America I found they were intimately united. The Americans combine the notions of Christianity and of liberty so intimately in their minds, that it is impossible to make them conceive the one without the other…They brought with them into the New World a form of Christianity which I cannot better describe than by styling it a democratic and republican religion…Christianity has therefore retained a strong hold on the public mind in America…In the United States…Christianity itself is a fact so irresistibly established, that no one undertakes either to attack or to defend it." **Alexis de Tocqueville**, 1835

"While most nations trace their origin to barbarians, the foundations of our nation were laid by civilizes men, by Christians." **Rev. Lyman Beecher**, Second Great Awakening, ~1835

"I know not how long a republican government can flourish among a great people who have not the Bible, the experiment has never been tried; but this I do know; that the existing government of this country never could have had existence but for the Bible. I… believe that if at every decade of years a copy of the Bible could be found in every family in the land its republican institutions would be perpetuated." **William Seward**, Secretary of State to Abraham Lincoln, 1836

"The Christian religion is the religion of our country. From it are derived our prevalent notions of the character of God, the great moral governor of the universe. On its doctrines are founded the peculiarities of our free institutions." **William McGuffey**, 1836, Foreword of McGuffey's Reader (seven volume series of textbooks for the schools loaded with scripture passages and scripture applications)

Why is it that, next to the birthday of the Savior of the World, your most joyous and most venerated festival returns on this day? Is it not that, in the chain of human events, the birthday of the nation is indissolubly linked with the birthday of the Savior? That it forms a leading event in the progress of the gospel dispensation? Is it not that the Declaration of Independence first organized the social compact on the foundation of the Redeemer's mission upon earth? That it laid the corner stone of human government upon the first precepts of Christianity, and gave to the world the first irrevocable pledge of the fulfillment of the prophecies, announced directly from Heaven at the birth of the Savior and predicted by the greatest of the Hebrew prophets six hundred years before? ***President John Quincy Adams***, July 4, 1837 (61ˢᵗ Anniversary of Declaration of Independence)

"I only look to the gracious protection of that Divine Being whose strengthening support I humbly solicit, and whom I fervently pray to look down upon us all. May it be among the dispensations of His Providence to bless our beloved country with honors and length of days; may her ways be pleasantness, and all her paths peace," ***President Martin Van Buren***, March 4, 1837, Inaugural Address (quoted Proverbs 3:17)

Martin Van Buren 1837-1841

"At the time of the adoption…of the [First] Amendment…the general, if not the universal, sentiment in America was, that Christianity ought to receive encouragement from the States….The real object of the First Amendment was not to countenance, much less to advance Mohammedanism, or Judaism, or infidelity, by prostrating Christianity, but to exclude all rivalry among Christian sects." ***Joseph Story***, Justice U.S. Supreme Court, *Familiar Exposition of the Constitution of the United States*, 1840

"I deem the present occasion sufficiently important and solemn to justify me in expressing to my fellow citizens a profound reverence for the Christian religion, and a thorough conviction that the sound morals, religious liberty, and a just sense of religious responsibility are essentially connected with all true and lasting happiness." ***President William Henry Harrison***, March 4, 1841, Inaugural Address

William Henry Harrison 1841

"When a Christian people feel themselves to be overtaken by a great public calamity, it becomes them to humble themselves under the dispensation of Divine Providence, to recognize His righteous government over the children of men...and to supplicate His merciful protection for the future." **President John Tyler**, April 4, 1841, proclaiming a National Day of Fasting and Prayer, following the death of President William Henry Harrison

"The schoolmaster and the missionary are found side by side." **President John Tyler**, December 6, 1842, 2nd Annual Message to Congress

"Our Puritan Fathers brought the Shorter Catechism with them across the ocean and laid it on the same shelf with the family Bible. They taught it diligently to their children...If in this Catechism the true and fundamental doctrines of the Gospel are expressed in fewer and better words and definitions than in any other summary, why ought we not now to train up a child in the way he should go?—why not now put him in possession of the richest treasure that ever human wisdom and industry accumulated to draw from? **New England Primer**, 1843 edition (The New England Primer was the primary textbook in schools from 1690 through at least 1930 [240 years]—when the last edition was printed)

"When little children were brought into the presence of the son of God, His disciples proposed to send them away, but [Jesus] said, 'Suffer little children to come unto Me.' [Matthew 19:14] Unto Me!... And that injunction is of perpetual obligation; it addresses itself to day with the same earnestness and the same authority which attended its first utterance to the Christian world. It is of force everywhere and at all times; it extends to the ends of the earth, it will reach to the end of time always and everywhere sounding in the ears of men with an…authority which nothing can supersede. 'Suffer little children to come unto Me.'" **Daniel Webster**, February 10, 1844, *Speech in Defence of the Christian Ministry and in Favor of the Religious Instruction of the Young*, presented before the U.S. Supreme Court

"The guaranty of religious freedom, of the freedom of the press, of the liberty of speech, of the trial by jury, of the habeas corpus… will be enjoyed by millions yet unborn.…Our prayers should evermore be offered up to the Father of the Universe for His wisdom to direct us in the path of our duty so as to enable us to consummate these high purposes." **President John Tyler**, December 3, 1844, 4th Annual Message to Congress

"Where can the purest principle of morality be learned so clearly or so perfectly as from the New Testament?" **Joseph Story**, Justice U.S. Supreme Court, *Vidal v. Girard's Executors*, 1844

James Knox Polk
1845-1849

"I fervently invoke the aid of the Almighty Ruler of the Universe in whose hands are the destinies of nations…I enter upon the discharge of the high duties which have been assigned to me by the people, again humbly supplicating that Divine Being, who has watched over and protected our beloved country from its infancy to the present hour, to continue His gracious benedictions upon us that we may continue to be prosperous and happy people…" **President James Knox Polk**, [descendant of John Knox, Reformer] March 4, 1845, Inaugural Address

"Sir, I am in the hands of a merciful God. I have full confidence in his goodness and mercy…The Bible is true. I have tried to conform to its spirit as near as possible. Upon that sacred volume I rest my hope for eternal salvation, through the merits and blood of our blessed Lord and Savior, Jesus Christ." **President Andrew Jackson**, May 29, 1845, a few weeks before his death

"That book [Bible], Sir, is the Rock upon which our republic rests." **President Andrew Jackson**, June 8, 1845

"My dear children, do not grieve for me; it is true, I am going to leave you; I am well aware of my situation. I have suffered much bodily pain, but my sufferings are but as nothing compared with that which our blessed Redeemer endured upon the accursed Cross, that all might be saved who put their trust in Him…God will take care of you for me. I am my God's; I belong to Him. I go but a short time before you, and…I hope and trust to meet you all in Heaven, both white and black." **President Andrew Jackson**, June 8, 1845, gathering of family and servants moments before his death.

1846 – 1848 Mexican War

"Independent of its connection with human destiny hereafter, the fate of republican government is indissolubly bound up with the fate of the Christian religion, and a people who reject its holy faith will find themselves the slaves of their own evil passions and of arbitrary power…God, in His providence has given us a Book of His revealed will…to teach us what we ought to do here, and what we shall be hereafter." **Lewis Cass**, Senator, Secretary of War, Secretary of State, 1846

"I accept with gratitude…your gift (Bible) of this inestimable Volume. It was for the love of the truths of this great Book that our fathers abandoned their native shores for the wilderness. Animated by its lofty principles they toiled and suffered till the desert blossomed as a rose. The same truths sustained them…to become a free nation, and guided by the wisdom of this Book they founded a government." **President Zachary Taylor**, *Frankfort Commonwealth*, 1849

"The only ground of hope for the continuance of our free institutions is in the proper moral and religious training of the children." **President Zachary Taylor**, 1849

Zachary Taylor 1849-1850

"Men, in a word, must be controlled either by a power within them, or a power without them; either by the word of God, or by the strong arm of man; either by the Bible or by the bayonet." **Robert Winthrop**, U.S. Speaker of the House, 1849

1840s Second Great Awakening Ends

"I dare not shrink; and I rely upon Him who holds in His hands the destinies of nations to endow me with the requisite strength for the task…The Sabbath day I always kept as a day of rest. Besides being a religious duty, it was essential to health. On commencing my Presidential career, I found that the Sabbath had frequently been employed by visitors for private interviews with the President. I determined to put an end to this custom, and ordered my doorkeeper to meet all Sunday visitors with an indiscriminate refusal." **President Millard Fillmore**, July 10, 1850

Millard Fillmore 1850-1853

"I cannot bring this communication to a close without invoking you to join me in humble and devout thanks to the Great Ruler of Nations for the multiplied blessings which He has graciously bestowed upon us. His hand, so often visible in our preservation, has stayed the pestilence, saved us from foreign wars and domestic disturbances, and scattered plenty throughout the land." **President Millard Fillmore**, December 2, 1850, Annual Message

"We owe these blessings, under Heaven, to the Constitution and Government...bequeathed to us by our fathers, and which it is our sacred duty to transmit...to our children." **President Millard Fillmore**, December 6, 1852

"If we and our posterity...live always in the fear of God and shall respect His Commandments...we may have the highest hopes of the future fortunes of our country. But if we...neglect religious instruction and authority; violate the rules of eternal justice, trifle with the injunctions of morality and recklessly destroy the constitution which holds us together, no man can tell how sudden a catastrophe may overwhelm us and bury all our glory in profound obscurity." **Senator Daniel Webster**, Addressing the New York Historical Society, 1852

"It must be felt that there is no national security but in the nation's humble, acknowledged dependence upon God and His overruling providence." **President Franklin Pierce**, March 4, 1853, Inaugural Address

Franklin Pierce 1853-1857

"The time has come for Christians to vote for honest men, and take consistent ground in politics or the Lord will curse them...Politics are a part of a religion in such a country as this and Christians must do their duty to their country as a part of their duty to God. God will bless or curse this nation according to the course Christians take in politics." ***Charles Finney***, circa 1855

1857 THIRD GREAT AWAKENING BEGINS (LASTED 60 YEARS ~ LATE 1857/EARLY 1920) SPIRITUAL LEADERS: DWIGHT L. MOODY; BILLY SUNDAY

"In entering upon this great office I must humbly invoke the God of our fathers for wisdom and firmness to execute its high and responsible duties." ***President James Buchanan***, March 4, 1857, Inaugural Address

James Buchanan 1857-1861

"The only ground of hope for the continuance of our free institutions is in the proper moral and religious training of the children." ***President Zachary Taylor***, July 4, 1859

APRIL 12, 1861 CIVIL WAR BEGINS

"The Declaration of Independence gave liberty not alone to the people of this country, but hope to all the world for all future time. It was that which gave promise that in due time the weights would be lifted from the shoulders of all men, and that all should have an equal chance…This is the sentiment embodied in the Declaration of Independence…I would rather be assassinated on this spot than surrender it." ***President Abraham Lincoln***, February 22, 1861 at Independence Hall, Philadelphia

"We are indeed going through a great trial [Civil War]…In the very responsible position in which I happen to be placed, being a humble instrument in the hands of our Heavenly Father…as we all are, to work out His great purposes…But if, after endeavoring to do my best in the light which He affords me, I find my efforts fail, I must believe that for some purpose unknown to me, He wills it…If I had been allowed my way, this war would have ended…But we find it still continues….We must believe that He permits it for some wise purpose of His own. We cannot but believe that He who made the world still governs it." ***President Abraham Lincoln***, October 6, 1862

"In giving freedom to the slave, we assure freedom to the free…We shall nobly save-or meanly lose-the last, best hope of earth. Other means may succeed; this could not fail. The way is plain…a way which if followed the world will forever applaud and God must forever bless." ***President Abraham Lincoln***, December 1, 1862, Second Annual Message

Abraham Lincoln 1861-1865

"The Commander in Chief…enjoins the…observance of the Sabbath…the sacred rights of Christian soldiers and sailors, a becoming deference to the best sentiment of a Christian people… demand that Sunday labor in the Army and Navy be reduced to the measure of strict necessity." ***President Abraham Lincoln***, 1862

"The atonement of Jesus Christ is the only remedy and rest for my soul." ***President Martin Van Buren***, 1862, during his last illness

"When everyone seemed panic-stricken…I went to my room and got down on my knees before Almighty God and prayed." ***President Abraham Lincoln***, 1863

"It is the duty of nations…to own their dependence upon the overruling power of God, to confess their sins…with assured hope that genuine repentance will lead to mercy….The awful calamity of civil war…may be but a punishment inflicted upon us for our presumptuous sins….We have been the recipients of the choicest bounties of Heaven…We have grown in numbers, wealth, and power as no other nation has every grown. But we have forgotten God. We have forgotten the gracious Hand which preserved us in peace, and multiplied and enriched and strengthened us; and we have vainly imagined, in the deceitfulness of our hearts, that all these blessing were produced by some superior wisdom and virtue of our own. Intoxicated with unbroken success, we have become too self-sufficient to feel the necessity of redeeming and preserving grace, too proud to pray to the God that made us! It behooves us then to humble ourselves before the offended Power, to confess our national sins and to pray for…forgiveness." **President Abraham Lincoln**, Proclamation of a *National Day of Humiliation, Fasting, and Prayer*, March 30, 1863

"…if you are ever tempted…to…put a bar between you and your family, your home, and your country, pray God in his mercy to take you that instant home to his own heaven." **Edward Everett Hale**, *A Man Without a Country*, 1863

"It is meet and right to recognize and confess the presence of the Almighty Father and the power of His hand equally in these triumphs and in these sorrows…I invite the people of the United States to…render the homage due to the Divine Majesty for the wonderful things He has done in the nation's behalf and invoke the influence of His Holy Spirit to subdue the anger which has produced and so long sustained a needless and cruel rebellion."

President Abraham Lincoln, National Day of Thanksgiving, Praise and Prayer, 1863

"I do not believe human society…ever has attained, or ever can attain, a high state of intelligence, virtue, security, liberty, or happiness without the Holy Scriptures; even the whole hope of human progress is suspended on the ever-growing influence of the Bible." ***William Seward,*** Secretary of State, circa 1864

APRIL 9, 1865 CIVIL WAR ENDS

"The last act of Congress ever signed by President Lincoln was one requiring that the motto…'In God We Trust' should hereafter be inscribed upon all our national coin." ***Schuyler Colfax,*** Speaker of the House of Representatives, 1865

"I do believe in Almighty God! And I believe also in the Bible." ***President Andrew Johnson,*** circa 1865

Let us look forward to the time when we can take the flag of our country and nail it below the Cross, and there let it wave as it waved in the olden times, and let us gather around it and inscribe for our motto. 'Liberty and Union, one and inseparable, now and forever.' And exclaim, Christ first, our country next." ***President Andrew Johnson,*** circa 1865

Andrew Johnson 1865-1869

"We are both at a period of life when it is our duty to relax our grasp on the world fast receding, and fix our thoughts, desires, and affections on One who knows no change. I trust in God that, through the merits and atonement of His Son, we may both be prepared for the inevitable change." **President James Buchanan**, circa 1868 near the end of his life

"If the next century does not find us a great nation…it will be because those who represent the…morality of the nation do not aid in controlling the political forces." **James Garfield**, U.S. Congressman chairing the Committee on Appropriations (previously a college President and preacher for the Disciples of Christ), circa 1875

"If the next century does not find us a great nation…it will be because those who represent the…morality of the nation do not aid in controlling the political forces." **President James Garfield**, 1876

"Hold fast to the Bible as the sheet anchor of your liberties, write its precepts in your hearts, and practice them in your lives. To the influence of this Book are we indebted for all the progress made in true civilization, and to this must we look as our guide in the future. 'Righteousness exalteth a nation; but sin is a reproach to any people.'" **President Ulysses S. Grant**, June 6, 1876, Letter to editor of the *Sunday School Times*

Ulysses S. Grant 1869-1877

"Moses spent 40 years thinking he was somebody; 40 years learning he was nobody; and 40 years discovering what God can do with a nobody." **Dwight L. Moody**, ~1876

"Looking for the guidance of that Divine Hand by which the destinies of nations and

Rutherford B. Hayes 1877-1881

individuals are shaped." **President Rutherford B. Hayes**, March 5, 1877, Inaugural Address

"I am a firm believer in the Divine teachings, perfect example, and atoning sacrifice of Jesus Christ. I believe also in the Holy Scriptures as the revealed Word of God to the world for its enlightenment and salvation." **President Rutherford B. Hayes**, circa 1878

"'Religion-the Only Basis of Society': How powerless conscience would become without the belief of a God…Erase all thought and fear of God from a community, and selfishness and sensuality would absorb the whole man. Appetite, knowing no restraint… would trample in scorn on the restraints of human laws…Man would become…what the theory of atheism declares him to be-a companion for brutes.'" **William Eller Channing**, 1879, lesson if McGuffey's 5th Eclectic Reader

"Let our people find a new meaning in the divine oracle which declares the 'a little child shall lead them,' for our own little children will soon control the destinies of the Republic. Our children will not be divided…concerning our controversies. They will surely bless their fathers and their fathers' God that the Union was preserved, that slavery was overthrown, and that both races were made equal before the law." **President James Garfield**, March 4, 1881, Inaugural Address

James Garfield 1881

"The deep grief which fills all hearts should manifest itself with one accord toward the Throne of Infinite Grace…We should bow before the almighty and seek from Him consolation in

Chester Arthur 1881-1885

our affliction." ***President Chester Arthur***, September 22, 1881, regarding the assassination of James Garfield

"I believe in the Holy Scriptures, and whoso lives by them will be benefitted thereby. Men may differ as to the interpretation, which is human, but the Scriptures are man's best guide...I did not go riding yesterday, although invited and permitted by my physicians, because it was the Lord's day, and because I felt that if a relapse should set in, the people who are praying for me would feel that I was not helping their faith by riding out on Sunday...Yes, I know and I feel very grateful to the Christian people of the land for their prayers in my behalf. There is not sect or religion, as shown in the Old or New Testament, to which this does not apply." ***President Ulysses S. Grant***, 1884, during his final illness

Grover Cleveland 1885-1889

"The goodness and the mercy of God which have followed the American people during all the days of the past year, claim their grateful recognition and humble acknowledgment. By His omnipotent power He has protected us from war and pestilence and from every national calamity; by His gracious favor the earth has yielded a generous return...by His loving kindness the hearts of our people have been replenished...and by His unerring guidance we have been directed in the way of national prosperity. To the end that we may with one accord testify our gratitude for all these blessings, I, Grover Cleveland, President of the United States, do hereby designate and set apart...a day of thanksgiving and prayer, to be observed by all the people of the land. On that day let all secular work and employment be suspended, and let our people assemble in their accustomed palaces of worship and with prayer and songs of praise give thanks to our Heavenly Father for all that He has done for us, while we humbly implore the forgiveness of our sins and a continuance of His mercy." **President Grover Cleveland**, 1887 Proclamation of a National Day of Thanksgiving and Prayer

"All must admit that the reception of the teachings of Christ results in the purest patriotism, in the most scrupulous fidelity to public trust, and in the best type of citizenship. Those who manage the affairs of government are by this means reminded that the law of God demands that they should be courageously true to the interests of the people, and that the Ruler of the Universe will require of them a strict account of their stewardship. The teachings of both human and Divine law thus merging into one word, duty, form of only union of Church and state that a civil and religious government can recognize. **President Grover Cleveland**, circa 1888

"It was never intended by the Constitution that the government should be prohibited from recognizing religion or that religious worship should never be provided for in cases where a proper recognition of Divine Providence in the working of government might seem to require it, and where it might be done without drawing an invidious distinction between religious beliefs, organizations, or sects. The Christian religion was always recognized in the administration of the common law of the land. The fundamental principles of that religion must continue to be recognized in the same cases and to the same extent as formerly." **Thomas Cooley**, *General Principles of Constitutional Law* (commentaries with shaped American law), 1890

Benjamin Harrison 1889-1893

"It is a great comfort to trust God—even if His providence is unfavorable. Prayer steadies one, when he is walking in slippery places—even if things asked for are not given." **President Benjamin Harrison**, circa 1890, Letter to his son, Russell

"The Pilgrims of Plymouth, the Puritans of Boston, and the Quakers of Pennsylvania all avowed a moral purpose, and began by making institutions that consciously reflected a moral idea." **Henry Adams** (grandson of John Quincy Adams) *History of the United States*, ~1890

"Above all, I know there is a Supreme Being who rules the affairs of men and whose goodness and mercy have always followed the American people, and I know He will not turn from us now if we humbly and reverently seek His powerful aid." **President Grover Cleveland**, 1893, Inaugural Address

Grover Cleveland 1893-1897

"There is no currency in this world that passes at such a premium anywhere as good Christian character...The time has gone by when the young man or the young woman in the United States has to apologize for being a follower of Christ...No cause but one could have brought together so many people, and that is the cause of our Master." **Governor (later President) William McKinley**, July 14, 1894, Christian Endeavor's International Convention

"Our faith teaches that there is no safer reliance than upon the God of our fathers...who will not forsake us so long as we obey His commandments and walk humbly in His footsteps." **President William McKinley**, March 4, 1897

William McKinley 1897-1901

"The more profoundly we study this wonderful Book [Bible], and the more closely we observe its divine precepts, the better citizens we will become and the higher will be our destiny as a nation." **President William McKinley**, circa 1897

"The light shineth in darkness, and the darkness comprehendeth it not (John 1:5; Wisdom is the principle thing therefore get wisdom and withal thy getting, get understanding (Proverbs 4:7); What doth the Lord require of thee, but to do justly, love mercy and walk humbly with thy God (Micah 6:8); The heavens declare the glory of God and the firmament showeth His handywork (Psalm 19:1). Inscribed on the walls of the **Library of Congress**, 1897

"One God, one law, one element, and one far-off divine event, to which the whole creation moves." *Alfred Lord Tennyson*, inscribed on the wall of the Library of Congress, 1897

FEBRUARY 15, 1898 – DECEMBER 10, 1898 SPANISH AMERICAN WAR

"*The New England Primer* was one of the greatest books ever published. It went through innumerable editions; it reflected in a marvelous way the spirit of the age that produced it, and contributed, perhaps more than any other book except the Bible, to the molding of those sturdy generations that gave to America its liberty and its institutions. **New England Primer**, 1900 edition (The New England Primer was the primary textbook in schools from 1690 through at least 1930 [240 years]—when the last edition was printed)

"I am only one, but I am one, I cannot do everything, but I can do something. What I can do, I should do and, with the help of God, I will do." *Edward Everett Hale*, Chaplain, U.S. Senate, ~1903

"No man can study the movement of modern civilization from an impartial standpoint and not realize that Christianity, and the spread of Christianity, are the basis of hope of modern civilization in the growth of popular self-government. The spirit of Christianity is pure democracy. It is equality of man before God-the equality of man before the law, which is the most God-like manifestation that man has been able to make." **President William Howard Taft,** missionary conference, 1908

"After a week on perplexing problems…it does so rest my soul to come into the house of The Lord and to sing and mean it, 'Holy, Holy, Holy, Lord God almighty'…(my) great joy and glory that, in occupying an exalted position in the nation, I am enabled, to preach the practical moralities of The Bible to my fellow-countrymen and to hold up Christ as the hope and Savior of the world." **President Theodore Roosevelt,** 1909

Theodore Roosevelt 1901-1909

"Progress has brought us both unbounded opportunities and unbridled difficulties. Thus, the measure of our civilization will not be that we have done much, but what we have done with that much. I believe that the next half century will determine if we will advance the cause of Christian civilization or revert to the horrors of brutal paganism. The thought of modern industry in the hands of Christian charity is a dream worth dreaming. The thought of industry in the hands of paganism is a nightmare beyond imagining. The choice between the two is upon us." **President Theodore Roosevelt,** 1909

"Every thinking man, when he thinks, realizes that the teaching of the Bible are so interwoven and entwined with our whole civic and social life that it would be literally impossible for us to figure ourselves what that life would be if these standards were removed We would lose almost all the standards by which we now judge both public and private morals; all the standards towards which we, with more or less resolution, strive to raise ourselves." **President Theodore Roosevelt**, circa 1910

"A God-fearing nation, like ours, owes it to its inborn and sincere sense of moral duty to testify its devout gratitude to the All-Giver for the countless benefits it has enjoyed." **President William Howard Taft**, November 7, 1912

William H. Taft 1909-1913

"The season is at hand in which it has been our long respected custom as a people to turn in praise and thanksgiving to Almighty God for His manifold mercies and blessings to us as a nation…In the year that has just passed…we have seen the practical completion of a great work at the Isthmus of Panama. '*Righteousness exaltheth a nation*' and '*peace on earth, good will towards men*' furnish the only foundation upon which can be built the lasting achievements of the human spirit.… Now, Therefore, I, Woodrow Wilson, President of the United States of America, do hereby designate…a day of thanksgiving and prayer, and invite the people throughout the land to cease from their wonted occupations and in their several homes and places of worship render thanks to Almighty God. In Witness Whereof, I have hereunto set my hand and caused the seal of the United States to be affixed. Done at the City of Washington this **23ʳᴰ DAY** of **OCTOBER**, in the year of our Lord one thousand nine hundred and thirteen." **President Woodrow Wilson**, 1913 (Proclamation of a Day of Thanksgiving)

Woodrow Wilson 1913-1921

1914 World War I Begins (Unites States Entered the War April 6, 1917)

"Christ came into the world to save others, not to save himself; and no man is a true Christian who does not think constantly of how he can lift his brother." **President Woodrow Wilson**, 1914

November 11, 1918 World War I Ends

"Its spirit [U.S. Constitution] is indubitably Christian." **H.G. Wells**, Outlines of History, 1920

1920 (Early) Third Great Awakening Ends

"What doth the Lord require of thee but to do justly and to love mercy, and to walk humbly with thy God." **President Warren G. Harding**, Inaugural Address, March 4, 1921

Warren G. Harding
1921-1923

"I have always believed in the inspiration of the Holy Scriptures, whereby they have become the expression to man of the Word and Will of God." **President Warren G. Harding**, circa 1921

"It's only through love that God can reach over from one human being to another. All real love is a divine thing." **H.G. Wells**, The Secret Places of the Heart, 1922

"There can be no peace with the forces of evil, Peace comes only through the establishment of the supremacy of the forces of good. That way lies through sacrifice…'Greater love hath no man than this that a man lay down his life for his friends.'" **President Calvin Coolidge**, 1923, Memorial Day Address

"Settlers came here from mixed motives…Generally defined, they were seeking a broader freedom. They were intent upon establishing a Christian commonwealth in accordance to the principle of self-government…It has been said that God sifted the nations that He might send choice grain into the wilderness. They had a genius for organized society on the foundations of piety, righteousness, liberty, and obedience of the law…Who can fail to see in it the hand of destiny? Who can doubt that it has been guided by a Divine Providence?" **President Calvin Coolidge**, 1923, Memorial Day Address

"I am interested in the science of government but I am more interested in religion…I enjoy making a political speech…but I would rather speak on religion than on politics. I commenced speaking on the stump when I was only twenty, but I commenced speaking in the church six years earlier-and I shall be in the church even after I am out of politics." **William Jennings Bryan**, U.S. Representative and Secretary of State, circa 1925

"People at home and abroad consider *Independence Hall* as hallowed ground and revere the *Liberty Bell* as a sacred relic…They are the framework of a spiritual event. The world looks upon them because of their associations of 150 years ago, as it look upon the Holy Land because of what took place there nineteen hundred years ago." **President Calvin Coolidge**, 150th anniversary of the Declaration of independence, 1926

Calvin Coolidge 1923-1929

"This great complex, which we call American life, is builded and can alone survive upon the translation into individual action of that fundamental philosophy announced by the Savior nineteen centuries ago. Part of our national suffering today is from failure to observe these primary yet inexorable laws of human relationship...Modern society cannot survive with the defense of Cain, 'Am I my brother's keeper?'" **President Herbert Hoover**, 1931

"Your Christmas Service held each year at the foot of a living tree which was alive at the time of the birth of Christ...should be continued as a further symbol of the unbroken chain of life leading back to this great moment in the spiritual life of mankind." **President Hebert Hoover**, 1932

Herbert Hoover 1929-1933

"We cannot read the history of our rise and development as a nation, without reckoning with the place the Bible has occupied in shaping the advances of the Republic...here we have been the truest and most consistent in obeying its precepts, we have attained the greatest measure of contentment and prosperity." **President Franklin D. Roosevelt**, October 6, 1935

"The Almighty...did prepare this American continent to be a place of the second chance... Millions have ...found...freedom of opportunity, freedom of thought, freedom to worship God." **President Franklin D. Roosevelt**, 1936 (50th Anniversary of the Statue of Liberty)

Franklin D. Roosevelt 1933-1945

"I hope that you have re-read the Constitution of the United States in these past few weeks. Like the Bible it ought to be read again and again." ***President Franklin D. Roosevelt***, March 9, 1937, Fireside Chat

SEPTEMBER 1939 WORLD WAR II BEGINS (UNITED STATES ENTERED THE WAR DECEMBER 7, 1941)

"As Commander-in-Chief, I take pleasure in commending the reading of the Bible to all who serve in the armed forces of the Unites States. Throughout the centuries men of many faiths and diverse origins have found in the Sacred Book words of wisdom, counsel and inspiration. It is a fountain of strength and now, as always, an aid in attaining the highest aspirations of the human soul." ***President Franklin D. Roosevelt***, January 25, 1941 (prologue to a special Gideons' edition of the New Testament & Book of Psalms distributed to millions of WWII soldiers)

"The belief in man, created free, in the image of God is the crucial difference between ourselves and the enemies we face…God of the free…grant us victory over the tyrants who would enslave all free men." ***President Franklin D. Roosevelt***, Flag Day 1942

"I say that loving our neighbor as we love ourselves is not enough-that we as a Nation and as individuals will please God best by showing regard for the laws of God. There is no better way of fostering good will toward man than by first fostering good will toward God. If we love Him we will keep His Commandments… In sending Christmas greetings to the armed forces and merchant sailors…we include our pride in their bravery on the fighting fronts…It is significant that Christmas Day our plants and factories will be stilled. That is not true of the other holidays. On all other holidays work goes on-gladly-for the winning of the war…So

Christmas becomes the only holiday in all the year, I like to think that this is so because Christmas is a holy day. May all it stands for live and grow throughout the years." **President Franklin D. Roosevelt**, 1942, Christmas Message

"I call upon every man, of all the Allies, to rise now to new heights of courage…with unshakable faith in the cause for which we fight, we will, with God's help, go forward to our greatest victory." **General Dwight D. Eisenhower**, Battle of the Bulge, 1944

"We must seek revival of our strength in the spiritual foundations which are the bedrock of our republic. Democracy is the outgrowth of the religious conviction of the sacredness of every human life. On the religious side, its highest embodiment is the Bible; on the political side, the Constitution. Former **President Herbert Hoover** during WWII (Joint statement with 5 Presidential widows)

"What then is the spirit of liberty? I cannot define it; I can only tell you my own faith…

- The spirit of liberty is the spirit which seeks to understand the minds of other men and women;
- The spirit of liberty is the spirit which weighs their interest alongside its own without bias;
- The spirit of liberty remembers that not even a sparrow falls to earth unheeded.
- The spirit of liberty is the spirit of Him who, nearly two thousand years ago, taught mankind the lesson it has never learned, but has never quite forgotten-that there may be a kingdom where the least shall be heard and considered side by side with the greatest."

- The use of history is to tell us...past themes, else we should have to repeat, each in his own experience, the successes and the failures of our forebears. **Judge Learned Hand**, U.S Court of Appeals, *The Spirit of Liberty*, 1944

"It is not easy to say 'Merry Christmas' to you, my fellow Americans, in this time of destructive war...but we will celebrate this Christmas Day in our traditional American way...because the teachings of Christ are fundamental in our lives...the story of the coming of the immortal Prince of Peace." **President Franklin D. Roosevelt.** 1944

"Almighty God has blessed our land." **President Franklin D. Roosevelt**, 1945, Inaugural Address

AUGUST 1945 WORLD WAR II ENDS

"The enemies of civilization who would have destroyed completely all freedom of religion have been defeated. All faiths unite in thanksgiving to Almighty God on our victory over the forces of evil...It has come with the help of God, Who was with us in the early days of adversity and... Who has now brought us to this glorious day of triumph. Let us give thanks to Him and...dedicate ourselves to follow in His ways." **President Harry S. Truman**, day after Japanese surrender ended WWII, 1945

Harry S. Truman 1945-1953

"We have just come through a decade in which the forces of evil in various parts of the world have been lined up in a bitter fight to banish from the face of the earth both of these ideals-religion and democracy...The right of every human being...to worship God in his own way, the right to fix his own relationship to his fellow men and to his Creator-these again have been saved for mankind." ***President Harry S. Truman***, to Federal Council of Churches, 1946

"Our…hopes of future years turn to a little town in the hills of Judea where on a winter night two thousand years ago the prophecy of Isaiah was fulfilled. Shepherds keeping watch by night over their flock heard the glad tidings of great joy from the angels of the Lord singing, 'Glory to God in the Highest and on Earth, peace, good will toward men.'…If we will accept it, the star of faith will guide us into the place of peace as it did the shepherds on that day of Christ's birth long ago…Through all the centuries, history has vindicated His teaching. In this great country of ours has been demonstrated the fundamental unity of Christianity and democracy." ***President Harry S. Truman***, Christmas Tree Lighting, 1946

"The choice before us is plain. Christ or chaos, conviction or compromise, discipline or disintegration. I am rather tired of hearing about our rights…The time is come…to hear about responsibilities…America's future depends upon her accepting and demonstrating God's Government." ***Senate Chaplain Peter Marshal***, 1947

"God of our Fathers…may it be ever be understood that our Liberty is under God and…to the extent that America honors thee, wilt Thou bless America." Prayed by ***Senate Chaplain Peter Marshal***, 1947

"Our liberty is under God and can be found nowhere else. May our faith be not merely stamped upon our coins, but expressed in our lives." ***Senate Chaplain Peter Marshall*** ~1947

"Attendance at the chapel is part of a cadet's training; no cadet will be exempted. Each cadet will receive religious training in one of the three particular faiths: Protestant, Catholic, or Jewish." **U.S. Corp of Cadets** [*U.S. Military Academy, West Point*], 1947

"It would not seem practical to teach…the arts if we are to forbid exposure of youth to any religious influences. Music without sacred music…would be …incomplete, even from a secular point of view." **Supreme Court Justice Robert Jackson**, 1948, *McCollum v. Board of Education*

"We have grasped the mystery of the atom and rejected the Sermon on the Mount…The world has achieved brilliance without conscience. Ours is a world of nuclear giants and ethical infants." **General Omar Bradley**, 1948

"All Midshipmen, except those on authorized outside church parties, shall attend Sunday services in the chapel." **U.S. Naval Academy**, 1949

"Never forget Americans that yours is a spiritual country. Yes, I know you're a practical people. Like others, I've marveled at your factories, your skyscrapers, and your arsenals. But underlying everything else is the fact that America began as a God-loving, God-fearing, God-worshiping people." **Philippine General Carlos Romulo**, 1949 (4th President of the U.N. General Assembly, served with General Douglas MacArthur in the Pacific)

"We believe that all men are created equal because they are created in the image of God." **President Harry S. Truman**, 1949, Inaugural Address

"When the U.S. was established...the motto was IN GOD WE TRUST. That is still our motto and we still place our firm trust in God." *President Harry S. Truman*, 1949

1950 Fourth Great Awakening Begins (Lasted 30 years ~ 1950/1980) Spiritual Leaders: Bill Bright; Billy Graham; Oral Roberts; Bishop Fulton Sheen

"The fundamental basis of this nation's laws was given to Moses on the Mount. The fundamental basis of our Bill of Rights comes from the teachings...of Isaiah and St. Paul. I don't think we emphasize that enough these days." *President Harry S. Truman* to Attorney General's Conference, 1950

June 15, 1950 Korean War Begins

"History fails to record a single precedent in which nations subject to moral decay have not passed into political and economic decline. There has been either a spiritual awakening to overcome the moral laps, or a progressive deterioration leading to ultimate national disaster." *General Douglas MacArthur*, Addressing the Salvation Army, 1951

"The First Amendment, however, does not say that in every and all respects there shall be a separation of Church and State... Otherwise the state and religion would be aliens to each other-hostile, suspicious, and even unfriendly. We are a religious people whose institutions presuppose a Supreme Being...When the state encourages religious instruction or cooperates with religious authorities by adjusting the schedule of public events to sectarian needs, it follows the best of our traditions. For it then respects the religious nature of our people and accommodates the public service to their spiritual needs. To hold that it may not would be to find in the Constitution a requirement that the government show a callous indifference to religious groups. That would be preferring those who believe in no religion over those who do believe. We find no constitutional requirement which makes it necessary for government to be hostile to religion…We cannot read into the Bill of Rights such a philosophy of hostility to religion." **William Orville Douglas**, Justice of the U.S. Supreme Court, *Zorach v. Clauson*, 1952

Freedom is a need of the soul, and nothing else. It is in striving toward God that the soul strives continually after a condition of freedom. God alone is the inciter and guarantor of freedom. He is the only guarantor. External freedom is only an aspect of interior freedom. Political freedom, as the Western world has known it, is only a political reading of the Bible. Religion and freedom are indivisible. Without freedom the soul dies. Without the soul there is no justification for freedom. **Whittaker Chambers**, [Journalist, author, former Communist defected to the West] 1952, *Witness*

"…every sincere break with Communism is a religious experience…A Communist (socialist) breaks because he must choose at last between irreconcilable opposites—God or Man, Soul or Mind, Freedom or Communism. Communism is what happens when, in the name of Mind, men free themselves from God. But its view of God, its knowledge of God, its experience of God is what alone gives character to a society or a nation, and meaning to its destiny. Its culture, the voice of this character is merely that view, knowledge, experience, of God, fixed by its most intense spirits in terms intelligible to the mass of men. There has never been a society or a nation without God. But history is cluttered with the wreckage of nations that became indifferent to God, and died...**Faith is the central problem of this age**. The Western world does not know it, but it already possesses the answer to this problem—but only provided that its faith in God and the freedom He enjoins is as great as Communism's faith in Man." **Whittaker Chambers**, [Journalist, author, former Communist defected to the West] 1952, Witness

"All that we call human history-money, poverty, ambition, war, prostitution, classes, empires, slavery-is the long terrible story of man trying to find something other than God which will make him happy. Christianity...is a religion you could not have guessed... It is not the sort of thing anyone would have made up. It has just that queer twist about it that real things have." **C.S. Lewis,** 1952, *Mere Christianity*

"My friends, before I begin...would you permit me the privilege of uttering a little private prayer of my own. And I ask that you bow your heads. Almighty God, as we stand here at the moment..." **President Dwight D. Eisenhower**, Inaugural Address, 1953

Dwight D. Eisenhower 1953-1961

"This is the work that awaits us all, to be done with bravery, with charity, and with prayer to Almighty God." **President Dwight D. Eisenhower**, 1953, Inaugural Address

JULY 27, 1953 KOREAN WAR ENDS

"The criminal is the product of spiritual starvation. Someone failed miserably to bring him to know God, love Him and serve Him." "We can see all too clearly the devastating effects of Secularism on our Christian way of life. The period when it was smart to 'debunk' our traditions, undermined…high standards of conduct. A rising emphasis on materialism caused a decline of 'God-centered" deeds and thoughts. The American home…ceased to be a school of moral and spiritual education. When spiritual guidance is at a low ebb, moral principles are in a state of deterioration. Secularism advances when men forget God." ***J. Edgar Hoover***, Director of the FBI, introduction to Elson's book, *America's Spiritual Recovery*, 1954

"As a former soldier, I am delighted that our veterans are sponsoring a movement to increase our awareness of God in our daily lives. In battle, they learned a great truth-that there are no atheists in the foxholes. They know that in time of test and trial, we instinctively turn to God for new courage…Whatever our individual church, whatever our personal creed, our common faith in God is a common bond among us." ***President Dwight D. Eisenhower***, on the American Legion "Back-to-God" program, 1954

"From this day forward, the millions of our school children will daily proclaim in every city and town, every village and rural school house, the dedication of our nation and our people to the Almighty. To anyone who truly loves America, nothing could be more inspiring than…this rededication of our youth, on each school morning to our country's true meaning. In this way we are reaffirming the transcendence of religious faith in America's heritage and future; in this way we shall constantly strengthen those spiritual weapons which forever will be our country's most powerful resource, in peace or in war." ***President Dwight D. Eisenhower***, signing Joint Resolution (Public Law 396) adding "One Nation Under God" to the *Pledge of Allegiance to the Flag*, 1954

"It was not the outer grandeur of the Roman but the inner simplicity of the Christian that lived through the ages." **Charles Lindbergh**, 1954

"I have just come from…the dedication of a new stamp…The stamp has on it a picture of the Statue of Liberty and 'In God We trust'…It represents…a Nation whose greatness is based on a firm unshakeable belief that all of us mere mortals are dependent upon the mercy of a Superior Being." **President Dwight D. Eisenhower**, April 8, 1954

"Well, I don't think anyone needs a great deal of credit for believing in what seems to me to be obvious…This relationship between a spiritual faith…and our form of government is…so obvious that we should really not need to identify a man as unusual because he recognizes it. Our whole theory of government finally expressed in our Declaration…said….Man is endowed by his Creator… When you come back to it, there is just one thing…man is worthwhile because he was born in the image of his god…Democracy is nothing in the world but a spiritual conviction…that each of us is enormously valuable, because of a certain standing before our own God. Any group that…awakens all of us to these simple things… is, in my mind, a dedicated, patriotic group that can well take the Bible in one hand and the flag in the other, and march ahead." **President Dwight D. Eisenhower**, November 9, 1954 (Address to the National Conference on the spiritual Foundation of American Democracy)

"Without God, there could be no American form of government, nor an American way of life. Recognition of the Supreme Being is the first-the most basic-expression of Americanism." **President Dwight Eisenhower**, "Back-to-God" program, 1955

"This is what I see in Billy Graham – A man who clearly understands that any advance in the world has got to be accompanied by a clear realization that man is, after all, a spiritual being." **President Dwight D. Eisenhower**, 1956

"Through the ages men have felt the uplift of the spirit of Christmas. We commemorate the birth of the Christ Child by…giving expression to our gratitude for the great things that His coming has brought about in the world." **President Dwight D. Eisenhower**, 1960

"The rights of man come not from the generosity of the state but from the hand of God." **President John F. Kennedy**, 1961, Inaugural Address

John F. Kennedy 1961-1963

"…Yet the same revolutionary beliefs for which our forebears fought are still at issue around the globe-The belief that the rights of man come not from the generosity of the state but from the hand of God." **President John F. Kennedy**, Inaugural Address, 1961

"To each of us is entrusted the heavy responsibility of guiding the affairs of a democratic nation founded on Christian ideals." **President John F. Kennedy**, to President of Brazil, 1961

"When we all-regardless of our particular religious convictions-draw our guidance and inspiration, and really, in a sense, moral direction, from the same general area, the Bible, the Old and the New Testaments, we have every reason to believe that our various religious denominations should live together in the closed harmony. The basic presumption of the moral law, the existence of God, man's relationship to Him there is generally consensus on those questions." ***President John F. Kennedy***, White House Rose Garden, 1961

"The guiding principle of this Nation has been, is now, and ever shall be IN GOD WE TRUST." ***President John F. Kennedy***, 1961

"Civilizations die from suicide, not by murder... So what does the universe se look like?...It looks as if everything were on the move either toward its Creator or away from Him. The course of human history consists of a series of encounters...in which each man or woman or child....is challenged by God to make the free choice between doing God's will and refusing to do it. When Man refuses, he is free to make his refusal and to take the consequences." ***Historian Arnold Joseph Toynbee***, Study of History, 1961

"We mark the festival of Christmas which is the most sacred and hopeful day in our civilization. For nearly 2,000 years the message of Christmas, the message of peace and good will towards all men, has been the guiding star of our endeavors...the birthday of the Prince of Peace." ***President John F. Kennedy***. 1962

"It is difficult for me to understand a scientist who does not acknowledge the presence of a superior rationality behind the existence of the universe...Viewing the awesome reaches of space...should only confirm our belief in the certainty of its Creator." ***Wernher von Braun***, Father of the American Space Program, in American Weekly, 1963

"We in this country, in this generation, are-by destiny rather than choice-the watchmen on the walls of world freedom. We ask, therefore, that we may be worthy of our power and responsibility, that we may exercise our strength with wisdom and restraint, and that we may achieve in our time and for all time the ancient vision of 'peace on earth, good will toward men.' That must always be our goal-and the righteousness of our cause must always underlie our strength. For as was written long ago, 'Except the Lord keep the city, the watchman waketh but in vain'" [Psalm 127:1 KJV] **President John F. Kennedy,** November 22, 1963, Speech written, but not delivered due to his assassination.

AUGUST 2, 1964 VIET NAM WAR BEGINS (UNITED STATES INVOLVEMENT)

"For nearly 200 years of our existence as a nation, America has stood for peace in the world. At this Christmas season–when the world commemorates the birth of the Prince of Peace–I want all men, everywhere, to know that the people of this great Nation have but one hope, one ambition toward other peoples: that is to live at peace with them and for them to live at peace with one another. Since the first Christmas, man has moved slowly but steadily forward toward realizing the promise of peace on earth among men of good will. That movement has been possible because there has been brought into the affairs of man a more generous spirit toward his fellow man. Let us pray at this season that in all we do as individuals and as a nation, we may be motivated by that spirit of generosity and compassion which Christ taught us so long ago." **President Lyndon B. Johnson,** December 18, 1964, Lighting of the Nation's Christmas Tree.

Lyndon B. Johnson 1963-1969

"The judgment of God is harshest on those who are most favored... If we fail now....we will have forgotten that democracy rests on faith...For myself, I ask only in the words of an ancient leader

(Solomon): 'Give me now wisdom and knowledge that I may go out and come in before this people.'" [2 Chronicles 1:10 KV] **President Lyndon B. Johnson,** 1965, Inaugural Address

"As all are born equal in dignity before God, all are born equal in dignity before man." **President Richard Nixon**, 1969, Inaugural Address

Richard M. Nixon 1969-1974

"To those of you who have advocated looking high we owe our sincere gratitude, for you have granted us the opportunity to see some of the grandest views of the Creator." **Commander Neil Armstrong**, Astronaut, 1969

"Some...challenge science to prove the existence of God. But must we light a candle to see the sun?" **Wernher von Braun,** *Father of the American Space Program*, to the California State Board of Education, 1972

"The Constitution is the supreme law of our land and it governs our actions as citizens. Only the laws of God, which govern our consciences are superior to it. As we are a Nation under God, so I am sworn to uphold our laws with the help of God." **President Gerald Ford**, 1974

Gerald Ford 1974-1977

1975 VIET NAM WAR ENDS

"I...call upon America to be more careful with its trust...Prevent those...from falsely using social justice to lead you down a false road...They are trying to waken you...We can only reach with determination for the warm hand of God, which we have so rashly and self-confidently pushed away." ***Alexander Solzhenitsyn***, Nobel Prize for Literature, 1975

"If we want to keep these freedoms, we may have to fight again. God forbid, but if we do, let's always fight to win…Face the flag, son…and thank God it's still there." ***Actor John Wayne***, 1977

"Christmas has a special meaning for those of us who are Christians, those of us who believe in Christ, those of us who know that almost 2,000 years ago, the Son of Peace was born." ***President Jimmy Carter***, 1977

Jimmy Carter 1977-1981

"And in despair I bowed my head. There is no peace on earth, I said. For hate is strong and mocks the song of peace on earth, good will to men. Then pealed the bells, more loud and deep, God is not dead, nor does he sleep. The wrong shall fail, the right prevail, With peace on earth, good will to men." ***Henry Wadsworth Longfellow***, *I Heard the Bells on Christmas Day*, [written during the Civil War] 1864 quoted by ***President Jimmy Carter***, 1979

1980 FOURTH GREAT AWAKENING ENDS

"With God's help, we can and will resolve the problems which now confront us. And after all, why shouldn't we believe that? We are Americans." ***President Ronald Reagan***, 1981, Inaugural Address

Ronald Reagan 1981-1989

"Our Nation's motto [In God We Trust]…reflects a basic recognition that there is a divine authority in the universe to which this nation owes homage." ***President Ronald Reagan***, 1981

"Why is a representative of government here? To welcome with humble pride a man whose mission in life has been to remind us that in all our seeking…the answer to each problem is to be found in the simple words of Jesus of Nazareth, who urged us to love one another." **President Ronald Reagan**, introducing Billy Graham

"Unfortunately, in the last two decades we've experienced an onslaught of such twisted logic that if Alice were visiting America, she might think she'd never left Wonderland. We're told that it somehow violates the rights of others to permit students who desire to pray to do so. Clearly this infringes on the freedom of those who choose to pray, the freedom taken for granted since the time of our Founding Fathers. To prevent those who believe in God from expressing their faith is an outrage…The relentless drive to eliminate God from our schools…should be stopped." **President Ronald Reagan**, September 25, 1982

"We can't have it both ways. We can't expect God to protect us in a crisis and just leave Him over there on the shelf in our day-to-day living. I wonder if sometimes He isn't waiting for us to wake up. He isn't maybe running out of patience. **President Ronald Reagan**, 1982, Alfred M. Landon Lecture Series

"Now, therefore, I Ronald Reagan, President of the United States of America, in recognition of the contributions and influence of the Bible on our Republic and our people, do hereby proclaim 1983 the *Year of the Bible* in the United States. I encourage all citizens, each in his or her own way, to reexamine and rediscover its priceless and timeless message." **President Ronald Reagan**, October 4, 1982 (Resolution also signed by Tip O'Neil, Democrat Speaker of the House and Strom Thurmond, Republican President of the Senate)

"Prayer is the mainspring of the American spirit, a fundamental tenet of our people since before the Republic was founded. A year before the Declaration of Independence in 1775, the Continental Congress proclaimed the first National Day of Prayer as the initial positive action they asked of every colonist. Two hundred years ago in 1783, the Treaty of Paris officially ended the long, weary Revolutionary War during which a National Day of Prayer had been proclaimed every spring for eight years." **President Ronald Reagan**, declaring a National Day of Prayer, January 27, 1983

"Sometimes, in the hustle and bustle of holiday preparations we forget the true meaning of Christmas…the birth of the Prince of Peace, Jesus Christ. During this glorious festival let us renew our determination to follow His example. **President Ronald Reagan**, December 20, 1983, Christmas Address

"Christmas is a time….to open our hearts to…millions forbidden the freedom to worship a God who so loved the world that He gave us the birth of the Christ Child so that we might learn to love. The message of Jesus is one of hope and joy. I know there are those who recognize Christmas day as the birthday of a wise teacher….then there are others of us who believe that he was the Son of God, that he was divine." **President Ronald Reagan**, 1983

"Each day your members observe a 200-year-old tradition meant to signify America is one nation under God. I must ask: If you can begin your day with a member of the clergy standing right here leading you in prayer, then why can't freedom to acknowledge God be enjoyed again by children in every school room across this land?" **President Ronald Reagan**, January 25, 1984, *State of the Union Address*

"Without God there is no virtue because there is no prompting of the conscience...without God there is a coarsening of the society; without God democracy will not and cannot long endure... If we ever forget that we are 'One Nation Under God,' then we will be a Nation Gone Under." **President Ronald Reagan**, August 23, 1984, Reunion Arena in Dallas, Texas

"God...should never have been expelled from America's schools. As we struggle to teach our children...we dare not forget that our civilization was built by men and women who placed their faith in a loving God. If Congress can begin each day with a moment of prayer...so then can our sons and daughters." **President Ronald Reagan**, February 7, 1984, National Association of Secondary School Principals

"The First Amendment of the Constitution was not written to protect the people from religion; that amendment was written to protect religion from government tyranny...But now we're told our children have no right to pray in school. Nonsense! The pendulum has swung too far toward intolerance against genuine religious freedom. It is time to redress the balance. Former Supreme Court Justice Potter Stewart noted if religious exercises are held to be impermissible activity in schools, religion is place at an artificial and state-created disadvantage...Refusal to permit religious exercises is seen not as the realization of state neutrality, but rather as the establishment of a religion of secularism." **President Ronald Reagan**, February 25, 1984, radio address

"I wonder if we could all join in a moment of silent prayer..." **President Ronald Reagan**, Inaugural Address, 1985

"I've always thought…that God had His reasons for placing this land here between two great oceans to be found by a certain kind of people." **President Ronald Reagan**, July 3, 1986 (relighting the Statue of Liberty)

"My first act as President is a prayer. I ask you to bow your heads. Heavenly Father, we bow our heads and thank You for Your love…Make us strong to do Your work, willing to heed and hear Your will…" **President George H. W. Bush**, Inaugural Address, 1989

George H. W. Bush 1989-1993

"The First Amendment does not require students to leave their religion at the schoolhouse door…It is especially important that parents feel confident that their children can practice religion…We need to make it easier and more acceptable for people to express and to celebrate their faith. If students can wear T-shirts advertising sports teams, rock groups or politicians, they can also wear T-shirts that promote religion…Religion is too important to our history and our heritage for us to keep it out of our schools…Nothing in the First Amendment converts our public schools into religion-free zones or requires all religious expression to be left behind at the schoolhouse door. Government's schools also may not discriminate against private religious expression during the school day." **President Bill Clinton**, James Madison High School, July 12, 1995

Bill Clinton 1993-2001

"I used to say I could live ten thousand years and never have an experience as thrilling as walking on the moon. But the excitement and satisfaction of that walk doesn't begin to compare with my walk with Jesus, a walk that lasts forever." ***Astronaut Charles Duke***, Prayer Rally at Texas Republican Convention, 1996

"As we face a new millennium, I believe America has gone a long way down the wrong road. We must turn around...If ever we needed God's help, it is now." ***Billy Graham***, receiving the Congressional Gold Medal, 1996

"I was taught to respect everyone for the simple reason that we're all God's children. I was taught, in the words of Martin Luther King, to judge a man not by the color of his skin, but by the content of his character. And I was taught that character is simply doing what's right when nobody's looking." ***Congressman J. C. Watts***, 1997, response to President Bill Clinton's State of the Union Address

"In the aftermath of September 11...Republicans and Democrats burst into that song of the same name by Irving Berlin on the steps of the U.S. Capitol...It was a slogan for peace..." ***Irving Berlin*** wrote, "God Bless America, Land that I love, Stand Beside Her, and Guide Her, through the Night with the Light From Above, From the Mountains, to the Prairies, to the Oceans White with Foam, God Bless America, My Home Sweet Home, God Bless America, My Home Sweet Home.!" ***Congressman Mike Castle***, Delaware, 2001

"I call upon all Americans to pray to Almighty God and to perform acts of service...Across our Nation, many selfless deeds reflect the promise of the Scripture: 'For I was hungry and you gave Me food; I was thirsty and you gave Me drink; I was a stranger and you took Me in.'" ***President George W. Bush***, declared a Day of Prayer and Remembrance, 2005

George W. Bush
2001-2009

"Let us reaffirm a fundamental truth: All children, born and unborn, are made in the holy image of God." **President Donald J. Trump**, February 5, 2019, State of the Union Address

Barak H. Obama 2009-2017

"America is a nation of believers, and together we are strengthened by the power of prayer." **President Donald J. Trump**, May 3, 2019

"Today, with one clear voice, the United States of America calls upon the nations of the world to end religious persecution. Stop the crimes against people of faith. Release prisoners of conscience. Repeal laws restricting freedom of religion and belief. Protect the vulnerable, the defenseless, and the oppressed." **President Donald J. Trump**, September 23, 2019, Address to the United Nations (First president to host a U.N. religious freedom meeting)

Donald J. Trump 2017-

Appendix III

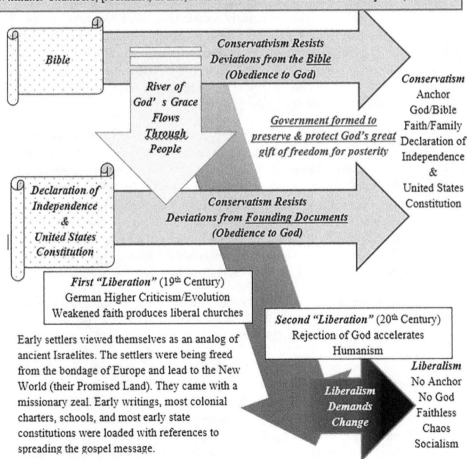

Both anchors of freedom (Bible & Founding Documents) must be restored to their originally intended authority. All men are driven by their deepest spiritual convictions (Christians and Humanists). Freedom has been 1) an unnatural condition since the Garden of Eden and 2) an unnatural condition in non-Christian countries. To destroy the American culture Spiritual separation from God must precede separation from freedom. Loss of appreciation for spiritual nature of freedom produces a loss of will to protect freedom and the anchors.

"It is impossible to rightly govern a nation without God and the Bible." **George Washington**

"Is it not that, in the chain of human events, the birthday of a nation is indissolubly linked with the birthday of the Savior? That it forms a leading event in the progress of the gospel dispensation? Is it not that the **Declaration of Independence** first organized the social compact on the foundation of the Redeemer's mission upon earth? That it laid the corner stone of human government upon the first precepts of Christianity, and gave to the world the first irrevocable pledge of the fulfillment of the prophecies, announced directly from Heaven at the birth of the Savior and predicted by the greatest of the Hebrew prophets six hundred years before?... **John Quincy Adams**, July 4, 1837

"*...it (Declaration) is still the preeminent support of free government throughout the world...* It is little wonder that people at home and abroad consider Independence Hall as **hallowed ground** and revere the Liberty Bell as a **sacred relic**... They are the framework of a **spiritual event**...*In its main features* the Declaration of Independence is a great spiritual document. *It is a declaration not of material but of spiritual conceptions.* Equality, liberty, popular sovereignty, the rights of man — these are not elements which we can see and touch. They are ideals. *They have their source and their roots in the religious convictions.* They belong to the unseen world." **Calvin Coolidge**, July 4, 1926

"Men, in a word, must be controlled either by a power within them, or a power without them; either by the word of God, or by the strong arm of man; either by the Bible or by the bayonet." **Robert Winthrop**, U.S. Speaker of the House, 1849

"If we and our posterity...live always in the fear of God and shall respect His Commandments...we may have the highest hopes of the future fortunes of our country. But if we...neglect religious institutions and authority; violate the rules of eternal justice, trifle with the injunctions of morality and recklessly destroy the constitution which holds us together, no man can tell how sudden a catastrophe may overwhelm us and bury all our glory in profound obscurity." **Senator Daniel Webster,** Addressing the New York Historical Society, 1852

Appendix IV

WHAT ARE THE 8 TYPES OF JIHAD? FORMER RADICAL MUSLIM EXPLAINS

By Samuel Smith, CP Reporter Apr 4, 2017

A *former Radical Muslim turned international Christian evangelist* has detailed different categories of jihad that she says is being carried out today to advance the Islamic agenda worldwide.

Isik Abla, who was raised and abused in a Muslim home in Turkey but now professes the name of Christ in over 150 countries around the world through her Virginia-based television ministry, spoke with The Christian Post last week to warn about the deception being used by radical Muslims to gain influence across the globe.

Although most people think of war and Islamic-related terrorism when they think of the term "jihad," Abla explained that there are actually eight different types of jihad. Even though Abla admits that she was involved in one of the forms of jihad before she left

Islam, she credited her friend Baroness Caroline Cox, a member of the United Kingdom House of Lords, with having taught her about the eight types of jihad.

"She has an amazing understanding about jihad," Abla said. "I knew these types of jihad before but I never categorized them. I just believed as Muslims, that we had to use every way to Islamize the world. When I got to meet her and become good friends with her, she was describing them just the way I was taught. I was part of it without knowing it. It makes perfect sense after hearing her."

1. Population jihad

According to Abla, "**_population jihad,_**" _also referred to as_ "**_cultural jihad,_**" _is the concept of populating the world with more Muslims than Christians, Jews or people of other religions or no religions._

Abla said that this not only refers to the _migration of Muslims_ and their invasion of foreign cultures, but it also is _a call for Muslims already embedded in Western countries to have more children than non-Muslims_. Abla explained that some mosque leaders even tell their congregations to have as many children as they can because "_Muslims must populate the world._"

"We are not only talking about refugees going to Western world from Islamic world with their families, but if you are also living in those countries, you need to make more children," Abla said. "It is taught in the mosques. Imams tell congregations to make children — 'Let's inherit the world through population.' I heard it before but I never thought of it as 'population jihad.'" Abla said that this is a "_very popular teaching in Islam and it is very powerful._"

"Muslims believe that when the end times come, at the end of the world, everyone is going to be a Muslim," she explained. "This is very sneaky because they sneak into the societies, cultures and countries before you know it. *This is more powerful than the violent side of Islam.*"

2. Media jihad

One of the most influential forms of jihad is "*media jihad*," which Abla said <u>allows Muslims to influence the way Westerners think or feel about Islam and particular political candidates</u>.

Abla asserted that <u>Muslims spend billions of dollars building partnerships with major television networks and other major media outlets</u>.

"<u>In the United States many media channels' partnerships are bought by Muslims</u>. There are so many Muslims behind the scenes in power because they invest money. <u>They invest billions into the Western world's media</u>. It is so crazy, mind blowing how much they invest into Facebook, Twitter, TV channels," she said. "Even in the political elections, [it's crazy] how much Muslims were investing into the campaigns to manipulate and change the atmosphere."

"You can take anything and make any person a monster or hero in the eyes of people through media," Abla told CP. "It is easy manipulate and brainwash people through media. It is the easiest way and most powerful channel as a weapon. We saw it in the previous elections. We see it in the world. They can get you to believe anything about any candidate that they want you to believe."

She also said that **one of the biggest media jihad initiatives is to promote the idea that "Islam is the religion of peace**." "Whoever says this is part of media jihad," she contended.

Another way in which Islam is trying to gain influence in the cultures of the Western world, Abla said, is by devout Muslims paying tuition for other Muslims to attend prestigious Western universities like Harvard, Yale, Oxford or Cambridge.

3. Education jihad

"These are going to be the people of the future to be in high positions," she explained. Abla admitted that she participated in "**education jihad**" when she was married to her first husband because his family was so involved with it.

"They pay their Harvard education, they pay Princeton, they pay Yale," Abla explained in an interview with CP in February. «So we were shoveling money to this kind of educational Jihad so those people could be in high places in power to dictate what needs to happen in the Western world [and] to Islamize the Western world. This is an ideology type of Islam and I was part of that."

"We were so ambitious ... to send these kids to those colleges," Abla further stated last week. "It was like almost tithing or giving an offering or sending a missionary. You are sending a missionary and you giving all your income to one kid to go to Harvard." Educational jihad is not only meant to help Muslims reach high standing in society but it also to help infiltrate the institutions.

"**Education jihad has two parts. One** is very powerful countries like Saudi Arabia, they invest into these colleges. They give millions of dollars a year. ... So they have a lot of saying into these colleges' curriculums," Abla claimed. "**The other way** is by sending these Muslim youths into these colleges. What happens is when they graduate, they don't have green cards but they have the highest chance of being hired by a company to get a green card."

4. Economic jihad

Abla also discussed "*economical jihad*," which can also referred to as "*financial jihad*." Much like "media jihad," Abla explained that wealthy and influential radical Muslims are investing in various businesses, banks, stocks and properties in the Western world.

"Right now, there are enormous amount of Muslims investors in the U.K. and America," she said. "They partner with the banks. They are populating and ruling over the economy." Abla contended that the goal behind this kind of investing is to obtain power within the culture.

"Anywhere that you invest money, you have cultural power. Anywhere you are a shareholder, you have cultural power. You have a voice when you invest your money. That voice is the voice of Islam," she argued. "When you invest your money in any field, you are basically buying people, you are basically buying companies. They are going to sooner or later going to mold into your ideology."

5. Physical jihad

"*Physical jihad*," or what Abla refers to as "*war against infidels*," is probably the most recognizable form of jihad, as terrorist groups like the Islamic State, Boko Haram and others are constantly in the news because they continue to kill nonbelievers and dissenting

Muslims in places like the Middle East and Africa and carry out attacks on soft targets in the West.

Abla explained that some Muslims are brainwashed into believing that Muslims are called to carry out wars against Christians, Jews and others until everyone dies or they become Muslims. Specifically, she pointed to Quran 2:171-173.

"*Quran is calling them evildoers. They are thinking Christians and Jews are not human beings. They are part of Satan's kingdom and when they kill Christians and Jews, they are destroying Satan's kingdom*," Abla said. "They were brainwashed and I was one of them. They were brainwashed with physical jihad to physically kill them. They believe in ethnic cleansing. So when you ask about physical jihad, it is not only war and defense, *it includes ethnic cleansing — genocide*."

Abla asserted that **Muslims are called to carry out jihad until everybody is either killed or recites the Muslim declaration of faith**.

Abla warned against efforts to bring "**sharia courts**," or **sharia councils**, to the United States like they have done in places in the United Kingdom.

6. Legal jihad

An estimated 30 sharia councils exist in England with the purpose of providing Muslim women with a way to get an Islamic divorce through religious scholars when their husbands don't approve of the divorce.

However, Abla and others have voiced concerns that the *sharia councils are being used to discriminate against women and provide unfair divorce terms*. "A number of women have reportedly been victims of what appear to be discriminatory decisions taken by sharia councils, and that is a significant concern," Prime Minister Theresa May *said* last year.

Uproar occurred in Texas when it was reported that an Islamic tribunal was established at a Sunni mosque in Irving, Texas. The town's mayor made headlines after voicing opposition to the mosque. Abla accused those trying to set up «sharia courts» in the United States of using democracy to «stop freedom."

"They take an action [under the guise] of human rights and religious freedom," she said. *"It is unbelievable. They use your law against you."*

7. Humanitarian jihad

Muslim humanitarian groups are using people's desperation to get them to convert to Islam and say the Shahada, according to Abla.

She warned that *displaced non-Muslims in high-need countries in Africa and other places throughout the world are being denied food unless they convert to Islam.*

"If you want to get help, you register as a Muslim. Even nominal Christians, they may be in so much need and register as Muslims to receive aid. Then they say that if you want to continue to get this aid, you need to come to Quran course once a week, you need to come to Friday prayer meetings," Abla explained. *"They start luring you little by little. First, you just fill out a piece of paper to get food. After three*

months, they say 'We change our rules, you need to come to prayer meeting.' After that, you need to put your kids into Muslim school."

Abla's claim comes as Open Doors USA warned recently that **Christians in Nigeria are being denied aid by Muslim humanitarian organizations.**

8. Political jihad

Muslims who hold power or public office in the West try to downplay the role of Islam when it comes to violence and terror, thus carrying out the "**political jihad**," Abla said.

As an example, she pointed to London Mayor Sadiq Khan's response to three bombings that injured over 30 people in New York City and New Jersey last September that was carried out by a man believed to be influenced by extremist ideology. Khan said that terrorist attacks like that are "part and parcel of living in a big city." In March, an attack in London claimed by Islamic State killed three pedestrians and a police officer and injured over 50 people.

"[He] said that this kind of attack should be expected," Abla said of the mayor, who is Muslim. "So this is a good example of being Muslim and having political power and making it seem like it is normal and desensitizing people to terrorism to stop giving reactions to Muslim terrorists."

"They say, 'We living a big city and attacks like this are normal.' I lived like terrorism is normal in the Middle East and a Muslim country. Politically bringing this to the Western world, with these people who are in power saying 'Islam is a religion of peace and terrorism is going to happen.' It becomes part of your life," Abla added. "When I was in the Muslim world, it was part of my life. I used to hear gunshots and machine guns. I grew up with PTSD. It became normal and it was part of my life but it was not part of my life when I came to America. Now, they are trying to make it part of your life."

http://www.christianpost.com/news/what-are-the-8-types-of-jihad-former-radical-muslim-explains-179338/page1.html

Appendix V

THE HIGH PRICE OF FORGETTING GOD

By Jerry Newcombe, D.Min., Author of *American Amnesia: Is America Paying the Price for Forgetting God, the Source of Our Liberty?* (Nordskog Publishing, Inc., 2018)

Recently a survey of Americans found an abysmal lack of knowledge of our history and some of the basics of American civics. The pollsters concluded: "A waning knowledge of American history may be one of the greatest educational challenges facing the U.S."

I once interviewed the late Mel and Norma Gabler of Longview, Texas, who reviewed textbooks from a Christian and conservative perspective. They told me of an old textbook that dedicated seven pages to Marilyn Monroe, but only a few sentences to George Washington. Our young people today know more about the trivia of today's celebrities than they do the men and women who sacrificed everything to bequeath our freedoms to us.

The High Price of Forgetting God

Karl Marx once said, "*Take away a people's roots, and they can easily be moved.*" Dr. Peter Lillback, with whom I had the privilege to write a book on the faith of George Washington, said in his book on church/state relations, *Wall of Misconception*, "*One of our great national dangers is ignorance of America's profound legacy of freedom. I firmly believe that ignorance is a threat to freedom.*"

Our loss of the knowledge of basic history and civics is a tragedy. We suffer from what I call *American Amnesia*. I even wrote a whole book about it. God is the source of our freedom—we have rights granted us by the Creator—but we forget this to our peril. In that book, I marshaled all sorts of quotes from great Americans through the years, showing that God is the foundation of our liberties.

Here's but a sample, as found in *American Amnesia*:

- *George Washington* said, "*It would be peculiarly improper to omit, in this first official act, my fervent supplications to that Almighty Being who rules over the universe....*" (p. 85)

- *Ben Franklin* told the Constitutional Convention, "*I have lived, Sir, a long time, and the longer I live, the more convincing proofs I see of this truth—that God governs in the affairs of men. And if a sparrow cannot fall to the ground without His notice, is it probable that an empire can rise without His aid?*" (p. 281)

- Whatever doubts on core Christian doctrines he later had, founding father *Thomas Jefferson* never abandoned the importance of our rights as God given. Etched in stone at his Memorial are these words: "*Can the liberties of a nation* be secure when we have removed a conviction that these liberties are the gift of God?"* The answer is No. (p. 278)

- During the dark days of the Civil War, **Abraham Lincoln** proclaimed April 30, 1863, as a national day of fasting and prayer. In his proclamation, he noted, *"We have grown in numbers, wealth, and power, as no other nation has ever grown. But we have forgotten God. Intoxicated with unbroken success, we have become too self-sufficient to feel the necessity of redeeming and preserving grace, too proud to pray to the God that made us! It behooves us then, to humble ourselves before the offended Power, to confess our national sins, and to pray for clemency and forgiveness." (p. 28)*

- **President Eisenhower** *said in 1955, "Without God, there could be no American form of Government, nor an American way of life. Recognition of the Supreme Being is the first—the most basic—expression of Americanism." (p. 8)*

- **Dr. Martin Luther King Jr.** *noted, "Religion endows us with the conviction that we are not alone in this vast, uncertain universe." (p. 76)*

- **Ronald Reagan** *said, "America needs God more than God needs America. If we ever forget that we are one nation under God, then we will be a nation gone under."* (p. 60)

American Amnesia: Is America Paying the Price for Forgetting God, the Source of Our Liberty? focuses on remembering our nation's Judeo-Christian roots, renewing our role as active citizens, and recovering our religious liberty in the face of a militant secularism.

The book is recommended by Dr. Peter Lillback, William J. Federer, Kerby Anderson, Star Parker, Joseph Farah, and others.

https://www.christianpost.com/sponsored/the-high-price-of-forgetting-god.html

Appendix VI

10 Reasons Why the Church Should Not Abandon Politics

By Jerry Newcombe, Wednesday, January 07, 2015

Recent events have raised the issue, Should the pulpit always avoid politics? It depends on what we mean by "politics;" it demeans the pulpit to use it for partisan politics. But here are ten reasons why I don't think politics and religion should (or even can) be completely separate:

1) The Word of God has something to say about all of life, beyond just the spiritual.

My long-time pastor, Dr. D. James Kennedy, once noted that the Church of Jesus Christ has always been opposed to abortion—-from the very beginning. It still is.

In the last generation, abortion has become a "political" issue. Does that mean, asked Dr. Kennedy, we should now ignore it in the pulpit? No, because the Bible is pro-life.

2) The Bible itself addresses the issue of governing in different texts.

There are biblical books dealing with political rulers—-1 and 2 Samuel, 1 and 2 Kings, Judges. In Genesis and in Daniel, we see godly men serving well in pagan courts, for the good of all. In Romans 13 and 1 Peter 2, we hear that God has established the civil magistrate, and we are to obey the government. In Exodus, we see Moses rebuking Pharaoh for mistreating the Hebrews.

3) The Scriptures also teach that on occasion, there may be a need for civil disobedience.

When the apostles were commanded to no longer preach the gospel, Peter said that we must obey God rather than man. If there is an either/or, then civil disobedience can be the right path. Many early Christians died for Christ rather than worship the emperor, clearly a false god.

4) Jesus said, "Render to Caesar the things that are Caesar's, and to God the things that are God's."

America is in the middle of a great spiritual battle. Our weapons are spiritual. In American Amnesia, Jerry Newcombe fights back against the atheistic deconstruction of America with historic, Biblical truth.

Nature abhors a vacuum. Someone will be involved in politics. Why should we abandon our role as citizens? According to Jesus, we have a positive duty to render certain obligation to the state.

5) When the Church does not speak out, evil can fill that void.

Silence in the face of evil can signal assent. We hold up those Christians who went against Hitler and the Nazis as heroes—-not the millions who acquiesced to them.

The December 23, 1940 TIME Magazine article called, *Religion: German Martyrs*, opens: "Not you, Herr Hitler, but God is my Führer. These defiant words of Pastor Martin Niemoller were echoed by millions of Germans. And Hitler raged: 'It is Niemoller or I.'"

6) The Church is called to be salt and light. Salt preserves and prevents decay.

Christians in society should help prevent corruption. As goes the pulpit, so goes the nation.

7) We pray, "Thy kingdom come, Thy will be done, on earth as it is in heaven."

That doesn't mean we should try and force the kingdom of God by use of the sword. When "Christians" did that in times past, we are still apologizing for it, as in the Crusades, the Inquisition, the Salem Witchcraft trials. But it does mean that Christians can apply biblical principles to government that result in good for all of us. And to be sure, someone's morality is always being legislated. It is not a question of "if," but of "what" and of "whose."

8) Christians bless everybody when we properly apply our faith to politics.

Our Constitution was an outgrowth of the biblical concept of covenant. University of Houston Professor Dr. Donald S. Lutz, author of *The Origins of American Constitutionalism*, said that Americans "invented modern Constitutionalism and bequeathed it to the world." And where did we get it? Says Lutz: "The American constitutional tradition derives in much of its form and content from the Judeo-Christian tradition as interpreted by the radical Protestant sects to which belonged so many of the original European settlers in British North America."

9) Politics may be the calling of some in the congregation. Therefore, ministers should encourage political involvement that is motivated by the desire to serve.

When the Member of Parliament William Wilberforce was converted in the 1780s, he sought counsel from Rev. John Newton, an ex-slave-trader. Should he leave politics and pursue the ministry? Newton advised him to stay because maybe God could use him where he was.

Wilberforce's crusade to free the slaves in the British Empire took him 50 years and was a direct outgrowth of his faith in Christ. I shudder to think if one of today's "no politics" ministers had counseled the young reborn Wilberforce. We might still have legal slavery in the Western world.

10) Religion and morality are "indispensable supports to our political prosperity."

So said Washington in his Farewell Address. John Adams said, "Our Constitution was made only for a moral and religious people. It is wholly inadequate to the government of any other." This was in a day when about 99% of the Americans were professing Christians. And on it goes.

I remember when I once interviewed former Secretary of Education William Bennett, who said, "Does anybody really have a worry that the United States is becoming overly pious? That our young people have dedicated too much of their lives to prayer, that teenagers in this country are preoccupied with thoughts of eternity?" In short, our problem today is not too much Christian influence on society, but not enough.

Dr. Jerry Newcombe is a key archivist of the D. James Kennedy Legacy Library and a Christian TV producer. He has also written or co-written 23 books, including The Book That Made America: How the Bible Formed Our Nation and (with D. James Kennedy), What If Jesus Had Never Been Born? His views are his own. www.jerrynewcombe.com

https://www.christianpost.com/news/10-reasons-why-the-church-should-not-abandon-politics.html

Appendix VII

IMPORTANCE OF THOUGHTFUL PLANNED VOTING

John Adams-We electors have an important constitutional power placed in our hands; we have a check upon two branches of the legislature... the power I mean of electing at stated periods [each] branch.... *It becomes necessary to every [citizen] then, to be in some degree a statesman, and to examine and judge for himself of the tendency of political principles and measures.* Let us examine, then, with a sober, a manly... and a Christian spirit; let us neglect all party [loyalty] and advert to facts; let us believe no man to be infallible or impeccable in government any more than in religion; take no man's word against evidence, nor implicitly adopt the sentiments of others who may be deceived themselves, or may be interested in deceiving us.

Samuel Adams-*Let each citizen remember at the moment he is offering his vote* that he is not making a present or a compliment to please an individual–or at least that he ought not so to do; but *that he is executing one of the most solemn trusts in human society for which he is accountable to God and his country.*

Nothing is more essential to the establishment of manners in a State than that all persons employed in places of power and trust be men of unexceptionable characters. The public cannot be too curious concerning the character of public men.

Matthias Burnett-Consider well the important trust . . . which God . . . [has] put into your hands. . . . To God and posterity you are accountable for [your rights and your rulers]. . . . <u>Let not your children have reason to curse you for giving up those rights and prostrating those institutions which your fathers delivered to you</u>. . . . [L]ook well to the characters and qualifications of those you elect and raise to office and places of trust. . . . Think not that your interests will be safe in the hands of the weak and ignorant; or faithfully managed by the impious, the dissolute and the immoral. Think not that men who acknowledge not the providence of God nor regard His laws will be uncorrupt in office, firm in defense of the righteous cause against the oppressor, or resolutely oppose the torrent of iniquity. . . . <u>Watch over your liberties and privileges–civil and religious–with a careful eye.</u>

Frederick Douglass-I have one great political idea. . . . That idea is an old one. It is widely and generally assented to; nevertheless, it is very generally trampled upon and disregarded. The best expression of it, I have found in the Bible. It is in substance, "<u>Righteousness exalteth a nation; sin is a reproach to any people</u>" [Proverbs 14:34]. This constitutes my politics–the negative and positive of my politics, and the whole of my politics. . . . I feel it my duty to do all in my power to infuse this idea into the public mind, that it may speedily be recognized and practiced upon by our people.

Charles Finney-[T]he time has come that Christians must vote for honest men and take consistent ground in politics or the Lord will curse them. . . . Christians have been exceedingly guilty in this matter. But the time has come when they must act differently. . . . Christians seem to act as if they thought God did not see what they do in politics. But I tell you He does see it–and He will bless or curse this nation according to the course they [Christians] take [in politics].

James Garfield-Now more than ever the people are responsible for the character of their Congress. If that body be ignorant, reckless, and corrupt, it is because the people tolerate ignorance, recklessness, and corruption. If it be intelligent, brave, and pure, it is because the people demand these high qualities to represent them in the national legislature. . . . *[I]f the next centennial does not find us a great nation . . . it will be because those who represent the enterprise, the culture, and the morality of the nation do not aid in controlling the political forces.*

Francis Grimke-*If the time ever comes when we shall go to pieces, it will . . . be . . . from inward corruption–from the disregard of right principles . . . from losing sight of the fact that "Righteousness exalteth a nation, but that sin is a reproach to any people" [Proverbs 14:34]. . . .[T]he secession of the Southern States in 1860 was a small matter with the secession of the Union itself from the great principles enunciated in the Declaration of Independence, in the Golden Rule, in the Ten Commandments, in the Sermon on the Mount. Unless we hold, and hold firmly to these great fundamental principles of righteousness, . . . our Union . . . will be "only a covenant with death and an agreement with hell."*

Alexander Hamilton-*A share in the sovereignty of the state*, which is exercised by the citizens at large, in voting at elections is one of the most important rights of the subject, and in a republic ought to stand foremost in the estimation of the law.

John Jay-_Providence has given to our people the choice of their rulers, and it is the duty, as well as the privilege and interest of our Christian nation, to select and prefer Christians for their rulers. The Americans are the first people whom Heaven has favored with an opportunity of deliberating upon and choosing the forms of government under which they should live._

Thomas Jefferson-The elective franchise, if guarded as the ark of our safety, will peaceably dissipate all combinations to subvert a Constitution, dictated by the wisdom, and resting on the will of the people.

William Paterson-_When the righteous rule, the people rejoice; when the wicked rule, the people groan._

William Penn-Governments, like clocks, go from the motion men give them; and as governments are made and moved by men, so by them they are ruined too. Wherefore governments rather depend upon men than men upon governments. Let men be good and the government cannot be bad. . . . But if men be bad, let the government be never so good, they will endeavor to warp and spoil it to their turn. . . . [T]hough good laws do well, good men do better; for good laws may want [lack] good men and be abolished or invaded by ill men; but good men will never want good laws nor suffer [allow] ill ones.

Daniel Webster-_Impress upon children the truth that the exercise of the elective franchise is a social duty of as solemn a nature as man can be called to perform; that a man may not innocently_ *trifle with his vote; that every elector is a trustee as well for others as himself and that every measure he supports has an important bearing on the interests of others as well as on his own.*

Noah Webster
In selecting men for office, let principle be your guide. Regard not the particular sect or denomination of the candidate–look to his character. . . . When a citizen gives his suffrage to a man of known immorality he abuses his trust; he sacrifices not only his own interest, but that of his neighbor, he betrays the interest of his country.

When you become entitled to exercise the right of voting for public officers, **let it be impressed on your mind that God commands you to choose for rulers, "just men who will rule in the fear of God."** The preservation of government depends on the faithful discharge of this duty; if the citizens neglect their duty and place unprincipled men in office, the government will soon be corrupted; laws will be made, not for the public good so much as for selfish or local purposes; corrupt or incompetent men will be appointed to execute the laws; *the public revenues will be squandered on unworthy men; and the rights of the citizens will be violated or disregarded.* If a republican government fails to secure public prosperity and happiness, it must be because the citizens neglect the divine commands, and elect bad men to make and administer the laws.

John Witherspoon-Those who wish well to the State ought to choose to places of trust men of inward principle, justified by exemplary conversation. . . .[And t]he people in general ought to have regard to the moral character of those whom they invest with authority either in the legislative, executive, or judicial branches.

http://www.wallbuilders.com/LIBissuesArticles.asp?id=80

About the Author

LLOYD H. STEBBINS, PH.D.

Dr. Lloyd H. Stebbins has been on a personal journey for about fifteen years, during which he experienced the convergence of several factors in his personal and professional life. Personally, he cared for his late wife around the clock for seven years. She suffered from a chronic neurodegenerative conditions similar to Alzheimer's disease that eventually cost her life. Despite the obvious tragedy and personal challenges, it was a monumentally life changing experience for him. Throughout tough times, when others often turned their backs, the Lord's presence was as real to the author as another person sharing the same sofa. The emotional and spiritual rewards evoked by taking care of a loved one too disabled to communicate any form of appreciation are so great as to defy description and are largely unknown in modern self-absorbed American culture.

That intense personal experience and others along with personal observations triggered the emergence of a heart wrenching concern for the fall of the family and the collapse of the American culture. The decades-long observations and concerns crescendoed in recent years. The path to family and cultural decay is traced and detailed in his book, *Wake Up America or Die! YOU Must Save America and the Family*. However, unlike other books, this focused history lesson spans just the first few chapters. The ten remaining chapters develop the "Awesome Remedy."

Earning dual academic qualifications in both the natural sciences, including chemical engineering, and business management enabled Dr. Stebbins to fully appreciate the spectacular successes of the scientific method of investigation and also to question its blind application to the social sciences. From its earliest beginnings, the public fascination with the scientific method spread rapidly throughout all western civilization and eventually dominated virtually all ordinary thought and behavior, albeit without the fancy scientific terminology. Today, science has become a faith, at least outside of the scientific world, which demands nearly absolute obedience. Such obedience comes at a very high social cost that leads to questioning the modern definition of *science* and subsequently shining a bright light on a refreshing earlier view of science that held until the last century and a half.

The dovetailing personal and professional experiences evoked a growing awareness that Judeo-Christian culture has drifted away from God in recent decades just a few steps behind the drift of the background secular culture. The ultimate inescapable conclusion is that virtually all modern social controversies are rooted in that drift. The resolution of the controversies is rooted in reversing the drift at least among Judeo-Christian believers and recapturing the real meaning of freedom which is a gift from the Creator, not from government.

Lloyd H. Stebbins, Ph.D.

Dr. Stebbins currently serves several universities as an adjunct professor teaching both natural science and business management courses. He can be reached at lsteb@brighthouse.com.

Dr. Stebbins publishing experience includes a book, co-authored with Dr. Judith Reisman, entitled, *America—Dark Slide; Bright Future* a doctoral dissertation and hundreds of articles for periodicals.

AMERICA—DARK SLIDE; BRIGHT FUTURE

You may also enjoy, Dr. Stebbins previous book co-authored with Dr. Judith Reisman. One man, little known today, did more to destroy the American Christian culture than any 100 more famous people you may choose to list. His name was Dr. Alfred Kinsey, purported to be the world's leading "sexologist" in his day (1930s – 1950s). His so-called "research" has been widely quoted in vast numbers of criminal trials, law journals, and thousands of scholarly articles in sociology and psychology journals.

Yet, decades later, Dr. Judith Reisman demonstrated and proved that Kinsey was a total fraud whose work would not qualify today as research by any definition. Rather, a present day researcher attempting to duplicate Kinsey's work would likely be arrested on hundreds of counts of child pedophilia. Although, Kinsey died in 1956, his devastating legacy lives in the legal, sociological, and psychological professions as well as in the Kinsey Institute at Indiana University. The institute and its progeny are responsible for virtually all the sex education materials used in the nation's public school systems.

How did it happen? Armed with an Ivy League doctoral degree, the atheistic Kinsey obtained tens of millions of dollars from the Rockefeller Foundation and was eagerly supported by one of the founders of the American Civil Liberties Union (ACLU) who had links to several justice on the United States Supreme Court. Kinsey lead the charge to revise the American Law Institute—Model Penal Code, later use to repeal or substantially weaken all morality laws. Throughout his career, he published books about the sex lives and habits of Americans using material derived from interviews with prostitutes and people in prison for sex-related offenses, fraudulently extrapolating his "findings" to the general American public. His work was widely accepted by an eager public at a time when the word "sex" was barely whispered in public.

The damage caused by Kinsey is incalculable. Nevertheless, the second half of the book provides, in easy-to-read language, a plan for Judeo-Christian believers to combat the devastation and restore traditional Biblical virtues and values that have stabilized America for 400 years. The plan begins and hinges on YOUR own family and a clear understanding of God's design and plan for the family. In a culture determined to destroy the family, the body of believers can and must fight back. It is easier than you might think.

Find the book at Amazon, Barnes & Noble, Books-A-Million and many other outlets. The book is available in paperback and online editions (Kindle/Nook).

CPSIA information can be obtained
at www.ICGtesting.com
Printed in the USA
FSHW020227050520
69888FS